ℯ Due

L

COME TO TEXAS

NUMBER NINETY-FOUR
Centennial Series of
the Association of
Former Students,
Texas A&M University

COME TO TEXAS

ATTRACTING IMMIGRANTS, 1865-1915

BARBARA J. ROZEK

TEXAS A&M UNIVERSITY PRESS
College Station

Copyright © 2003 by Barbara J. Rozek
Manufactured in the United States of America
First edition

The paper used in this book meets the minimum requirements
of the American National Standard for Permanence
of Paper for Printed Library Materials, z39.48–1984.
Binding materials have been chosen for durability.

Library of Congress Cataloging-in-Publication Data

Rozek, Barbara J., 1945–
Come to Texas : attracting immigrants, 1865–1915 / Barbara J. Rozek.—1st ed.
p. cm.—(Centennial series of the Association of Former Students, Texas A&M
University ; no. 94)
Includes bibliographical references and index.
ISBN 1-58544-267-4 (alk. paper)
1. Immigrants—Goverment policy—Texas—History. 2. Immigrants—Texas—History.
3. Texas—Emigration and immigration—History. 4. Texas—Emigration and
immigration—Goverment policy—History. I. Title. II. Series.

JV7098 .R69 2003
325.764'09'034—dc21
2002154227

CONTENTS

ILLUSTRATIONS

PREFACE

Out on the road, one bumper sticker reads, "I wasn't born in Texas, but I got here as fast as I could." I observed this message in August, 1992, after living in the state for twenty-five years and having come to call myself an "adopted Texan." The sticker brought a chuckle to my lips, but also a tug at my heart. I had come slowly to absorb much of the mentality that comes with longtime residence in the state. I had even begun teaching Texas history at a local community college, challenging my students, and myself, to understand more about the state's past. Symbols inundate those making associations with Texas—boots, cowboys, oil wells, the state's outline on freeway overpasses— and I had become very comfortable with these mythological associations.

But the realization grew that this bumper sticker was a 1992 version of the marketing that took place between 1865 and 1915 when Texans of many different stripes and vocations used their energy, enthusiasm, and rhetorical skills to entice others to come to Texas. During the research phase for this book, I was repeatedly amazed at the amount of work done by earlier Texans to encourage migration here. The variety of documents they produced also broadened my concept of what it means to try to convey a message. They wrote and wrote and wrote—they produced volumes. The energy committed to the task and the enthusiasm evident on the page made me stop and ask why? I haven't answered that question yet, at least not to my complete satisfaction, but this book is an effort to show the attempts made by the Texans of the late nineteenth century to encourage a migration toward Texas. Their unbounded belief in the power of words to change people's place of residence triggered something for me that I can't quite explain.

Saying thank you is a very rewarding exercise that comes at the end of a long process in creating a book. Individuals who contributed to the final process represent a wide spectrum of people who all had in common an encouraging word, or two, or three, when this author struggled through the multiple phases of creating a book: dreaming about the idea, research, writing, rewriting, indexing.

The joy of research comes from the multiple experiences one has during the process and the numerous sources that are unearthed. Many libraries contributed to that joy and to them I would like to express by gratitude. Archivists and librarians often responded to my statement that I was looking for material on immigration into Texas by saying, "I don't think we have anything." But then together we would tease out a wide variety of material. For their existence as institutions, my thanks go to the Rosenberg Library and its "Texas Room" for a wide range of materials on Texas and specifically Galveston; to the Texas Seaport Museum in Galveston; to the Texas State Library for its crucial government documents and multiple visual images made available through the photographic department; to the Center for American History at the University of Texas at Austin for their newspaper collection and Texas holdings; to the DeGolyer Archives at Southern Methodist University, especially for access to their Railroad Collection; to the Woodson Archives at Rice University; and to the Houston Metropolitan Research Center of the Houston Public Library. I am especially indebted to Fondren Library at Rice University, both for its extensive secondary sources dealing with southern history and for the willingness of the employees of the Inter-Library Loan Department to search for items not available on campus. Earlier drafts of portions of this work have been graciously published by the *East Texas Historical Journal,* the *Gulf Coast Historical Journal,* and the Texas State Historical Association. My thanks to them for early support of my research and publication efforts.

The experience of being a scholar at Rice University created challenges to my growth as a person and as an historian. There are many people at Rice whom I want to thank. The History Department made funding available for my continued studies. The financial and emotional support made it possible for this "returnee" to academia to keep going. Informal and formal discussions with other history graduate students opened my eyes to a myriad of new possibilities and ideas. I appreciate the time and energy devoted to my studies by Professors Edward Cox, Matthew Mancini, Harold Hyman, Alan Matusow, and Chandler Davidson. A special thank you goes to my dissertation advisor, John B. Boles. As a scholar, his knowledge and analytical skills are preeminent. As a "cheerleader," his enthusiasm for my research helped propel me further and further into my topic. And as a person, his caring attitude spurred this student to try her best. Thank You.

Earlier in my career as an historian, three other scholars encouraged my work. Cary Wintz of Texas Southern University as director of a National Endowment for the Humanities summer experience for teachers suggested that I pursue graduate studies. Two very special professors in the history department at Valparaiso University during the 1960s fostered my interest in the history of the United States and especially the topic of immigration. They were Willis Boyd and Daniel Gahl.

Many others contributed their expertise or encouragement on my pathway as researcher and writer. They include Louis Marchiafava, Donely E. Brice, Michael R. Green, John Anderson, Robert Robertson, Casey Greene, Kristin Jacobsen, George Ward, Elizabeth Turner, Lynda Crist, Ken Williams, Sam Watson, Patricia Kell, Rick and Judy Etchells, and the editorial staff at Texas A&M University Press. A research fellowship from the Texas State Historical Association helped ease the cost of scholarship.

While researching and preparing to write this book (a full-time task), I was also a full-time mother and wife. A home base provided the focus for renewing my energies. A special thank you goes to my children—Paul Scott, Douglas Martin, and Janelle Lynn—for keeping me grounded on the importance of being with people. An extended thanks to my husband Ken—payer of the bills, personal helpmate, and computer guru. Friends who valued me as an individual also sustained me through their encouragement. They believed in me when, at times, I had doubts. Thank you Anna, Judy, Bonnie, Sharon, and Gay. And finally, thanks to my parents, LaVerne and Thomas Wadzuk, for their willingness, while I was young, to buy me books, encourage my love of reading, and support my educational dreams.

COME TO TEXAS

CHAPTER 1

WORDS OF ENTICEMENT

"Come to Texas"—a refrain heard throughout all of Texas history—held a special urgency in the fifty years after the Civil War. With enormous tracts of land to settle, Texans longed for help in that task. In a loud, bold, persistent voice that was also multidimensional, the residents of Texas broadcast their need. Just how did they do this? They wrote letters to their families and friends. They published promotional brochures. They met in conventions to develop plans for enticing newcomers. In some cities, like Galveston, their internal improvement efforts demonstrated their interest in pulling immigration into the state. Corporations, like the railroads, developed advertising agencies and immigrant homes to lure migrants. Even the state government, for a time, supported a Bureau of Immigration to encourage the agricultural development of its vast lands. While not typically working cooperatively, various avenues evolved over time that facilitated the effort to entice immigrants to "Come to Texas."

Words often became the common denominator for these efforts: words to explain; words to entice; words to make people feel welcome. Texans of the late nineteenth century believed in the power of words written down. Word of mouth might succeed in a primitive sort of way, but words on paper could really convey the message—at least that is what many Texans strongly believed. They envisioned a movement energized by the power of rhetoric. They aggressively acted on this belief, creating together an overwhelming tide of publications. Their efforts were seemingly rewarded as the population of Texas steadily increased between 1865 and 1915.

The energy and interest Texans displayed at attracting newcomers drives this story. Some Texans put pen to paper and sent letters. Some Texans turned scribbled notes into published pamphlets. Other Texans established government agencies that in turn produced words of enticement on paper. Some citizens joined with their local neighbors and created booster brochures. This story is one of activists, railroads, community developers, individual farmers, committee members, politicians, and business leaders. Just as importantly it is an account of the influence carried by a terse restrictive clause in the state's

1876 constitution. This Texas story begins with a burning desire to solve the state's perceived labor problem as the Civil War comes to an end. It continues through to the establishment of a federal immigration station in Galveston harbor. In between are many unique examples of the way Texans worked to say, "Come to Texas."

IMMEDIATE POST-CIVIL WAR ENERGIES

Robert E. Lee formally surrendered to Ulysses S. Grant on April 9, 1865. The gradual end of military conflict between the northern and southern states produced a season of uncertainty for all southerners, including Texans. With slavery no longer an option, what would be the nature of labor relations between blacks and whites? What would be new? What would remain of the old?

One strand of calm, unchanging experience amid all the chaos was the agricultural foundation of southern society. The rhythm of planting and harvesting, especially the planting and harvesting of cotton and corn, dominated southern daily existence. With the constancy of agricultural production and the uncertainty of most other peripheral yet crucial issues, the South in 1865 struggled to stand stable and strong one day at a time.

In 1865, on the nineteenth of June—a day now celebrated by black Texans as "Juneteenth"—slaves in Galveston officially learned of their freedom. This special event arrived midway in the growing season—more than halfway through the development of the cotton crop. Many concerns fed an intense panicky feeling immediately after emancipation. Lawlessness throughout the state seemed epidemic.[1] Blacks on the move shook the expectations of whites. Population shifts from rural to urban areas intensified the sense of change taking place.[2] Political questions and military occupation heightened personal and individual fears.[3] Texans looking for solutions hoped to set aright a floundering economy. Those immediate months and years following the close of the Civil War found Texans with a mingled sense of fear and hopefulness for the future. As they scrambled to redraw the rules of black/white labor relations, they also searched for alternatives to black workers.

Blacks were a significant portion of the Texas population. The census records 182,566 slaves in Texas in 1860, listing twenty-five thousand of that number as mulattos. They thus comprised about 30 percent of the state's population. Using these figures, one historian notes that the black population was increasing at a rate much faster than the white population, the blacks having grown by 212 percent in the decade between 1850 and 1860 and the whites by 173 percent. The Civil War years saw additions to these totals as many slave-owning southerners fled other areas of the South for the relative safety of Texas. Another scholar labels these individuals who were finally freed in 1865 as "uprooted slave immigrant[s]."[4]

No matter how the blacks arrived in Texas or when they arrived, they were treated upon emancipation with the same contempt found throughout the South. Blacks entered the free labor force at a "time of massive disruption." In the midst of uncertainty, whites made multiple assumptions about the previous slaves. They presupposed the black person would not work unless coerced physically. Some assumed that blacks would just fade away in time—become extinct through natural demise. Others believed that blacks made the best common laborers but definitely needed to be controlled. Blacks were thus both praised and damned for their supposed characteristics.[5]

Racism permeated the atmosphere of the time as well as the written documents. One farmer from Maury County complained that blacks didn't want to work for white men. He also projected onto the future by saying, "I fear that next year they will not work at all." With such apprehension of failure it would not be surprising that pessimism was in the air. Another Texan wrote, "Negroes will never make neat and careful farmers. . . . Negroes know nothing of the value of time." Then angry with black geographical mobility, he added to the racial stereotypes saying, "Negroes rove from place to place. They love change, and a month's work at a place, and are reluctant to make a year engagement." By comparison he went on to say "White people love home, take interest in making it pleasant, comfortable—as the spot from which issue all their money and comforts." Expectations became concrete assumptions and then solid fact for many white citizens. The black worker was held down by the whites' economic and political power. Rather than work to change black/white perceptions or relationships, many southerners turned elsewhere. Elsewhere was where the grass seemed greener, at least in terms of hard-working, highly motivated individuals willing to be farmers in a new land. Immigration was seen by many as "the" answer to the labor problem.[6]

"The thinking among us do not believe the great mass of free persons are to be relied on for the *continuous production* of cotton; hence the obvious utility of the enterprise you desire to inaugurate of inducing emigration from Europe to our cotton lands," wrote a man from Montgomery County, Texas. He went on to note that competition with northern and western states existed and had previously promoted "injurious and false reports" about Texas. Overcoming negative publicity was thus, for this citizen, an essential part of attracting immigration to his state. He also encouraged people to simply come to Texas and check things out for themselves.[7]

In racist fashion the press in Texas, as well as the press across the South, repeatedly linked the value of the immigrant to the white's belief in the lack of the "Negro's" ability. The argument for white immigration allowed southerners and Texans a way to express in print their intolerant attitudes left over from slavery and to meld that view with current racist assumptions about the superiority of white workers. By raising up the call for supposed hard-working white immigrants, the press could "put down" by comparison the failure of blacks to work hard in their freed status. To compare the two—white immigrant and black ex-slave—was to praise the one while devaluing the other. W. H. Neblett of Grimes County disparaged black workers, writing, "The negro, working for a part of the crop or as a renter, failed to exert himself at the critical periods of his crop, and either lost a portion or permitted it to suffer from weeds and grass until it made but little." Another observer noted, "In a great majority of instances the negroes have worked listlessly, and to kill time instead of grass and weeds."[8]

Often the best indications of strongly held beliefs are found in personal communications, for the letter requires less circumspect language than the formal press. Thomas Affleck, a Washington County plantation owner, vigorously condemned black workers in his correspondence. "The bulk of them, including almost all of the young & able-bodied, [are] already worthless," wrote Affleck. Very pessimistically he claimed, "We have no hope of working our plantations by free negro labour" and the "negroes are becoming daily more unwilling to work—with a very few exceptions; and daily verging nearer & nearer insolence." Another Texan, James Harper Starr of Harrison County, derisively explained in one of his letters that blacks were fast on the track to becoming as "indolent as were their ancestors on the banks of the Niger."[9]

Relatively newer Texans made similar observations. Having arrived in Texas in 1858, a lawyer wrote back to kin in Virginia seven years later: "I do not believe that the negro can be used successfully unless he can be compelled to labor regularly and from the beginning to the end of the year. I have no confidence in moral suasion in the case of a negro who is at best not above a half savage. . . . The retrogradation of the negroes commenced at the moment of their liberation and will continue until the race is exterminated." A Mississippian recently turned Texan wrote home "the negroes, here as elsewhere, are disposed to be idle." Frustrations abound in such personal letters revealing expectations of whites upon the black workers.[10]

By contrast, the white immigrant seemed to receive nothing but praise. One editorialist wrote, "We shall soon have our troublesome labor question settled by having an abundance of intelligent white men to till our rich soil."

Another journalist noted the arrival of Swedish immigrants to Austin and proclaimed, "Let them come. There is plenty of room for all foreigners desirous of homes in our state. All hard-working industrious people, of whatever nationality, who will come to this country, are now more than welcome."[11]

Getting hard-working laborers to Texas became a passionate goal. The option of cooperative organization appealed to many Texans. Enthusiasm for such cooperative endeavors is clearly seen in the newspapers of the time. Let's organize a "Labor and Immigrants Aid Society," said J. S. Thrasher, a Texas planter, in an August, 1865, letter to the *Galveston Daily News.* In a very sensible proposal Thrasher pointed to the fact that most people have private businesses that keep them from spending large amounts of time on securing needed immigration. The answer could be the formation of a group that would fund a central secretary to handle correspondence, the collation of information from around the state, and its distribution to potential migrants. Some of these efforts at association died on the vine. But Thrasher's suggestion seems to have become a concrete effort about a year later. The 1867 *Texas Almanac* identifies the incorporation by the 1866 legislature of a "Land, Labor, and Immigration Company." Thrasher, who had previously written several letters to the *Galveston Daily News,* was on the nine-member executive committee developing this company.[12]

The publication of Thrasher's letter in the *Daily News* also spurred a public correspondence between Thrasher and W. R. Baker of Houston. Baker set the tone for the dialogue by suggesting that there was no sense in bemoaning the past. He looked to immigration from Europe, from other states, and even from Canada as part of the solution, but he asked how best to achieve that goal. Thrasher, in reply, answered loud and clear, "the secret of successful effort—*organization.* We must have organized action in this great field."[13]

Calls for statewide coordination of immigration efforts continued to appear in the newspaper throughout the decade after the Civil War.[14] The suggestions varied, but the goal of peopling Texas with new farmers and laborers remained central. The *Galveston Daily News* reported on activities of such successful planters as Mr. Cherouze and Mr. Lawrence. Cherouze's trip to Europe in order to obtain white labor received full coverage in the paper. *Flake's Bulletin,* another Galveston newspaper of the time, also reported on efforts at association. In a reference to "Emigrants' Aid Societies" being discussed by Mayor Leonard, the editor said that more than talk was necessary. "There must be those who will undertake the organization, and put its machinery in motion. The object is to secure the greatest possible number of the better class of emigrants—those for which other States are competing." This reference to other states was meant to act as a spur to state pride. It was an argument used repeatedly during the subsequent years. What did Flake see as the task of this organization? He wrote, "What is essential is two or three energetic, shrewd and conscientious salaried officers, who will devote their whole energies to the work of settling the State with the hardy yeomanry of oppressed Europe." With unknowing prescience, Flake's suggestion of lecturers and paid immigration agents was a precursor to the Texas Bureau of Immigration, established in 1870 with exactly this mode of operation in mind.[15]

Yet another, albeit different, approach to cooperative action was the work of legislators in the 1866 Texas congress. According to one historian, these representatives "thoroughly understood" the needs of Texas for responsible laborers and people to till the soil. They encouraged each congressman to gather information of current conditions in his home district. These reports would then be provided to Willard Richardson, editor of the *Galveston Daily News*. As editor of the *News,* Richardson also used the presses to produce the most comprehensive state *Almanac* of the time. According to Richardson, the legislators cheerfully contributed what he described as accurate and helpful information for immigrants. His *Almanac* was a 360-page work with 108 pages devoted to these county descriptions. The legislators thus demonstrated their belief that authoritative, correct information would have a strong pull on the prospective immigrant. This particular *Almanac* for 1867 offers an interesting window into Texas society in 1866. It reinforces the picture of planters' hopes for a substitute labor force to replace or supplement the freedmen. For example, the account for Washington County quoted a recent clerk of the county, J. H. Randle, as stating that German immigrants within the last year had purchased over 10,000 acres of land in the county involving ninety different tracts of land. This information directly followed the statement by the Washington County reporter that "Our population is fast increasing; can not say at what rate; but the result will be to make this beautiful county a white man's country."[16] Racism obviously propelled some Texans in their desire to attract European immigrants to do the planters' work.

Tremendous energy, especially through written admonitions in newspapers, stimulated ideas for collective action to entice immigrants. This positive encouragement by the Galveston newspaper helped to foster interchange of information among Texas communities through the columns of the paper. This interaction served to dispense ideas throughout the state, since the *Galveston Daily News* was the preeminent paper in Texas. A July 20, 1867, letter to the editor began, "As your paper is an advocate of immigration, and thus working for the welfare of the State, and as this movement is for the same, you will please publish the following Resolutions." Other examples of cooperative action and newspaper publicity exist. In Walker County, a group had formed the Waverly Immigration Society. Among their goals was the importation of Polish workers that they "cordially recommend . . . as good laborers to the country." This immigration society announced the group's formation with election of a president, secretary, and agent all selected for the purpose of helping their local community. By using the newspaper with a statewide readership, they were also showing a willingness to share with others the benefits of the structure they had in place. Another individual seeking to encourage migration announced in his letter to the editor that he had 30,000 acres of land along the Concho River available in tracts of about 320 acres each that he was "willing to lease . . . for a term of five years, without charge, to actual settlers who will cultivate them." He urged individuals and colonies to take advantage of his offer. In his mind, many soldiers during the recent war had traveled into the southern states and seen for themselves the advantages of agriculture in that area. He was sure they were ready to make a move and he thus offered his land.[17]

Yet another individual who heavily invested energy and time into promoting immigration to Texas in the postwar years was Thomas Affleck. A Scottish immigrant, Affleck moved to Texas in 1858 after living in Ohio and Mississippi. He developed a reputation for agricultural interests, propagating plants for his nurseries, publishing articles and books such as his *Southern Rural Almanac and Plantation and Garden Calendar,* and generally keeping abreast of the latest developments in the field of agriculture. Affleck owned a large plantation known as Glenblythe near Brenham in Washington County. Before the war he was a successful planter with a very large cadre of slaves. By 1865 Affleck, well-educated and heavily involved in agricultural development, had adopted the full complement of anti-black racial attitudes common among white southerners. Using his wealth, his writing skills, and his experience at organizing work, Affleck developed extensive and well-thought-out proposals for importing white workers from Europe.[18]

While Affleck seemed to be open to new approaches and developing ideas when it came to agricultural techniques, he kept strictly to a racist belief in black inferiority. He had no qualms about expressing those opinions either, and did so frequently. An August, 1865, *Galveston Daily News* article quoted him as referring to "the animal nature of the negro." He later wrote in a letter to the *News,* "I never had, nor yet have, any confidence whatever, in free negro labor." He held out absolutely no hope in a prosperous Texas based on freed black labor. Probably those strong racist views nurtured the immense energy he poured into promoting white immigration. The common phrase-ology of the time—a desire for a white man's country—also filtered into his language. Envisioning that totally white land, he used the flip side of his racist beliefs to endorse the hard-working Scottish and English farmers. For Affleck, these European workers were all that the black failed to be. And in prejudicial fashion he extolled the virtues of these white Europeans to his fellow Texans. From his viewpoint the Scots were "cautious, prudent, persistent people" who would faithfully and thoroughly carry out any contract they signed.[19]

Affleck's first goal was to travel to Scotland, then find and bring back twenty-five to thirty families to Glenblythe. In paternalistic fashion he planned to settle them on his land in "cottages" (a new name for the slave quarters?), furnish them with tools and animals, and allow them to work un-der their own selected foreman. He had heard of the movement to break up plantations into small farms and agreed that such was a possibility, but he pre-ferred the larger enterprise. Plantation economy suited his sense of efficiency and organization. When later listing the advantages of immigrating to plan-tations in Texas, Affleck told his Scottish and English listeners of the almost "pre-packaged" opportunity available through his plan. Affleck went to Scot-land and energetically pursued his proposals among the common folk. He published in Scotland a twelve-page pamphlet entitled *Texas and Her Re-sources,* which he must have given away free of charge. He filled six pages with descriptions of what he called his "adopted State" and then followed with six pages clarifying his proposition. In unique fashion he pointed to comparisons with other emigration opportunities in Australia, Canada, and various west-ern states in the United States. He also stretched the truth, although his read-ers were probably not aware of it, when he referred to cotton picking as "light, pleasant and paying work."[20]

While on his European trip he wrote back to the *Galveston Daily News* chronicling his work and sharing his hopes for the future. He bemoaned the unofficial nature of his trip wishing he held a formal position representing the state government, assuming he could accomplish more as an official ambassa-dor of Texas. He anticipated speaking to the state legislature upon his return and suggesting a plan for aiding immigrants.[21]

Once back in his beloved Texas, Affleck met with fellow planters and pre-sented his ideas to anyone who would listen. He continued to write letters to the Galveston newspapers. Planning the incorporation of a company to en-courage immigration, he printed a six-page circular entitled *Immigration and Labor* dated May 21, 1866. These pamphlets circulated throughout south and east Texas suggesting how other farmers could participate in the enterprise.

Two months later he added another twist to his extensive scheme by issuing a two-page letter plus printed blank contracts for potential shareholders in a plan to export livestock to Europe. Cattle and immigration may seem distant interests, but for businessman Thomas Affleck they were very much complementary and he meant to explain that to fellow Texans. The main reasoning behind the plan was the key issue of transportation. Getting white laborers to Texas required expensive passage by ship. Affleck's solution meant sending livestock out of Texas to English ports and in return shipping back the very much needed white laborers. He admitted that his idea was an experiment but "one well worth trying." And he backed up his ideas with his own personal investment of time, energy, and money.[22]

Affleck's efforts illustrate one person's interest in immigration into Texas, and they illustrate his belief that concerted action could make that possible. The uncertainty of the postwar months and years left some people apathetic and doubtful about the future. But that same uncertainty propelled individuals like Thomas Affleck to step into action, doing something based on deeply held racist beliefs. Realizing that change was happening, Affleck came up with a plan and worked to implement it.[23]

While private individuals presented plans for stimulating immigration in 1865 and the years following, government also participated in this ongoing effort. No matter what the governmental authority in power at a specific time, assumptions of geographic mobility were a constant. During the nineteenth century, Texas rather quickly experienced a succession of different governmental authorities. Before 1835, Mexico held legal jurisdiction over the area now known as Texas. From 1836 to 1845 this same area became the independent Republic of Texas. Although incorporated into the United States of America in 1845, Texas later seceded from that Union and joined the Confederate States of America in 1861. By 1865, Texas again came under the power and authority of the United States government as the state was forcibly corralled back into the Union. While legal control may have changed over time, all governmental entities, except for Mexico from 1830 to 1834, encouraged population movements to the state. Statistics also document that the political and legal entity of Texas grew in size as people immigrated into the territory. Anglos moved onto Mexican land and eventually established an independent Republic. Additional people from overseas and from the states and territories of the United States migrated into the area. After Texas became a state within the United States, settlers continued to move into the state, swelling its population and tapping into its resources. Texas history has always been a history of immigration.

In the decade between 1865 and 1875 the issue of immigration was not the central concern for Texas or for the other southern states. Known historically as the era of Reconstruction, this long decade churned with changes in the black labor force, intrusion of northern influence on politics, and violence based on racist concepts of society. Texas existed squarely within this reconstruction tradition. Immigration fits into this larger picture as a minor but very significant side issue. Political decisions about suffrage, education, internal improvements, pardons, business incorporations, taxation, revenue, budgets, and land laws had to take into consideration the flow of people into and within the state. The Texas legislatures and constitutional conventions debated immigration concerns throughout this decade and the rest of the century.

Central to the early immigration efforts was the proposed supplanting of black freed people with white laborers. However, the issue became more complex as the years 1867, 1868, and 1869 arrived. The need to populate the great empty territories of Texas also received attention. The desire to create an influx of settlers, especially agricultural people, expanded. Cooperative efforts remained a possibility. However the main arena shifted to the political theater in the ten to twelve years after Appomattox.

Typically, Reconstruction history chronicles the initial control of southern state governments by Confederate leaders followed by radical Republican control followed again by the reinstatement of conservative Democratic Party–led governments. Texas participated in these reconstruction shifts. However, in spite of successive state constitutions in 1866, 1869, and 1876, Texas legislatures showed a rare continuity throughout the Reconstruction era in supporting formal efforts at enticing immigration to the state. Studies of other southern states reeling from the economic consequences of the Civil War are needed. To what extent they also urged in-migration has not been documented to date. While each political party throughout the South sought increased membership through migration, Texas's experience was more complex due to its frontier, public lands, and immense size.[24]

Between 1866 and 1869 the state legislature, functioning under the authority of the 1866 constitution, passed several pieces of legislation directly dealing with immigration issues. A Commissioner of Statistics was charged "to organize a system for the promotion of immigration to the State of Texas." His duty was "to collect information in regard to the mineral resources, productions, and populations of the State, and to prepare and publish such documents as may be calculated to furnish correct information about all the counties of the State, and inviting immigration from other States and countries." Information-gathering tasks were perceived as one step in providing reliable data for the state's public relations efforts. This ordinance reflects an interest in encouraging immigration and suggests the belief that immigrants typically made decisions based on adequate information. People were obviously choosing among alternative locations and Texas wanted to be one of the places under consideration.[25]

This 1866 session of the legislature also saw the passage of acts incorporating companies dealing with immigration. The legislature chartered the "Texas Land, Labor and Immigration Company" with its stated goal "to promote immigration to Texas, to facilitate the purchase and settlement of lands by immigrants, and to introduce laborers and skilled operatives into the State." A few weeks later, the state legislature incorporated the "Western Texas Colonial Land Immigration Company," which intended to "develop the resources of the State by disseminating reliable information, inducing emigration from other States and from Europe, furnishing labor, extending facilities to emigrants, and directing and determining the investment and employment of capital and enterprise to the State."[26]

When the First Reconstruction Act in 1867 effectively discredited the 1866 Texas constitution, Texans were forced to create a new basic law for the state. The resulting 1869 constitution, acceptable to the northern Republicans, also valued government action to entice immigrants. It made specific provision for a Bureau of Immigration. A Superintendent of Immigration could be appointed by the governor for a four-year term at an annual salary of two thousand dollars. The legislature was given power to appropriate money "for the purpose of promoting and protecting immigration." This portion of the 1869 constitution obviously and enthusiastically encouraged future legislation dealing with immigration.[27]

Debate during the long and involved constitutional convention of 1868–69 included a multitude of subjects and issues of interest to Texans. Black suffrage and civil rights were primary concerns among others. For the purposes of this narrative, a detailed analysis of the convention's activities is not necessary. But it is most helpful to follow the events during the convention that influenced immigration recruitment in order to document the constancy of interest in bringing people to Texas. At the first full session of the constitutional convention, Governor Pease's address was read to the assembled delegates. The governor referred to many important issues including crime, enfranchisement, school taxes, and state debts. One of his hopes was "that you will adopt efficient measures to encourage immigration to our State from foreign countries, and to give aid and encouragement to such works of internal improvements as the necessities of our people require." Subsequent supporters of immigration, following the lead of Governor Pease, often combined their interest in peopling the state with support for internal improvements that would facilitate transportation and commerce.[28]

Relative to the issue of immigration the governor's address also included the following optimistic observation:

> We have reason to congratulate ourselves on prosperous seasons, and the prospect of abundant crops. The freed people are doing well, far better than their most ardent friends anticipated under all the circumstances by which they have been surrounded. The prejudice against them is gradually giving way to a better feeling. Many of those who prophesied ruin to the country from their emancipation are now compelled to admit that there is still some hope for the future.[29]

While not everyone would have agreed with Governor Pease, the sense of emergency and immediacy during those first few months at the Civil War's end had dissipated.

Among the many committees established by the convention was one designated for immigration. Its chair was Edward Degener, representative for the western counties of Bexar, Wilson, Kerr, Bandera, Medina, Uvalde, Kinney, Maverick, Edwards, and Zavala. Degener was a German by birth, had served in German legislative bodies, and immigrated to Texas in 1850. He was a wholesale grocer in San Antonio. There were six other members of the committee. Julius Schuetze represented Fayette and Bastrop Counties. He was Prussian born, immigrated to Texas when he was seventeen, and was currently serving as a Bastrop County judge. H. H. Foster of Colorado County was a twenty-eight-year-old farmer and one of the convention's native Texans. George W. Smith representing Bowie, Davis, and Marion Counties was only a three-year resident of Texas serving as a major in the Union occupation army in San Antonio. He was from New York State. Erwin Wilson represented Brazoria County, where he was a fifty-eight-year-old farmer. He was originally from Tennessee, though he had lived in Texas for over eighteen years. Nothing biographical is known about John Morse other than he was white and represented Shelby, San Augustine, Sabine, and Newton Counties. Stephen Curtis was the one black man on the committee. He was sixty-two years old, born in Virginia, and represented Brazos County. The forceful figure on the committee was its chair, who also sat on the Committee on Division of the State, the Political or Legislative Committee, and the Committee on Apportionment.[30]

The Committee on Immigration presented its report on June 18, 1868. It included the proposed wording of the constitutional provision followed by an extra five pages explaining their recommendations. The rationale for a bureau of immigration, the report said, came from the past tradition of the nation's interest in and encouragement of immigration. Noting population growth in the western territories of the United States, the committee's report then stated that, "the American slave States could not keep time with their successful sister free States." Pointing to recent political changes while adding the valuable advantage of the mild southern climate, the committee said it was now time for Texas to induce immigration southwestward.[31]

Money appropriated for the bureau was to be spent in three ways: "to defray the expenses of the Bureau of Immigration . . . to support agencies in foreign seaports . . . [and] to pay in part or in toto the passage of emigrants from Europe to this State, and their transportation on railroads in this State." The committee explained that, as a rule, agencies in the United States did not suggest options to the potential immigrant in his or her home country before those migrants purchased tickets via a more "circuitous route." The perceived need for funds to support the immigrants' actual travel came from the committee's understanding of "the unavoidable difference between freights from Europe to Northern seaports and our shipping places." These legislators were very aware of the disadvantages under which the southern states, including Texas, labored in terms of direct shipping routes with Europe. Debate ensued over various portions of the committee's recommendations. The ultimate constitutional provision eventually allowed for state financial support of the actual travel expenses. As to the issue of placement of Texas immigration agencies, the final provision expanded the potential inherent in the constitutional article by including the opportunity to establish agencies in seaports of the United States in addition to foreign seaports.[32]

The committee recommended the donation of land to immigrants. They proposed that the head of a family should receive 160 acres while a single male would be entitled to eighty acres "free of all costs whatever, other than the expense of surveying the same." The members saw this as a gift dependent upon the immigrants living there for at least three years and also noted that such occupation enhanced "the value and increased taxability of the lands bordering on the new location." They saw investment in attracting people as ultimately increasing the state's revenues. Their ability to see the long-range picture is something not often shared by legislators burning with interest over the moment's concerns.[33]

Finally, the report anticipated some objections to its proposals. Noting that just one type of immigration was being encouraged by this constitutional provision, i.e. foreign immigration, they tried to explain:

> It is not the wealthy foreigner, nor the merchant; not the industrial nor the experienced American citizen; immigrating from another State to Texas, who is in need of the protecting and assisting hand of the Bureau of Immigration, but such class of foreign labor to whom the trifling outlay for ocean transportation is a serious consideration.
>
> What we are in need of, is a hard working thrifty population, which clings to the soil it has once undertaken to cultivate, without nomadic propensities and of unquestionable *loyalty to the Government of the United States.*[34]

This explanation seems to present a fairly narrow focus toward peopling the state. Such a view was not to remain the only one over the many years ahead in the late nineteenth century.

Violence was part and parcel of life in many parts of Texas. This was the case during the war years and in the immediate postbellum era. Texas still had a frontier—sparsely settled land touched by marauding Indians. Black/white tensions also existed as the freed slaves sought to carve out their position in Texas society. Government between 1865 and 1870 was often inadequate and laws frequently not enforced. Early on, newspapers noted the gruesome stories of violence and editorialized over them. Ferdinand Flake, an avowed Republican of German birth, wrote about this lawlessness regularly in his newspaper's columns. However, on November 28, 1866, he pointed out that overstating this tendency to violence could and would have negative results. He wrote that such statements would "prevent immigration, hinder our trade, destroy our good name, and mar our general prosperity." As a typical newspaperman of the time he assumed a booster mentality for his adopted state and hoped that the growth of the state would not be harmed by the reports of lawlessness.[35]

Another Galveston booster was Willard Richardson of the *Galveston Daily News;* he also saw the connection between slowed immigration rates and reports of violence. His response was to blame the Republicans. In an editorial column of August, 1868, he wrote, "The object of the crime report of the Convention is to prevent emigration to Texas. The radicals have not given up the hope of ruling the State through the negro . . . they do not want white people to come in for fear their programme may have to be changed." Richardson added, "Already the first crime report of the Texas Convention has been translated into foreign languages, to be scattered in Europe for the purpose of keeping emigrants away from Texas." What better can we expect from the radicals, Richardson sarcastically continued.[36]

This criticism of radical Republicans in Texas rested on two reports. Governor Pease presented one report to the United States House of Representatives (May 11, 1868). Another came from the constitutional convention as a report by the Special Committee on Lawlessness (July 25, 1868). The Committee on Reconstruction in the federal House printed the Pease communication, and thus it was available nationwide for publication in various newspapers and magazines. In seven separate documents covering twenty-eight pages, Pease disputed the military's report that peace existed in Texas and begged for assistance in holding down violent occurrences throughout the state. The other report emanated from the Texas convention. It had a more limited initial impact, but according to Richardson still had tremendous influence overseas. Both reports distressed those seeking to present Texas in a positive light as the place for future settlers.[37]

How did the two political parties "line up" on the issue of encouraging immigration to Texas? Did they try to undermine each other's work? Or did they see immigration in a positive light but argue about who should be attracted to the state and how that encouragement should be facilitated? These are difficult questions to answer. No crystal-clear picture emerges. A look at official party platforms as bare bones political statements suggests both parties held an interest in immigration. Their motives covered a full spectrum from desire for economic development to an increase in their party membership to transportation improvements to power in the legislature.

Meeting in Bryan on July 7, 8, and 9, 1868, the Democratic Party adopted a platform that included the following plank:

> That we need more population, labor, and capital, as well as peace and civil government, for the development of the resources of our great State, and that our true policy is to invite immigration and capital from the Northern States and Europe, and to assure them of a friendly welcome, and we declare that statements that immigrants from the Northern States are not received with friendship and cannot expect security for life and property amongst us are made by the Radical party for political effect and are wilful [sic] perversions of the truth.

The Republican Party met in Austin on August 12–14 of the same year and its official platform had no separate statement about immigration. This meeting reflected the decisions of the moderate Republicans in office. A smaller group of Republicans, commonly referred to as the radical wing of the party, bolted this convention and held a separate meeting on August 14–15. Lead by E. J. Davis, E. Degener, and James P. Newcomb, this "other" Republican convention adopted among its eight resolutions the statement, "that the establishment of just and liberal provisions in our organic law, placing our State among the most progressive of the Union, with a rigid and exact enforcement of the laws, will encourage emigration, promote prosperity, and at an early day suppress lawlessness and violence." The tone of their plank suggests the belief that as people immigrate into the area, the violence will subside. They thus saw the suppression of violence and the encouragement of immigration as complementary concerns. From the platforms in 1868 it would seem both parties were concerned about their image around the country as well as within the state itself. Even as they jockeyed for position and voter support, both parties seemed to be supportive of population movements into the state.[38]

During the succeeding years, the official voices of both parties continued to support immigration. The 1869 Radical Republican convention, spoke of, "condemn[ing] the demagogical use of the term of "carpetbagger" and other terms of reproach applied to strangers who may come among us, designed to keep alive the prejudices of the ignorant and deter immigration." Two later conventions of the Democrats in 1869 and 1871 expressed positive feelings about immigration, especially white immigration. A small group of Democratic journalists met and wrote into their platform the statement, "we are in favor of encouraging European and American immigration, and pledge them our protection, irrespective of both place and political principles." The larger Democratic State Convention held in Austin January 23–26, 1871, included as one of its ten resolutions: "The Immigration of the white races from all quarters of the world should be encouraged . . . uniformly in favor of a liberal policy toward all persons of foreign birth, who in good faith seek a home in our favored land."[39]

Activity in the constitutional convention of 1868–69 also raises another historical question whose answer remains cloudy. Was there a connection between those who favored immigration to Texas and those who voted the question of division of the state? Texas came into the Union with the option to divide its large landmass into smaller states if it so desired. This possibility has been entertained throughout the history of the state, but received special interest at the 1868–69 constitutional convention. Frustration over violence in the state intensified feelings separating eastern and western counties. Western counties felt the need for frontier control against Indian raids and lawbreakers. The eastern counties struggled with racial violence as black/white tensions intensified after the war. Some representatives of each section saw a division of the state as one way to cope with the perceived failings of the other section.

While the division issue was a complex political maneuver involving many disparate issues and supported by many Texans, some have suggested that differing sectional interests in bringing immigrants to the state played into the story. Yet voting records do not seem to indicate a clear-cut division by sectional representatives. Others have noted the argument that racial concerns were involved in the division issue. Yet again voting records note that of the nine black delegates at the 1868–69 constitutional convention, five voted for division and four voted against. One other piece of documentation provides an interesting insight. During the division debate at the 1868–69 convention, a printed copy of a proposed Constitution of the State of West Texas was laid on every delegate's desk one January morning. Article ten of that proposed document dealt with immigration. Its two sections look remarkably similar to the ultimate provision for a Bureau of Immigration incorporated in the final version of the 1869 constitution. It would seem that those hoping for a separate state of West Texas held similar if not identical views on immigration with those who were working to formulate a constitution facilitating readmission of the whole state of Texas to the federal Union.[40]

The long and involved deliberations of the Texas constitutional convention finally came to an end in February, 1869. Debate over ratification kept journalists, politicians, and citizens wrangling with each other through the summer and early fall. At the polls in November and December, Texas citizens ratified the document and then proceeded to elect Edmund J. Davis as governor. Once all the paperwork and bureaucratic recordkeeping were complete, Texas rejoined the Union on March 30, 1870, in full partnership with all other states.[41]

Immigrants continued to move into Texas from 1865 to 1870. Just what specifically pulled them to this locale or pushed them out of their previous homes cannot be clearly explained. But it is obvious that the sentiment extant in much of Texas at the conclusion of the Civil War favored in-migration. Immediate concerns over substitutes for the freed blacks developed into ongoing energy at luring farmers to Texas, pushing back the lawless frontier, and stimulating economic growth. Discussion of immigration did not center on questions of whether or not immigration was desirable. Instead debate focused on how to facilitate this movement to Texas. Belief in cooperative action dominated this discussion. At first individuals encouraged the banding together of like-minded people. Eventually duly elected representatives developed constitutions and laws providing for governmental coordination of immigration efforts. In 1860 Texas had 604,215 people, of which 420,891 were white. Despite the horrors, death, and destruction from warfare in the intervening ten years, that population figure rose in 1870 to 818,579 people, and of that total number 564,700 were white and 253,475 were black.[42] Texas and Texans saw the influx of people during the first decade after the Civil War as a positive movement. Their legislative body, governmental agencies, and private initiatives continued to nurture that feeling through the first five years of the 1870s.

CHAPTER 2

———•❖•———

A BUREAU OF IMMIGRATION

As the decade of the 70s opened, the governor and the legislature of Texas identified a need and created an executive agency for the purpose of encouraging immigration and supporting immigrants as they moved to the state. The formal enabling legislation (May 23, 1871) gave flesh and body to Article 11 of the state constitution. The governor could appoint a superintendent for a four-year term of office and offer a salary of $2,000. The superintendent could then select up to four salaried representatives for the bureau. One of these agents would work in Great Britain, another on the continent of Europe, and two others would represent the bureau in the United States: "one for the Northern and one for the Southern States." In addition, the governor could designate individuals as unpaid lecturers or agents to supplement the cadre of salaried officials.[1]

The full appropriation of $30,000 for the Bureau of Immigration included such line items in the budget as a yearly report to the governor, publication of informational pamphlets, and salaries for the superintendent and his four agents. The superintendent's task was to "take all the steps which he may deem advisable and proper for the encouragement of immigration, and for the protection of immigrants." This included help "in the procurement of their transportation from the coast into the interior; in the guarding them against fraud and chicanery and peculation; in their temporary location in proper and reasonable places of board and lodging on their arrival." The legislation stated that the assistance of other state officers would be forthcoming as needed. Superintendents of the Bureau interpreted this provision to mean that officials around the state could thus be a source of help in collecting information.[2]

A belief in the value of the written word can be seen in Section 4 where the law states, "it shall be the duty of the Superintendent to collect and compile, from all the sources within his reach, such suggestions, references and statistics as are best calculated to give a correct idea of the material and social condition of our State, and to diffuse correct information of the advantages of this State to immigrants." Distributing information about Texas was central to the mission of the Bureau of Immigration. Dissemination of information meant publication of pamphlets, writing articles for distribution to newspapers, and preparing data for submission to journals. That the state of Texas directed much of its efforts to foreign-born people is obvious from the provision that such pamphlets could and should be published in "one or two of the principal languages of Europe." These booklets must describe the "developed and undeveloped agricultural and mineral resources of the State of Texas; the nature of her climate, soil, geographical features and advantages; her manufacturing capacities; her public improvements."[3]

The law was both specific and clear in its purpose. Typical of many laws, however, there was no real indication in its actual wording of the social influences or needs that propelled the legislators to frame such a law and provide for its implementation. In searching for their rationale and/or motivation, one hint exists in a message by Governor Edmund Davis to the legislators at the outset of their 1871 session. According to Davis, "the impression which is abroad, that an era of peace and quiet and prosperity has commenced here, is attracting an unusual stream of immigrants, and of a more intelligent class than heretofore. With immigration is also coming capital to invest in internal improvements." Davis's address reflects typical thinking of the time. In simple equation form it would read: People equals money. Peace on the land means people will come. Peace on the land means money comes with them. The Bureau of Immigration continued in operation throughout the existence of the 1869 state constitution. But when the new constitution of 1876 emerged as the supreme law of Texas, the bureau became a relic of the past. Section 56 of the 1876 document stated, "The Legislature shall have no power to appropriate any of the public money for the establishment and maintenance of a Bureau of Immigration, or for any purpose of bringing immigrants to the State."[4] The story of the 1875–76 debate over the Bureau's existence will be related later. Here, we pause to describe the work of the Bureau from 1870 to 1876.

The 1869 constitution provided for a bureau with a superintendent and gave the legislature the power to appropriate revenue of the state for its operation. Utilizing this proviso, Governor Davis must have appointed Gustav Loeffler as superintendent and given him the go-ahead to begin operations even before enabling legislation was passed. Correspondence between Davis and Loeffler in August 1870 suggests that Loeffler believed people would come from the northern United States and then also from Europe when the Franco-Prussian War ended. In these early months of government under Governor Davis, Loeffler established headquarters in the port city of Galveston and reported to the governor that he had already organized a settling of five hundred Germans. The sense of urgency felt by the governor is evident in Davis's first address to the Texas House of Representatives. He noted that as peace moved over the land, more and more people would view Texas as a destination. He added that Texas's cheap lands with mild climate by their very existence would provide a lure. But he urged immediate attention to the organization of the formal Bureau of Immigration since, "we wish at once to turn the tide of immigration in this direction." This "at once" mentality may explain the governor's quick appointment of Loeffler to head up the state agency.[5]

The first superintendent for the Bureau of Immigration was born in Germany in 1828. As a young man he traveled originally to New Orleans but then quickly moved to Houston, Texas. He married Julia J. Fisher, a Houston native, and together they had ten children. He settled in that growing city and according to the 1873 *City Directory* had become a cotton factor. An earlier postbellum directory listed him as a "merchant" sharing offices with E. R. Wells & Co., a dry goods dealer in the city. Loeffler must have been active in the large German community, for in 1866 he served as president of the Houston Turn-verein, a social and athletic club common in cities with sizable German populations. There is no indication of what specific qualifications prepared him for the job other than his foreign birth, but he held the office of superintendent for almost four years. In 1874 he returned full-time to the cotton business as a dealer and exporter, finally retiring to San Antonio where he died in 1877.[6]

Loeffler's first report to Governor Davis, published in 1870, identified his working format for disseminating information. "I considered that the collecting of statistics showing price of land, production of the soil, means of communication in the different parts of our State, for the purpose of publishing the same to the world, was one of first importance." With that in mind he sent out a "circular" requesting information. He cast a wide, fairly unscientific net over the state to landowners, farmers, and business people. His unsystematic approach to mining the field for information reflects ignorance of the time in scientific surveying techniques. But it also reflects the enthusiasm for the task and the intense interest by Loeffler in his mission. In one paragraph of the circular he asked for responses based on these questions:

Are you willing to sell land to immigrants? How much have you for sale? Where is it situated? What is the character of the land? Has it water and timber, and in what proportion? Is it in a healthy locality? What is chiefly raised in the neighborhood? How far to market? Is it in the neighborhood of a railroad or navigable stream? Are the titles good? What are your school facilities? What is your price, and how the terms of payment? Will you rent land—if yes, what are your conditions? If you desire help from immigrants, what will you pay to farm laborers, what to mechanics? What nationalities do you prefer? What inducements are offered to immigrants in your settlement?

Not only was the net cast broadly, but the information requested was wide-ranging as well.[7]

Loeffler intended to provide concrete, specific information for the immigrants. He assumed their first thoughts were questions about land, schools, and labor opportunities. He knew that the farmer was concerned about transportation access for marketing his crops, the potential to buy or rent land, the legal concerns to property ownership, and future healthfulness of his family. A key interest for almost all the immigrants to Texas in this time period was availability of land. Late-nineteenth- and early-twentieth-century immigration more frequently revolved around job openings in cities or industrial areas. This is not to negate that some immigrants to Texas between 1865 and 1914 were job hunting and/or urban oriented, but the large mass of people who came to Texas had land opportunities in mind.

The superintendent also saw his position as liaison between the immigrants and the transportation companies. He negotiated with the rail and shipping companies in order to obtain special rates for immigrants and their luggage. He reported some success with companies in Texas and in the port of New Orleans. By mentioning Canada in his report he hinted at a potential source of immigration through that country. Loeffler referred to the numerous letters received by him requesting information, and this surely influenced his request within his formal report that the bureau be furnished with maps of the many Texas counties.

Patterns of seasonal migration that continued throughout the later part of the nineteenth century emerge here. For example, no immigrants were identified as arriving in July and August of 1869. Summer travel was both uncomfortable and could be dangerous, with epidemics not unusual, so settlers avoided traveling at that time. The heaviest migrations into the state most typically came in the late fall and early winter months. Loeffler reported immigration totals through the port of Galveston for fall, 1869:

September	1700
October	1100
November	2900
December	4100

Of these figures, Loeffler stated that 3,300 were from Europe, thus at least one-third of all immigrants at that time came directly from overseas. Loeffler ended his first report with a request that the legislature develop laws and provisions so that the work of the bureau could be carried out.[8]

His request probably encouraged legislators to pass the May 23, 1871, act formalizing the bureau's structure and purpose. A year and a half later Loeffler submitted his second report. The size of this printed report—twenty-seven pages versus the three pages of the first report—reflects the bureau's greater activity. The agency was past the stage of gearing up for activity and was in full swing now. Loeffler's major distress was the failure to get a pamphlet about the state into publication. After collating information and writing the document he begged for the money to have it printed. As a prod to congressional action he pointed to the fact that other states and various railroads were distributing pamphlets in Europe. Texas, according to Loeffler, was missing a golden opportunity being seized by others. He praised the newspapers for printing any and all information he could supply, thus suggesting that he received more cooperation from the news media than from the legislature.[9]

Loeffler appointed four bureau agents—all on the state payroll. They moved to their assignments and began their tasks. As representative to the southern and western states J. H. Lippard began work in New Orleans, but quickly moved to St. Louis, Missouri. Loeffler referred to Lippard as the "right man in the right place." William H. Parsons set up offices in New York City as the Commissioner of the Northern and Eastern States and reportedly directed immigrants to Texas, emphasizing settlement in groups. Dr. Theodore Hertzberg was working in Bremen, Germany, and had good success utilizing European newspapers for his message. Great Britain also had a representative of the Texas Bureau of Immigration in the person of John T. McAdam with headquarters in Manchester. McAdam had "already sent over three hundred persons to Texas, most farmers, and many men of means" according to Loeffler's report. Governor Davis's hope that people coming to Texas would bring money into the state was materializing—at least as Loeffler's report seemed to reflect.[10]

Loeffler's continual push for adequate financial help meshes with the very caring image he and his bureau portrayed in the pages of the report. "All immigrants arrived have been properly taken care of, and no serious cause of complaint reported. Through their own carelessness it occurred now and then that a portion of immigrants' baggage remained behind or was miscarried, and whenever this was made known to me the proper steps for its recovery were taken, and always resulted in the obtaining of the missing articles." He thus conveyed the image of a caring father facilitating the introduction of people into the state. His official report reflects the energy and enthusiasm with which he tackled both the "people part" of the job and the administrative needs.[11]

The main body of the 1872 report was followed by eight separate sections, or "addenda." Superintendent Loeffler included a copy of his circular to county officials, as well as a short printed schedule of favorable rates for transportation and lodging that the Texas Bureau of Immigration had been able to identify and share with potential settlers. He also included a facsimile of the certificate used by the bureau to verify immigrant status for those lower transportation rates. Statistics inserted in the report stated that a total of 41,598 people arrived at the Galveston port in the year 1872. And finally there were several letters from bureau agents reporting on their various work. The Texas Legislature couldn't have asked for a more detailed account of the small bureau's activity, though surely they must have wished that the calls for increased funding were not a part of the report.[12]

New and ingenious approaches to the "immigration problem" came to the surface through the letters of these bureau agents. John Lippard, working in St. Louis, felt visual aids would complement and stimulate the printed word. He explained how he traveled from Missouri to Texas collecting various agricultural products. Then he returned to St. Louis, putting his Texas goods on display a full six weeks before the more northern climate would allow maturing of the same foods. The local papers as well as the national journal *Industrial Age* cooperated in reporting his activities. The visual aids were thus turned into written material, of which Lippard duly "circulated a large number." He proudly proclaimed that this "one act awakened more inquiry concerning the advantages and resources of Texas than anything else I had done." In addition, Lippard parlayed that idea into discussions with the *Industrial Age* Printing Company to produce a weekly paper entitled the *Saint Louis Texan.* He must have felt strongly about the paper's potential, because he advanced $800 of his personal money to initiate the endeavor. His enthusiasm runs throughout his letter, as when he suggests that the bureau has accomplished so much "in so short a time with the limited means on hand."[13]

Dr. Theodore Hertzberg's communication from Germany also brimmed with enthusiasm. He echoed Lippard's statement "I am proud of Texas" with his own version of that feeling as he wrote, "I can proudly say to-day that my road is clear before me, and that the State of Texas will not long remain the *lonely* star in the Union as regards European immigration, but she will soon shine as *the lone star,* receiving the greatest percentage of the transatlantic immigration." Hertzberg's innovative idea involved the collection of $2.50 from each head of a family that had migrated from Europe in the last twenty-five years to Texas. That money, once collected, would serve as the funding for a "Texas paper" to be published in German and French on the continent of Europe. As the bureau agent lodged in New York, William Parsons followed the pattern of his fellow agents by utilizing any means at hand to disseminate information about Texas. Since official documents were not available yet from the bureau itself, he submitted articles to various New York papers and they published his information. He cast abroad his name and address, suggesting anyone interested write him for further information. He claimed to "have set in motion a vast amount of individual migration and several co-operative associations." Both Parsons and Hertzberg mention competition for immigrants by other states. The repetition by several agents of the "competition scare" suggests that whether the place was Germany, New York, or St. Louis, the movement to encourage population migration was definitely part of the tenor of the times.[14]

The bureau continued its work in 1873 with some shift in personnel, continually struggling as an under-financed government bureaucracy. Loeffler pragmatically admitted to using what resources he could find at hand, such as a *Texas Almanac* and map, *Brady's Glimpses of Texas,* and "a pamphlet gotten up by the Texas and Pacific Railway Company." Always aiming at publication of information and its distribution, Loeffler placed ads in current journals. Loeffler purchased a full-page advertisement for the Texas Bureau of Immigration in a business reference work entitled *Frensz's Tariff Investigator of the United States, Enumerating Steamboat, Sail Vessels, Express, Steamships, Immigration, Canal, Railroad, Telegraph.* Published in 1873, *Frensz's Tariff Investigator* was thirty-six pages long and aimed to provide the latest business information for merchants.[15]

The Bureau of Immigration advertisement proudly and clearly identified a schedule, "Showing favorable rates obtained by this Bureau from Steam and Sailing vessels, Railroad Companies and Boarding Houses for the transportation and accommodation of immigrants to our State." In capitalized boldface type the notice stated "ALL RAILROAD AND STEAMSHIP COMPANIES IN TEXAS CONVEY IMMIGRANTS AT HALF PRICE." This coup by Loeffler had involved considerable effort, and he worked to extend those rates to interstate transportation lines. The major burden in transportation was interstate or overseas travel, so the goal of lowering those fees was a primary one for Loeffler. Reduced intrastate rates were one step in that direction. The bureau was to play an active role here, because in order to procure the half-fare rates an immigrant had to obtain "a certificate from this Bureau or its Agents . . . proving the bearers to be *bona fide* Immigrants to Texas."[16]

This published schedule specified rates company by company and identified costs for cabin and steerage passage. For example, the Liverpool and Texas Steamship Company offered cabin passage at $125.00 and steerage for $40.00. Sailing vessels commanded charges of $75.00 and $28.25 respectively with some reduction in fares for children. The ad quoted rail rates from New York as well. The Missouri, Kansas & Texas Railroad offered a $40.00 fare from New York to Dennison City, Texas, but also offered connections from other cities such as St. Louis and Chicago. Various other railroads were listed. Notations included the amount of free baggage allowed for each paying ticket.[17] Luggage limits could be a major concern especially for someone within the United States seeking to relocate with household and farm equipment.

The bureau's advertisement aimed at comprehensiveness. In addition to transportation fees, the page schedule also enumerated costs at boarding houses in New Orleans, Galveston, and Houston. Some hotels offered to carry baggage "at reduced rates." Loeffler noted certain lodging houses that could accommodate German, French, or Bohemian speaking guests most comfortably. The schedule listed the specific names of individuals who could be of assistance at the various transportation hubs such as New York, St. Louis, Galveston, or New Orleans. Names and addresses of bureau agents in these various places were included. The ad concluded with the statement that "further information of Texas as a field for the capitalist, merchant, farmer, and every other willing worker, will be cheerfully given by Gustave Loeffler, Sup't of Immigration for the State of Texas." Then followed the explicit disclaimer, "Agents of this Bureau are strictly forbidden to exact pay for their services from Immigrants."[18]

This extensive effort by the Bureau of Immigration illustrates several crucial points about the "immigration business." First, transportation was a central focus for the immigrant. Expenses entailed in long-distance moving could be prohibitive. The bureau assumed that part of its mission was to help lower those costs. This specific ad offered "special reduction for large numbers together." Large families that traveled with neighbors from one location could save substantially. Second, a multitude of matters faced the immigrant, creating what might seem at times as a morass of details—luggage, meals, lodging along the way, and length of the trip. Loeffler and the bureau offered concrete information to alleviate this distress. In addition, the ad addressed what was probably the ultimate fear for immigrants: being taken advantage of by un-scrupulous people along the way. One specific provision in the state's legisla-tion stated that the bureau should help immigrants "in the guarding them against fraud and chicanery and peculation." Loeffler's disclaimer as to the motives of bureau agents was an effort to quell some of those fears. In its to-tality, this ad demonstrates the extent of the bureau's work and reflects its per-ceived mission. Loeffler and his cohorts wanted to provide help and support to the potential immigrant. The *Frensz's* ad suggests they did this primarily through concrete specific information to facilitate transportation.[19]

Frensz's Tariff Investigator demonstrates one activity of the bureau. Another possibly more widespread delivery of information existed in almanacs, a com-mon publication of the day. The interaction of the Texas Bureau of Immi-gration with these statewide publications is best illustrated by an 1871 an-nouncement in the *Galveston Daily News* where the editor tells his readers about the progress toward publication of the sixteenth edition of the *Alma-nac*. He wrote, "As usual, much of our space will be devoted to such subjects as will be of peculiar interest to immigrants, such as the price and production of lands in the several portions of our State. . . . Instances will be given show-ing that the poorest immigrants may become the owners of good farms of their own in two or three years by ordinary industry and economy." The *News* announcement included the statement, "We also hope to receive from Mr. Loefler [*sic*], the State Commissioner of Immigration, some interesting infor-mation connected with his department." Loeffler was usually more than will-ing to oblige, because publication in such works multiplied the number of people he could reach with his collected information.[20]

Yet another example of bureau activity illustrates the continued emphasis on transportation as well as the trend of the future in cooperating with the growing railway systems. Loeffler maintained constant contact with the rail-roads and employed these connections to further his need to disseminate in-formation. In 1873 the Texas and Pacific Railway actively promoted its west-ward building program through publication of a pamphlet entitled *Notes on Texas and the Texas and Pacific Railway*. Published at the company's head-quarters in Philadelphia, *Notes on Texas* proclaimed the advantages of the Texas and Pacific Railway as an "inter-oceanic railway." The so-called Ap-pendix to the thirty-two-page pamphlet extended for fifteen more pages. It read like an almanac. Under the title "General Facts, Useful to newly arrived Immigrants and those Contemplating Emigration," paragraphs covered such subjects as Texas laws, minerals, industry, crops, and potential locations.

Without formally using Loeffler's name, the booklet listed a schedule of rates by ship and rail supplied by "The Commissioner of Immigration for the State of Texas."[21]

Included in *Notes on Texas* were hints on "How to Select a Location" and reports on "What a Man of Small Means can do in Texas." Trying to dispel notions to the contrary, the pamphlet exclaimed in italics, *"and the fact has been abundantly proven, that white men can labor effectively every day, and all day long, in the exhilarating breezes of our favored land."* Assessing the immigration to Texas up to this point in time, the railroad pamphlet claimed that it "has been almost exclusively of whites, and mostly from the other late slave holding States; but, during the last twelve months, a large number of immigrants have come into northern Texas, from Kansas, Illinois, Indiana, Iowa, and Minnesota."[22] Loeffler was pleased with this pamphlet. Its glowing picture of Texas's potential connected railroad growth to population growth to the ultimate growth of the state. He admitted in a bureau report to using it in the absence of a yet-to-be-funded government publication.

Loeffler utilized a variety of means at hand to dispense current Texas information, but his pet project remained a specific brochure published by the state agency for distribution by its agents. Frustrated, Loeffler pleaded with the Texas Legislature for funds to publish such a document, which by this time was ready to roll off the presses if only financially supported. *Texas: The Home for the Emigrant, From Everywhere* was first published under the direction of Loeffler and later reissued and updated by his successor Jerome B. Robertson. The 1875 edition consisted of forty-three pages pointing to the emphasis on practical current information for distribution through Bureau channels.[23]

Not only did Texas set up a governmental agency to encourage immigration, it also continued to legislate on other issues tangential to immigration. The state incorporated many railroad companies over the years. In an indirect way these chartered railroads then influenced movement of people into the state by hiring workers, shipping people and freight, and advertising the sale of their lands. The Texas Legislature gave legal status to such companies as the "European and Texan Immigration Association" and the "Texas Land and Immigration Company." Real estate agents, land developers, and town boosters all contributed to a variety of organizations interested in attracting immigrants to specific plots of land in Texas. State legislation in the form of homestead laws provided an additional lure to potential immigrants and remained on the books up through the turn of the twentieth century. These statutes were seen by lawmakers to be "of essential value to the State in securing an industrious and law-abiding population."[24]

Yet another close link in the overall scheme of attracting people to Texas was the establishment of a geological survey and a state agency to keep updating this type of information. Governor Davis and later Governor Coke both sought passage of the needed legislation. This extensive activity would imply, on the part of the Texas government, an active, involved role in the state's economic development. The government did not take a hands-off or laissez-faire attitude toward economic growth. Rather it actively sought capital, people, and entrepreneurial skills to help develop the state's potential.[25]

The Bureau of Immigration continued to function during both the Davis and Coke administrations. Through this governmental agency significant collective efforts to influence immigration to Texas were made from 1870 to 1876. The Texas Bureau of Immigration officially had begun under enabling legislation in 1871. As a small arm of the executive branch, it continued to function until 1876 as a governmental agency attracting people to Texas. While persevering in its efforts, political unrest swirled around it and other state agencies. The political scene found Republicans and Democrats fighting for control of the legislature and the governorship. Republican strength waned as Democratic politicians became more numerous and potentially more influential.

The newly elected Thirteenth Legislature that met in 1873 contained a majority of Democrats bent on changing the Republican agenda of the previous three years. The issues were many and controversial. Educational programs, suffrage requirements, internal improvements, budgets, and appropriations claimed the attention of these lawmakers. Debates raged over these topics. In the midst of this storm the Bureau of Immigration continued to function with no major shift in its policies or stated purpose. Cosmetic changes occurred as a new administration took over the governor's mansion. When a Democratic governor took office in January, 1874, he exercised the option to place his own appointees into government positions. For the Bureau of Immigration this meant the replacement of Gustav Loeffler with Jerome B. Robertson as superintendent.

A great deal is known about Jerome B. Robertson but very little about his work as superintendent of the Bureau of Immigration. Born in Kentucky, Robertson had his first contact with Texas when he served in a volunteer company of eighty-six men responding to Texas's President Burnett's call for help against the Mexicans in 1836. After serving in the cause of Texas Independence, he was permanently furloughed in June 1837. Robertson returned to Kentucky to settle his affairs there and then moved to Texas, his newly adopted state. His early years in Kentucky had included an apprenticeship to

Jerome Bonaparte Robertson, shown here in post–Civil War civilian clothes (precise date unknown), served as the second superintendent for the Texas Bureau of Immigration from 1874 to 1876. Courtesy Harold B. Simpson, Hill College History Complex, Confederate Research Center, Hillsboro, Texas.

a hatter and then some experience with the hatter's trade in St. Louis. He also attended Medical School at Transylvania University in Kentucky as well as studied medicine under the tutelage of a doctor in Owensboro. In this way Robertson earned the title of doctor and practiced medicine on and off throughout his lifetime. A military title seemed to be his preference however. He served in many capacities on the Texas frontier and in the Confederacy held the rank of general upon the cessation of hostilities. He is probably remembered most as a leader of Hood's Brigade, fighting under Lee in the eastern theater. He succeeded General John B. Hood to that position in September 1862.[26]

In addition to his medical and military careers, Robertson served in several capacities as public servant and politician. Living in Washington County, he was a member of the Texas state house from 1847 to 1849 and the state senate from 1849 to 1851, after earlier working as coroner and postmaster of his

county. One source labeled him "a rabid secessionist" in the 1861 state secession convention. After fighting in the Civil War, he was paroled and returned
to Independence, Texas, where he attempted to support himself and his family as a physician. Robertson had married Mary Elizabeth Cummins in
March, 1838, and together they had three children, two of whom survived in-
fancy. Mary died in April, 1868, and Robertson remained a widower for the
next ten years. In those years after the War, Robertson became active again in
his local Masonic order. He also encouraged and helped organize the Hood's
Texas Brigade Association, which officially formed in May, 1872. He served in
multiple capacities in this association of confederate veterans and had a special interest in collecting the history of his brigade.[27]

Governor Richard Coke in 1874 appointed Robertson as the Democratic
administration's choice for head of the Bureau of Immigration. Robertson
held that position for two and a half years until the bureau was dissolved.
Throughout his tenure in office he maintained the confidence of Governor
Coke if not of the legislature. In an extensive message to the Texas legislature
in 1875, the governor praised efforts at increasing the Texas population and ap-
plauded the superintendent's efforts. He said, "General Robertson has labored
faithfully and incessantly, and it is believed, considering the slender resources
at his command, most efficiently for the promotion of immigration." That
Robertson later served as an emigration agent for the Houston and Texas Central Railroad would indicate he carried this interest into the years after the demise of the bureau and used the same skills to continue making a living.[28]

The striking aspect of the 1874 changeover in the Bureau of Immigration
remains the continuity it demonstrates in Texas's interest in attracting immigrants. No dramatic break with Loeffler's efforts were suggested or made.
Robertson carried forward the same goals of the bureau's first superintendent.
Robertson saw transportation as key to the success of importing new people
into the state. So he continued to work for reduced rail and steamship rates.
He also felt strongly the need to provide good specific information. The publication of the pamphlet *Texas: The Home for the Emigrant, From Everywhere*
remained central to the bureau's mission.

The 1874 report of the superintendent of immigration expressed the frustration of a governmental executive agency trying to accomplish its goals and
purposes with little or no funding by the legislature. Letter writing remained
a constant challenge and burden within those funding parameters. The fact
that both Loeffler and Robertson referred to the large number of incoming
requests for information and their agency's struggle to keep up with dispensing information in reply tells us much about the people of the time. Letter

writing was a finely tuned skill of even barely literate individuals. People wrote letters to family and friends. But they also wrote to the stranger asking for help and/or information. In the pre-electronic world of nineteenth-century United States, paper and pencil served a valuable function in making connections. Loeffler referred to letters "from every State in the Union—even from California . . . Europe and the Canadas." Robertson later wrote that the "demands . . . for information . . . have steadily increased . . . and are now one hundred per cent greater than they were at my last annual report." Postage and stationery required a significant portion of each year's budget. In the absence of copies of these many letters—incoming or outgoing—we can only wonder how they were worded or exactly what they said. The repeated emphasis by both superintendents of the bureau on concrete, correct, and up-to-date information suggests that recipients of letters from the bureau received the most current information available at the time.[29]

Both Loeffler and Robertson made sustained efforts to get something into publication. A published document would serve several purposes. It would facilitate the transferal of information without long letter writing. While the downside of that formal nature might be the lack of a personal touch, it would be compensated by the comprehensiveness of the information and the documents' authoritative appearance. Secondly, it would demonstrate the efficiency and energy of Texas to publish such a document. And thirdly, it would be a source of information more easily and more widely passed on to friends and family.

The bureau did eventually get its own brochure into print. When finally it rolled off the press, the fairly nondescript pamphlet published by the Bureau of Immigration said reams in the title alone: *Texas: The Home for the Emigrant, From Everywhere.* The family image evoked by the word "home" trumpeted the main purpose of the bureau. In facilitating the growth of families and homesteads, the bureau meant to dispel the frontier image of the state's past, emphasize stability and a sense of place, while encouraging the influx of newcomers. The inclusivity expressed by the phrase "from everywhere" also projected an image of arms reaching out to embrace the multitudes.[30]

No sketches or photographs graced the forty-three-page document. Multiple tables, charts, and testimonials made up the substance of this Bureau of Immigration publication. In this format the pamphlet also succeeded in presenting an image of official information, unprejudiced by private business interests looking to make money from the immigrants. The tenor of the pamphlet can be seen by the repeated use of assumed authorities on topics of interest. For example, one section read, "For the information of the readers hereof, I insert a letter from Col. John James, a practical sheep-grower, and a substantial and reliable citizen of thirty years residence in the State, whose statements may be relied on as correct." Such affidavits sprinkle the pages for a readership that would value such authoritative statements.[31]

In *Texas: The Home for the Emigrant, From Everywhere,* tables and statistics were used to attract potential immigrants. Numbers provided annual temperatures, amount of rainfall, and humidity totals. All of these figures were marshaled to tell the story of a healthful climate, with plenty of rain for crops, and temperate weather for year-round work. A farm ledger list was reproduced to give a hint of the typical costs in production and the rhythm of farming in Texas. Statistics showed the commerce at Galveston's port, with emphasis on imports and exports, especially cotton. Inclusion of such information pointed out the extent of trade in the state and the access to markets for Texas farmers. Yet another list gave counties by name and the increase in their population from 1850 to 1870.[32]

This no-frills report was filled with advice for the immigrant: Consider renting first upon arrival. Buy land after you have scouted out the area, in order to make the best-informed decision about purchase. Travel by wagon is an option to be considered, because you can bring your animals and livestock with you. If you end up with an extra horse or mule or wagon, you will surely find a market for them. If you are a lawyer or a physician you "ought not to be advised to come to Texas, unless [you] can come with the additional determination to seek employment in tilling the soil." Write to a county clerk for specific information on that county. If he can't help you he will put you in touch with a "reliable citizen" who can. "Should the immigrant wish to raise sugar, rice, cotton, corn and stock, let him settle in *lower* Central Texas. Should he wish to raise cotton, corn and stock, let him settle in *middle* Central Texas. Should he wish to raise cotton wheat corn and stock, let him settle in *upper* Central Texas." Travel in groups—such travel lowers initial rail costs, since railroads offer group rates. Come to Texas in the fall—this is the best time so that preparations can be made for making a crop the first year here.[33]

Choices were presented to the potential immigrant. Information to whet everyone's appetite filled the pages of *Texas: The Home for the Emigrant, From Everywhere.* Many items presented in the pamphlet may have encouraged the immigrant to develop a new concept of the potential in Texas. For example, the longer growing seasons and opportunity to plant more than one crop in a year probably caused some who wintered in snow-laden countries to consider moving south. Statements about current taxes must have made many pause over higher tax rates in their homeland. Potential for receiving a homestead of 160 acres must assuredly have lured some to trek to Texas.[34]

Reassurances were also a part of the bureau's pamphlet. It labeled as an "erroneous opinion" that northern and western men were not wanted in Texas, or safe in Texas. The pamphlet printed sections of the state constitution to demonstrate the availability of homesteads and their exemptions from forced sale for debts. This information demonstrated the liberality of the state government and its desire to make settlers secure in their homes. Another way of reassuring the immigrant was to point to the negatives in Texas, showing them to be in reality a positive. Describing the notorious "northers" everyone had heard about as "winds coming suddenly from the north" changing the temperature "from the temperate to and below the freezing point in a few hours," the pamphlet went on to show the positives of such northers. It referred to "their purifying effect of the atmosphere and beneficial effect on the health of the people." Addressing these kinds of fears, the bureau's information sought to reassure potential immigrants that while change is inherent in the experience of moving, that change need not be a negative experience.[35]

Texas: The Home for the Emigrant, From Everywhere did not explain labor-hiring conditions in Texas. Comment existed about the use of Mexicans as shepherds for the livestock, but no mention was made in the booklet of black workers. The only reference to women's needs was made by a man in the sheep growing region who wrote, "wool-growers . . . are not likely to have many neighbors. Therefore, men having families, used to society, must have a residence in a village as near to his business as he can find a suitable location. Otherwise, the females in the family are lonesome, being often left alone, while the men are attending to the flocks." City living was not described. The assumption throughout the document was that people would settle on the land and raise crops or livestock.[36]

It would be interesting to compare later editions of this work, if the Bureau of Immigration had existed beyond 1876. Would their approach have changed over the years? Would their heavy emphasis on bare statistics have continued? Would urban life have been extolled as yet another opportunity for the immigrant? Would certain immigrant nationalities have been discountenanced? Would references to blacks and Mexicans have changed? Unfortunately, we don't have that luxury of comparison. This pamphlet stands alone as "the" government document of the era. Later, private enterprise would enter the scene producing veritably hundreds of fliers, booklets, maps, and pamphlets extolling the virtues of life in Texas. But *Texas: The Home for the Emigrant,*

From Everywhere was the government's effort at attracting the immigrant to its borders.

Robertson's sense of frustration over budget constraints propelled him to use an earlier technique: comparing Texas's efforts with those of other places in the United States and abroad. Praising the work of Wyoming's Board of Immigration he claimed that the territory of Wyoming was "better known to potential immigrants" than Texas. He praised the aggressive efforts of many western states, and in appealing to state loyalty Robertson was in his own way shouting at the legislators to see the impact of their parsimonious behavior.[37]

In addition to the "competition scare" efforts, Robertson resorted to bottom-line economics to argue his case. "Nor is the pecuniary benefit from immigration remote; for the immigrant, as soon as he arrives among us, begins to bear his proportion of the expenses of the State government, to the extent of his poll, State and county taxes (leaving out the value of the increased productions by his labor); he lightens the burthen of those who were here before him." The rhetoric continued, "Double the population of Texas, and we will hear no more of high taxes."[38] The tactic of speaking to lawmakers' pocketbooks would seem a good one, but in reality it did not seem to sway the legislators at all. In fact, as Robertson continued to plead for better funding, the push for a convention, which ultimately met in 1875, to formulate a new constitution was in full swing. That convention, dominated by those wanting retrenchment in government spending, ultimately spelled doomsday for the Texas Bureau of Immigration.

Superintendent Robertson and Governor Coke continued throughout the 1874–76 period to support government involvement in the effort to attract immigration to Texas. In one of many booster speeches, Governor Coke referred to "an immigration policy which shall make known to the world the unrivaled advantages of Texas." In spite of Democratic Party calls for cuts in state spending, Governor Coke encouraged liberality in connection with the Bureau of Immigration as he worked to stir up patriotism for state endeavors:

The one thing needful in Texas is population. We want labor, thrifty industrious men and women. . . . The eyes of the world are now turned to Texas; her vast resources, the unequaled inducements she offers to immigrants, is beginning to be appreciated; our railroad communications now tap the hive where the population swarms, and Texas is easy of access; the tide of immigration now pouring into her borders is strong and swelling; now is the propitious time by wise legislation to

inaugurate a policy which shall to the fullest extent utilize our splendid opportunities to make Texas the home of the immigrant from every quarter of the world.

Still struggling with the elected representatives over the budget, the governor
sent yet another message to the congressmen stating, "The estimate for the
Bureau of Immigration, I am satisfied, is not as liberal as it should be. . . . I
recommend that this appropriation be increased to an amount commensurate
with the important part this bureau should perform in settling and developing the State."[39]

Continued underfunding hampered bureau work. But Governor Coke
continued to cheerlead for Robertson and the Bureau of Immigration. What
kind of immigrant was Coke imagining as being attracted to Texas? He spoke
about their coming from "rural districts," thus seeing them primarily as agriculturalists. They "would bring with them resources" and would be "of the
most desirable character, intelligent reading persons." He envisioned a literate
immigrant—a self-starter who could read. Coke sensed the value of the written word as propaganda as well. He encouraged, "As near as it can be done, we
must place immigrants on our standpoint, give them our knowledge and experience of Texas, and to make them come to Texas for homes, and prefer
Texas as we do to any other country." We must "as far as possible put them in
possession of the reasons which influence us, and this can only be done by a
judicious, liberal advertisement of Texas, as she is."[40] Coke pointed to the inter-relatedness of immigration to the entire economic development of the
state. For Governor Coke it was critical to broaden the legislators' view of
the world. He spoke about markets and a reliable labor force. He pointed to
the economic power of merchants with many customers and the value of
cheap transportation for those commercial goods. One major benefit, according to the governor, was increased political power in the national arena when
the state's population increased, since representation in Congress would increase also. Coke wanted the congressmen to see the value of a little money
invested now reaping large rewards in the future.[41]

That the population of Texas increased over the years 1865 to 1876 is
recorded in the statistics compiled by census takers. That the Bureau of
Immigration was instrumental in a significant way in affecting that movement cannot be so easily documented. What can be shown, however, is the
steady activity of a state agency—the Texas Bureau of Immigration. The belief in concerted action, a carryover from the immediate years after the Civil
War, propelled the efforts to establish a Bureau of Immigration in addition
to efforts at providing tax money to run such an agency. A confidence in the

value of written information also permeated the efforts of this governmental body to influence the direction of migration to its territories. Both a belief in cooperative effort and a value placed on written words motivated the Texas Legislature to experiment with a governmental agency aimed at attracting people to Texas. This experiment came to a decisive end when Texans chose to ratify a new constitution in 1876.

CHAPTER 3

CLOSING THE GOVERNMENT DOOR

The Legislature shall have no power to appropriate any of the public money for the establishment and maintenance of a Bureau of Immigration, or for any purpose of bringing immigrants to the State.
Article 16, Section 56, 1876 Texas Constitution

With this succinct wording, the state of Texas through its formally elected representative body officially closed a governmental door to encouraging immigrants to populate its immense territory. It did not categorically deny an interest in attracting people to Texas, but it did clearly state that no government money could be spent in any such endeavor. How did Texas move from its 1869 constitutional provision allowing for a special governmental bureaucracy, facilitating and coordinating immigration, to this blanket prohibition? The bottom line in all the decision making seems to be money—the state budget. Anger over perceived heavy taxation crystallized a coalition that saw government money spent for the purposes of attracting immigrants to Texas as an extravagance the state could ill afford. The central story revolves around the decision to revise the state's constitution.

Much agitation existed in 1873 and 1874 over the issue of a new constitution for Texas. As the Republican-controlled legislature lost seats to the Democratic Party, a rising tide of public opinion turned away from the 1869 constitution. When the Texas voters in 1873 ultimately voted Republican governor, Edmund Davis, out of office and Democratic governor, Richard Coke, into office, the noise increased. One scholar suggests that Democrats saw the 1869 constitution as "the last reminder of radical control in Texas" and felt an absolute political duty to destroy it.[1]

Yet Governor Coke did not automatically join in the call for a new constitution. Upon his election, he shared concerns about changing the current constitution and encouraged the legislature to consider preparing amendments to improve it. He chronicled the changes around the state with characteristic optimism by saying, "new population with new ideas are filling the country, new industries are springing up. Enterprise and rapid improvement is the order of the day." In this way he gave credit to the tide of immigration moving into the state and its potential influence. Finally in early 1875 Governor Coke accepted the stirrings within his party and encouraged the legislature to issue a call for a special constitutional convention. In his address to the Texas congress he wrote, "The present constitution of Texas is by universal consent admitted to be in many essential particulars an extremely defective instrument . . . and the time and temper of the people are propitious for the work of constructing a new constitution."[2]

On September 6, 1875, a constitutional convention began to meet in Austin. With ninety elected delegates, twenty-one standing committees were formed. Of these committees one worked to formulate the state's direction on the issue of immigration. There were ten men on the committee, with Jacob Waelder as its chair. See table 1 for a list of the members of the committee and some of their biographical information.

All the men were married. Davis was the only black on the committee and one of only five in the whole convention. He was also the committee's only Republican member. Half of the committee members also held Grange

Table 1
STATE IMMIGRATION COMMITTEE MEMBERS

Person	Occupation	Age	County	Nativity Represented	Arrival In Texas
Jacob Waelder	Lawyer	55	Bexar	Germany	1852
Julius E. Arnim	Farmer	47	Lavaca	Prussia	1850
Joe P. Douglass	Merchant Farmer	45	Cherokee	Alabama	1857
Caton Erhard	Druggist	53	Bastrop	Germany	1839
Wm. C. Holmes	Physician	34	Grayson	S. Carolina	1867
J. L. Johnson	Farmer Minister	51	Franklin	Tennessee	1845
Sam B. Killough	Farmer	62	Robertson	Tennessee	1837
B. D. Martin	Farmer	51	Hunt	Virginia	1860
Bird B. Davis	Farmer	48	Wharton	N. Carolina	1858
Jonathon Russell	Farmer	51	Wood	Alabama	1847

Source: Walsh & Pilgrim's Directory of the Officers and Members of the Constitutional Convention.

COME TO TEXAS + 42

membership—Douglass, Holmes, Johnson, Martin, and Russell. In trying to analyze the committee's make-up, it is difficult to see any significant trend. Three of the ten were born in Europe. None were native Texans, but then there were only four of those in the entire convention.[3]

The issue of Granger influence on the constitutional convention is of primary importance. One past historical argument runs as follows: A large number of the constitutional delegates were members of the Patrons of Husbandry. The final constitution did not provide for a Bureau of Immigration or include any encouragement of immigration to the state of Texas. Thus, the Grangers must have been against immigration, i.e. the farmers in Texas did not like immigrants. While the argument progresses logically, it misconnects motive and outcome.[4]

The Grange, or Patrons of Husbandry as it was formally called, was a growing force in Texas life and "easily the largest interest group" in Texas politics. The State Grange organized in October 1873 and "spread rapidly in Texas" with a membership between forty thousand and fifty thousand farmers. It "ranked second in size only to that in Kentucky." Although the actual discussions during meetings of local Grange groups were normally closed to outsiders or outside reporting, the Grange outlook on topics of the day did filter into newspapers. These accounts help to flesh out the Grange "position" on political topics.[5]

While no one monolithic position existed among Grangers, trends can be identified. Governmental budgets, taxes, and spending programs grabbed the attention of Grange members. Most of these members were farmers working to eke out a living from the Texas soil. Their hopes for future agricultural production were often thwarted in their minds by the excessive intrusion of government in their personal affairs, by the lack of good, cheap transportation for their products, and existence of oppressive centralized government. As these farmers viewed the rising taxes of the Governor Davis–dominated Twelfth Legislature and the subsequent allocations under Governor Coke, they saw future disaster in big government spending. According to historian Seth Shepard McKay, members "all over the state were outspoken in favor of retrenchment and reform." Thus as a group in the constitutional convention Grange members favored less taxation, lower government spending, and less government bureaucracy. But to suggest that they voted en masse is misleading.[6]

The debate over supporting government expenditures to entice immigrants to Texas was not a battle between the Democrats and the Republicans. The convention was overwhelmingly a body dominated by Democrats, with only fourteen Republicans out of ninety delegates. The vocal discussions on the convention floor were most frequently debates among Democrats with differing opinions, rather than interparty squabbles. The floor debate on the immigration provision follows that pattern, both in the final recommendations of the immigration committee and in the convention debate itself.[7]

The first notice taken of the immigration issue at the convention was on the fifth day, September 10, 1875. W. W. Whitehead, a Democrat representing Tyler County, introduced a resolution that was referred to the Committee on Immigration. Whitehead first moved to Texas in 1851 from Alabama. He was a married man and listed his occupation as farmer and doctor. At the time of the convention he was forty-seven years old and held Grange membership. His resolution requested the Committee on Immigration to refrain from inserting any provision for a Bureau of Immigration into the final constitution.[8]

A second resolution relating to immigration came from Caton Erhard. Introduced on September 30, it was also referred to the same committee. The resolution reflected Erhard's personal experience as an immigrant as well as his sense of history in trying to clarify the rationale for his viewpoint. He encouraged the continuation of the Bureau of Immigration as a state agency requiring inclusion in the constitution. He assumed such an agency would continue to publish written materials including "good and disinterested advice." He noted that many immigrants were not native speakers of English. Then in an effort to create empathy with those potential immigrants, he said that such written materials were crucial, "the necessity of which all those will appreciate who ever were in any foreign country." Looking at the subject historically, he reminded the delegates that the Preamble to the United States Declaration of Independence included a grievance against King George accusing him of failing to pass laws to encourage immigration to the then colonies of Great Britain. Mr. Erhard went on to note that Texas during the Republic days had induced immigration by giving land to newcomers "being well aware their newly-acquired Republic would be valueless without immigration." Suggesting a tradition in Texas of encouraging immigrants to move to the state, Erhard saw the Bureau of Immigration as fitting perfectly within that past heritage.[9]

Just a few days after Erhard's resolution was referred to the Committee on Immigration, the committee reported to the full convention its majority decision. After debating the resolutions referred to them in committee, they recommended, "the people ought not *to be taxed for any such purposes,* and therefore respectfully recommend that a clause be put in the organic law restraining the Legislature from ever appropriating money for such purposes."

The report was received and placed on the docket for later discussion. Two members of the Immigration Committee served notice that they would be submitting separate minority reports. Only five of the ten members signed the majority report, leaving us to wonder what were the opinions of the other three supposedly in the majority. Of the five who signed—Russell, Killough, Arnim, Holmes, and Douglass—all were white and Democrats. Three were Grangers. Four of the five had originally lived in another of the southern states, while one, Arnim, was foreign-born. The official position of the majority members claimed taxes as their central concern. Nowhere in the short report is there a statement against foreigners or newcomers. Nowhere does the majority report use racial antagonism or party allegiance to define its position. The minority reports submitted later were much fuller in their presentations and help give at least a partial insight into the discussions made behind closed doors as the committee was hammering out its report.[10]

The chairmanship of the Immigration Committee originally belonged to Jacob Waelder. When he found himself at odds with the majority of the committee members, he must have stepped down from that leadership position. The name listed as chair for the majority report was that of Jonathan Russell. Waelder submitted a minority report on October 5. His report made several relevant points. First, while he conceded the lack of success on the part of the current Bureau of Immigration, he expressed the sincere desire to continue the information-sharing tasks of that agency. He suggested the formation of a Bureau of Agriculture, Statistics, and Immigration. This state agency would obtain, collate, and disseminate Texas information. Waelder valued written information "coming from a public officer, by authority of the State" claiming it would have greater influence on strangers than any other document prepared by some private organization or company. Second, he tried to develop support from other legislators by showing how such information would not only be helpful for immigrants, but would also inform Texans of their state's resources and potential. This idea of information for internal use had not been emphasized before by earlier legislation on immigration.[11]

Waelder valued concrete and specific information written down and disseminated for Texans and Texans-to-be. Another angle to his argument against adoption of the majority resolution involved the issue of fairness and "justice," as he perceived it, as well as diverse needs throughout the state. One short section of this minority report by Waelder gives us a slight window into one of the arguments that may have colored the immigration debate. Waelder wrote, "If all sections of the State do not need, or desire increase of population, there are other sections whose prosperity would be enhanced thereby."

Maybe here were shadows from the 1869 constitutional convention fight over division of Texas into two or more states. That debate showed that certain areas of Texas had needs different from other sections and saw state division as a solution for those differences. It is an obvious observation that the western and northwestern portions of Texas were in greater need of people to fill up their unused lands than were eastern and southeastern counties. Saying this, however, says nothing about perceived desires by plantation owners in these eastern and coastal regions for replacement labor for the ex-slaves. It says nothing about desires to break up large plots of land into smaller tenant farms and the hiring of labor to produce a crop on those lands. Maybe the committee argument revolved around varying perceptions of the need for more settlers in different areas of the state.[12]

Waelder's minority report not only opposed the majority report's absolute prohibition against expenditure of state funds, but subtly suggested a novel approach to the issue. His suggestion shifted the focus of the old Bureau of Immigration's efforts from direct solicitation of immigrants to publication of information meant for a wider readership. He thus attempted to broaden the appeal for such publications by broadening the audience. He refrained from direct support for the current agency known as the Bureau of Immigration, insisting rather on the continuation of efforts to disseminate information that would attract people to Texas.

A second minority report, submitted October 6, came from Caton Erhard. He presented a carefully worded tentative article for a constitution that included a bureau "which shall have supervision and control of all matters connected with immigration." Erhard must have felt the money issue was the primary argument to be refuted, for most of his efforts were directed to that subject. He boldly tackled the subject of taxes. Instead of lowering taxation, Erhard maintained that the destruction of the bureau and the failure to make any other provisions would result in "an increase of taxation" due to the decrease in immigration to the state. The earlier Davis theory that more bodies means more money and spreads the tax base was being revived by Erhard in his own way. He was suggesting that a larger population would widen the state's tax base and thus relieve tax burdens on all.[13]

Yet another stand taken by Erhard refuted the statement presented by some in the convention that immigration would happen naturally and needed no additional assistance. Erhard perceived this view as shortsighted. Again drawing on arguments similar to late 1860s dialogue, Erhard contended, "By individual effort we may perhaps partially carry out the wishes of the people; by combined effort we *most certainly* will." For him concerted effort far outweighed any benefits of false economy in allowing the state immigration agency to disappear and expect private individual efforts to supplant that work. For Erhard this would be taking a big step backward. Erhard continued to address the money issue directly.[14]

Like Waelder before him, Erhard accepted negative reaction to the perceived inefficiency of the past bureau administration. But he pushed the point by saying that "a fair trial of an immigration bureau has never been had in this State." Erhard then presented a resolution calling for a constitutional provision allowing a Bureau of Immigration with power and money "for the purpose of promoting and protecting immigration, and for the maintenance of said bureau." No portion of the resolution suggested state aid to support assisted travel for potential immigrants and neither was there a specific reference to pamphlets or written material. Erhard's minority report was accepted and referred for later discussion. The first extensive debate on the floor of the convention began on October 14. One legal historian refers to the debate over the continuation of a bureau as "passionate" with "eloquent" speeches proclaiming all aspects of the issue.[15]

Delegate Waelder initiated the debate with his amendment seeking to delete any prohibition of appropriation of money by the state. According to the newspaper account of the day's proceedings, he was concerned about how such a provision would be viewed by those outside Texas. He feared potential settlers would perceive a hostility by Texans toward foreigners and therefore decide to migrate to other developing states in the west. Caton Erhard offered yet another amendment, suggesting that "immigration shall be encouraged by the Legislature by all means within their power." Convention delegates tabled both amendments, leaving the subject of immigration to be debated at a later time.[16]

The major floor debate took place on Tuesday, October 19. Jonathan Russell, representing Wood County in the northeastern section of the state, introduced the majority decision of the Committee on Immigration rejecting any provision for a special bureau. Jacob Waelder quickly offered a substitute article calling for the establishment of a bureau of agriculture, statistics, and immigration. According to McKay, who bases his analysis of the convention's proceedings on a newspaper account of the day, Waelder then addressed the assembled body at length, attempting a seemingly coy negative remark with the hope of crystallizing support for state aid to immigration. Waelder claimed that past immigration had helped to steadily build up many counties in the state, but then suggested that there did not seem to be much of a desire for immigration at present. Surely Texans would not want to exclude such people from participating in future state development, hinted Waelder.[17]

At this point in the early moments of the debate, the *Journal* proceedings record that John H. Reagan, a lawyer, farmer, Granger, and resident of Texas since 1839, then spoke to the issue with some support for Waelder's proposal. Reagan reportedly sought to amend Waelder's proposal for the newer bureau by inserting the phrase, "provided, that the moneys expended by this bureau shall be for the collection and dissemination of information on these subjects, and that no money shall be paid out for bringing immigrants to the State." The wording of Reagan's amendment suggests two things. First, there seemed to be support for some kind of central agency for collecting and disseminating information. Second, there was little or no support for direct state aid to immigrants.[18]

Reagan's compromise sought to encourage immigration but limit that encouragement to written words. Reagan's moderate position, if it had been adopted, would have provided the state of Texas much flexibility over the next eighty years. It would have allowed the expenditure of money for immigration encouragement, as succeeding legislative bodies saw fit to apply money to specific times and places. Reagan was a respected member of the Texas elite, having served as postmaster general of the Confederacy. At the time of his participation in the constitutional convention he was also waiting to serve as congressman-elect to the U.S. House of Representatives.[19]

The issues on this debate seemed to revolve around three schemes: one, government money to be spent on a specific bureau of immigration to facilitate the bringing of immigrants to Texas; two, government money to be spent on accumulating and dispensing information about Texas to entice immigrants to come; and three, no tax money to be appropriated for any effort to attract people to the state. Erhard spearheaded the first scheme, Waelder proposed the second, and J. Russell of Wood County, serving as chair of the Committee on Immigration, pushed for no money, no bureau, no governmental support to encourage immigration. Reagan's suggestion thus became a compromise possibility that entered consideration as option four.

The debate escalated and political oratory intensified the battle lines. Waelder had earlier suggested that probably no interest in immigration existed at the present time in Texas. R. Sansom from Williamson County got hooked on that baited statement. He claimed that people were not opposed to immigration (probably the very statement Waelder was hoping would come from the lips of the antibureau faction), but rather to any separate bureau for that purpose. Sansom pointed to his earlier suggestion that a clerk be utilized at the state comptroller's office for the collating of statistical information relating to agriculture and mining interests. In this way Sansom admitted the need for viable information, but he expressed his personal unwillingness to spend extensive state money on the project.[20]

More debate followed. John Henry Brown, a printer from Dallas County, supported some moderate efforts at providing written information for immigrants but felt that climate, soil, good government, and low taxes would, in and of themselves, attract people to the state. While arguing for the demise of the bureau, Brown insisted on clarifying that J. B. Robertson, the current head of the Texas Bureau of Immigration, was not the object of this debate. Brown registered admiration for the work of Robertson and shared hopes that Robertson's expertise might find a useful outlet in the future.[21]

The next speech was a lengthy one by Henry C. King of Kendall County—a county situated just northwest of San Antonio. King's argument approached the subject from a sectional perspective. He noted that the "western half of Texas is comparatively unpeopled." But he quickly added that no matter the locale, the subject of immigration is one "in which the whole State as a body politic, is virtually interested." In attempting to enlarge the vision of the constitutional delegates, his arguments covered a broad spectrum. He used statistics to say, "it is well known that immigrants will bring with them about $500 per capita, or about $1,500 to each head of a family." He pointed out that these families typically buy land, become producers, and then, obviously taxpayers.[22]

According to King, Texas needed people. He asked the assembled group, "Now, how are we to get them?" With options of waiting for the natural process of slow in-migration or utilizing an aggressive information campaign, King supported the latter:

> I venture to say, Mr. President, that there are but few members of this Convention who are not in receipt of many letters from one quarter of the country or another, making inquiries about Texas. They want to know all about the climate, soil, products, society and the respective advantages of different localities, and they generally exhibit, by the character and number of the questions they ask, as much ignorance of Texas as anxiety for exact information.

The importance of the written word was central to King's argument. He spoke of the "streamlet" coming to Texas "as compared to the swelling tide" heading to other parts of the nation. Assertively, he then said, "They would all come to Texas if they knew the facts."[23]

Supporting the idea of governmental money to collect and distribute information about Texas, King went on to decry any attempt to place the majority report resolution into the constitution:

> Adopt such a declaration in your organic law, and what does it announce to the world? Why that Texas has departed from its traditional policy; and you may say to the stranger, . . ."We do not want you in Texas, stay where you are, or go elsewhere for a home." I hope this Convention will not place the State in such an attitude before Christendom!

He ended his speech warning, "We will commit a grave blunder if we place the State in an attitude of hostility to immigration."[24]

The debate, as happens in many committee or convention debates, seemed to focus on two different questions, unfortunately mixing them and muddying the issue. While the Bureau of Immigration as set up by the 1869 constitution allowed for the expenditure of state money to actually assist in transporting immigrants into and around the state, such moneys were never appropriated or used in that way. Tax money was spent to collect information and publish it, as well as to provide expenses for Texas immigration agents in the United States and in Europe. This distinction, concerning past legislation establishing the Texas Bureau of Immigration, got lost amid the emotion of convention debate.

The last extended speech before final vote on the measure came from W. T. G. Weaver of Gainesville. He resided in Cooke County, located on the far northern border of Texas along the Red River. Weaver was not a Granger but a lawyer who had come to Texas at the age of three from Illinois with his family. His vociferous speech asserted "there never was a day when the people of Texas were not ready with open arms to welcome immigrants without reference to their nationality." In glowing political rhetoric he spoke of the "liberal spirited people of Texas" and boldly pronounced, "It is not foreign immigration they oppose—it is the institution created by the Constitution of 1869, known as the Bureau of Immigration." Then chronicling the salaries of Bureau employees, Weaver stated that Texans did not want to pull that kind of money "out of their [own] pockets . . . to hire immigrants to come here."[25]

Weaver expressed the hope that he was preaching at the funeral of the Bureau of Immigration. Then in a much louder voice, with passionate overtones, he continued, "But again we are told that it will advertise Texas. *Advertise Texas!* Why, sir, her name, fame, and territory are parts of the world's greatest history; her natural resources, her fertility . . . are known wherever civilization extends. . . . Why sir, you might as well talk of sending a dispatch to China, that gold has been discovered in California. It is known in all Christian lands, and Stanley is telling it today, perhaps, in Central Africa that Texas has more wealth in her bosom than a hundred Californias." Weaver praised all those immigrants who had come before, especially the industrious, hard-working Germans in the middle portion of the state. But he went on to say that these same immigrants would do a better job of encouraging further immigration among their fellow countrymen through the sending of their letters or newspapers, land agents' circulars, and almanacs. For Weaver, a Texan's task was to, "stand in the Gulf shores and say, welcome to this Canaan of fair and happy lands. We say that millions of hospitable homes and rich acres are waiting for your hands without price when you come, *but not one cent to hire you to do so.*" A few moments later the proposal to accept Waelder's ideas as amended by Reagan was defeated by a vote of thirty-three yeas and forty-seven nays. The convention thus accepted the full majority report and moved on to the next day's business.[26]

The issue still sputtered for a few more times on the convention floor. F. S. Stockdale, a lawyer and stock raiser from Calhoun County, moved on October 20 to reconsider the vote of the previous day. There seems to have been lengthy but unrecorded debate and a decision was made to place the issue on the calendar for October 27, one week later. Due to other debates, the immigration discussion was postponed one more day and the motion to reconsider was taken up on October 28. The motion lost by a vote of forty-five to thirty-one. The October 19 decision stood.[27]

Who supported this major change in outlook? Was the discussion over immigration a debate involving ethnic hatreds? party politics? black versus white viewpoints? Or was it a case of Grange opposition to newcomers in Texas? A definite "NO" must be registered against the idea that farmers who also happened to be Grange members were against immigration. It might prove helpful to buttress this point by going outside the constitutional convention itself and looking at various Grange activities around the time of the convention. In August, just one month before the convention met, the Patrons of Husbandry held their second annual state meeting in Dallas. Their elected leader was William W. Lang, whose title within the organization was Worthy Master. His address to the assembled group, reported in full in the published *Proceedings,* did not make any specific reference to immigration or immigrants, but it did state, "Greater economy in all national and State expenditures is imperatively demanded."[28]

Those same *Proceedings,* however, included a fascinating submission by

A. B. Kerr, a Texas Grange member from Fayette County. In a letter addressed to the Worthy Master and Grange Members, Kerr reported his efforts during the past year over the signature, "A. B. Kerr, Immigration Agent." His report to fellow Grange members bubbled with enthusiasm, both for the Grange and for his perceived mission representing that group. He documented his appointment by Governor Coke on the recommendation of the superintendent of the Texas Bureau of Immigration to the position of immigration agent for the state and reported on the beginning of his travels east. He wrote, "I did this the more cheerfully, without fee or reward, save an interest in common with every true Patron in the State, believing that great benefits would result both to our people and those coming among us." Then in true booster fashion he spoke of the extensive land resources of "our great empire State" envisioning them cultivated and contributing to the state's economic growth. Seeing Grange interests as synonymous with the state's development, Kerr viewed the influx of these farmers as inaugurating "a scene of prosperity without parallel in the annals of this Republic."[29]

Then this Grange member and state-certified Immigration Agent chronicled his work on the east coast. "I set about making arrangements for immigrants to reach our borders with as little expense as possible, and first tried to negotiate terms with the different railroads leading North and East, and I am happy to say, found them wide awake to their own interest and disposed to make the very best terms in their power." Kerr thus negotiated for lower fares on the road from Richmond, Virginia, to Galveston. He issued a circular which he "distributed through the Grange organizations, and otherwise, in several States." His advertising announcement included the statement, "having all the facilities offered by the State, the Texas State Grange, and the Railroads leading to Texas, I am prepared to transport emigrants upon better terms than ever heretofore offered, and furnish land for rent or purchase in any county desired; or give them 160 acres of public land." His circular gave a Virginia address with the promise that immigration certificates, instructions, and information would be forthcoming to anyone who wrote. According to Kerr, this published notice "had the desired effect, creating a heavy correspondence" which Kerr claimed he was continuing to answer.[30]

With all the enthusiasm of a neophyte, Kerr then urged the state Grange to support this work financially. He wrote, "my belief is that a small amount of money could not be better appropriated by the organization, than in sending out labor in this prolific field; say, sufficient to pay the board bill of the agent, the agent volunteering his time free, while the railroads would meet him with free passes." Kerr's report reflects his early successes and his assumption that the Grange as an association shared his opinion on immigration. The enthusiasm with which he presented his plan to send agents out among those living on "old worn out farms" resonates throughout the report. He envisioned the influx of people translating into the erection of looms and tanneries and grain mills—all of which would aid farmers in their agricultural pursuits. His report expressed the essence of cooperation that so epitomized the visionary work of the Grange and the later Farmer's Alliance.[31]

No further comment is made regarding immigration in those published *Proceedings* of 1875. And there is no indication of Kerr's work in cooperation with the Texas Bureau of Immigration in the records of the Bureau. But Kerr's report to his fellow Grange members surely indicates positive interest on the part of the Grange in bringing immigrants to Texas—and in the case of Agent Kerr, a willingness to put his pocketbook where his ideals stood.

Records from the yearly meetings of the state Patrons of Husbandry indicate the existence of a Committee on Immigration during many years of its formal organization. In addition, elected leaders of the organization addressed the Grange assemblies over the years in support of immigration. Prominent Grange members belonged to various other organizations supportive of the same goal. For example, William Lang, who long served as the statewide Grange leader, resigned his Grange position in July, 1880, to take the presidency of the South Western Immigration Company and then began extensive involvement through a private corporation to secure people for Texas. All in all, such circumstantial evidence strongly suggests an attitude of support for immigration "per se" by Grange men and women. The Texas Grange was not unique in efforts to encourage immigration. "Nearly every state grange in the South and many of the local granges undertook some scheme in this direction."[32]

The argument that blacks participated in the convention endeavor to eliminate state support of immigration must also be laid to rest. Documentation for such a position is, however, much more slender in size. First, it can be noted that of the five black delegates at the convention, only one voted to eliminate state support for a Bureau of Immigration. Second, no black delegates took the opportunity to speak before the assembly either for or against this issue. The mere fact that blacks had such small representation in the convention meant that whatever their voice might have been, it was not going to be heard very loudly, if at all. Third, it is worthy of note that the Committee on Immigration did have one black delegate, Bird Davis, and he went on record as not supporting the majority report as it was presented to the assembly.

Concerning black views, one final tangential bit of evidence comes from outside the convention records. In the decade after the Civil War, blacks held various meetings and conventions around the state. Topics for discussion included concerns over violence against blacks, restrictions to black suffrage, and difficulties providing for education for all of Texas's citizens. At one such convention held in Brenham, Texas, on July 3–4, 1873, several of these topics were discussed and a final address printed for public distribution. Along with other issues, this convention placed itself in solid support of internal improvements and then wrote into its document the following statement:

> This we also consider an appropriate occasion to disabuse the minds of our fellow-citizens of foreign birth, of the desire that has been attributed to us to lay obstacles in the way of the immigration of their brethren in Europe to this State. We indignantly deny that we cherish any so unworthy or selfish feeling. We look on the Americans as the trustees of this soil for the oppressed of all nations, and we welcome the downtrodden immigrant from wherever he may come with open arms.[33]

Similar support of immigration was surely not embraced by the entire black population of Texas. But there is nothing in the recorded events of the constitutional convention itself to indicate black versus white antagonism on the subject.

The vote tally (October 19) on making the majority report of the Committee on Immigration a part of the proposed constitution provides no clues as to whether the delegates themselves supported the idea of encouraging immigration to the state. But it does give a clear picture of who voted to prohibit governmental expenditures to carry out that possible goal. The final vote was forty-four yeas, and thirty-nine nays. In actuality the vote was fairly close. If a two-thirds or three-fourths vote had been necessary, Section 56 as presented might not have passed. Among those voting in the affirmative, i.e. to prohibit establishment of a bureau and expenditure of state money, Grangers contributed twenty-eight votes of the total forty-four. Only one Republican voted "yes," and he was a black delegate from Harrison County, David Abner. Listed among those voting against the measure were seven Grange members. Out of the thirty-nine "no" votes, eleven were Republican Party members and of those eleven, three were black delegates. Thus twenty-six Democrats voted against the measure while forty-three Democrats voted in the affirmative.[34]

Another interesting way to view the final vote tally is to assess those who spoke on the convention floor regarding the measure (see table 2). Whether

Table 2
PARTICIPANTS IN FLOOR DEBATE ON IMMIGRATION

Delegate	Grange Membership	Political Party	Vote
Waelder		Democrat	No
Erhard		Democrat	No
Reagan	Yes	Democrat	No
Russell	Yes	Democrat	Yes
McLean	Yes	Democrat	Yes
Sansom		Democrat	Yes
Brown		Democrat	No
King		Democrat	No
McCormick		Democrat	No
Wright		Democrat	Yes
Whitfield	Yes	Democrat	No
Weaver		Democrat	Yes

Source: Journal of the Constitutional Convention of the State of Texas, 1875 *and* Walsh & Pilgrim's Directory of the Officers and Members of the Constitutional Convention.

looking at tally votes or speeches on the floor of the convention, the final result proclaimed loud and clear that taxpayer's money was not to be spent in any effort to attract people to Texas.

The constitutional convention adjourned on November 24, 1875. The date set for voter ratification of this new constitution was the third Tuesday of February, 1876. If it met voter approval, the proposed constitution was to become the basic law of the land on the third Tuesday in April. A battle over ratification consumed the winter months. In the newspapers, at political party gatherings, and in speeches around the state prominent Texans debated many portions of the proposed constitution presented by this very dollar-conscious convention. Fortunately for the democratic process, copies of the proposed constitution flooded the state because the convention made provision for over forty-nine thousand printed copies, including three thousand in the German language, three thousand in Spanish, and one thousand in Bohemian.[35]

In addition to providing copies for distribution, the constitutional convention also appointed a group of twelve delegates to prepare a special address explaining to the people in Texas the motives of the signers. This published address was distributed across the state as well. As the weeks moved closer to the February polling date, all the different issues debated on the floor of the convention were pulled out and debated again through the media and by word of mouth. The concern over Section 56 did not attract nearly the attention of the other provisions, but it did elicit some response. Interestingly, the address submitted by the convention made no mention at all about the immigration section. It did note that the final document was not perfect, but submitted it as "a vast improvement on the present one" and a document that "will bring great relief to the people."[36]

The statewide debate over ratification of the 1876 constitution reflected a continuation of the debate that had been going on during convention deliberations. Newspapers around the state had been keeping Texans aware of the issues. Local discussions in political meetings, in saloons, and over evening meals are long lost to recorded history. However one historian notes that most of the newspapers around the state "with a few exceptions, condemned the action of the convention in refusing to permit further aid to immigration."[37]

Sampling material in the *Dallas Weekly Herald* for October 23, 1875, provides one example of a single paper's multiple coverage of the issue. In one article that day they reported in outline format the accomplishments of the convention and its actions during the preceding week, including reference to the passage of the immigration provision. In another article entitled, "Brief Comments on 'Texas Notes'" the journalist announced the arrival of several families to Collin County. According to the writer, "these intelligent farmers from Illinois" contribute a fresh spirit "which is everywhere infused by the example they set before the Texas farmer." With such praise for newcomers, the news article optimistically portrayed the potential for growth in northern Texas. Then, in an editorial article on the constitutional convention's activity, the paper's editor objected to the total prohibition against money to encourage immigration. The writer stood in favor of "some method by which the markits [sic] of Texas should be thrown broadcast over the whole country, to let people in the older states and Europe who are seeking new homes, know the character of our country and the inviting field for the immigrant." The editor made reference to the multiple letters that his newspaper had been receiving requesting information about Texas. He viewed these letters as a clear rationale for encouragement of statewide efforts relating to immigration. Finally, attacking the decision to include Section 56 in the constitution, the editor wrote that it would be a mistake to "wholly ignore the subject, and say in effect that we do not want emigrants." This would be, "in our opinion, unwise and suicidal. We have a vast territory to people."[38]

Other papers were not unhappy about the proposed section in the constitution. The *State Gazette* in Austin supported the provision. The *Jefferson*

Jimplecute "heartily approved the decision" according to one reference, saying that expenditures for a bureau were not productive for Texas. But opposite views were also printed in other areas of the state. The *Houston Age* saw decisions on the immigration issue as just one more "parsimonious policy" that would ultimately destroy the chances for ratification of the final document. The *Mexia Ledger* seemed to voice the same opinion in regards to potential ratification.[39]

The statewide debate continued after the formal November 24, 1875, convention vote supporting the constitution as a total package. The Republican Party state convention met in Houston, January 12–14, 1876, and came out clearly against the document. Their resolution stated, "we denounce the Constitution framed by the late convention at Austin . . . (it) is unfriendly to immigration, so much needed to develop the great natural resources of our young and fertile State." The Democratic Party convention, held a week earlier in Galveston, adopted a platform in 1876 omitting earlier planks from previous years that had supported immigration and state support for internal improvements. They also did not formally endorse the constitution and thus sidestepped the issue altogether.[40]

The *Galveston Daily News* included a variety of articles informing their readership about the issue. In December they reported an interview with Webster Flanagan, an important politician in the Republican Party. When asked about the new constitution, he said, "as a citizen I am against it. I think it cripples immigration, education and internal improvements." While no editorial comment was then directed at Flanagan, the paper that same day included a front-page article lauding the new constitution. They specifically pointed to the inclusion of the Homestead Exemption that helped those economically able to purchase property and to a new clause "exempting current wages from garnishment" for the daily laborer. In supporting this last provision the paper saw the poorer classes of people given a measure of security formerly only available to the more well-to-do. Then it added that this clause "will give a strong impulse to the immigration of journeyman mechanics and every description of productive laborers, exactly the kind of population that is now most wanted." The *News* editor felt the clause "will go far toward removing the regrets of those who are disappointed and vexed at the failure of the convention to provide expressly for a distinct immigration bureau." A later article by the *Galveston Daily News* reported opinion from the *Fredricksburg Sentinel* that was vehemently opposed to ratification. The hill country newspaper was quoted as saying, they were "an advocate of the development of the resources of the State" and they condemned "the stingy, picayunish policy that prohibits the expenditure of a few thousand dollars per year for the support of an honest and efficient bureau of immigration" and the "petty, mean, beggarly spirit" displayed by the results of the convention. After much debate the constitution became the law. The voters in Texas adopted it "by a landslide margin of 136,000 votes to 56,652" and Section 56 thus became the law of the land in Texas.[41]

An epilogue to this story exists and deserves to be noted, for it provides an inkling of the future direction of Texas in relation to any formal efforts to attract immigration. Of first note is the passage of Joint Resolution No. 9 by the houses of the Texas legislature on August 28, 1876.

> Whereas, The Constitution inhibits this State from expending money in the interest of immigration, and whereas an impression prevails that the people of this State are indifferent or opposed to immigration from the older States of the Union, and from foreign nations, and whereas the Texas Land and Immigration Company of St. Louis, a corporation organized under the general statutes of the State of Missouri, composed of men of known integrity of character, business reputation, possessing ample means, have undertaken to carry on a free communication with the other States of the Union, and with foreign countries, furnishing information of the great resources of the State of Texas, her climate, soil, minerals, and advantages presented for the investment of capital in manufactures, and other advantages to the immigrant; therefore,
>
> Section 1. *Be it resolved by the Legislature of the State of Texas,* That the people of Texas extend a cordial invitation to the good and industrious immigrant to come and make his home among us, and that we will extend to him a hearty welcome, and that the State officers are authorized and requested to furnish the agents and officers of said company such official documents at their disposal as will aid the said company in the work of securing immigration to this State; *provided,* the same be done without any cost to the State.[42]

A later legislative decision also indicates residual and legal interest in state involvement concerning migration. The Sixteenth Legislature, meeting in 1879, utilized Article Twelve of the 1876 constitution for authority to pass several laws relative to private corporations in Texas, i.e. their creation and regulation. In part, the law lists over twenty-seven "purposes for which private corporations may be formed," and number twenty-two reads, "The promotion of immigration."[43] These two acts by the Texas Legislature—one a joint resolution in 1876 and the other a representative law passed in 1879—point to the direction of future state efforts to attract immigration.

Reconstruction politics took place on top of shifting sand. For Texas this meant three different constitutions in a ten-year period. The "radical" constitution of 1869 "involved the centralization of power in Austin, especially in the hands of the governor." Its provisions for a four-year term for the governor and his ability to appoint most state executive positions were just a few of the perceived negative aspects that propelled the calling of yet another constitutional convention. Delegates in 1875 "wrote a constitution reflecting their dislike for centralized, activist, expensive state government." The years between 1865 and 1875 "deepened the negative attitude most white southerners held toward government." A formal Bureau of Immigration fell to this attitude. Texas shared with most other southern states the tug and pull of politics during the decade after the Civil War. Texas stands out as unique, however, in its internal battle over the best approach to peopling its extensive lands.[44]

While the 1876 constitution included an absolute prohibition, it also created, in some sense, a vacuum. After pulling out official government support for the movement to encourage immigration, the politicians and private citizens of the state essentially held one of two views. Some believed nothing needed to be done to attract people to Texas, assuming immigrants would come of their own accord. Others believed that concerted effort of some kind, independent of direct government support, was necessary. Among these latter groups were business enterprises such as railroads, real estate agents, land developers, and various entrepreneurial industries, as well as booster organizations touting the claims of their community, town, or city. The activity of these many groups makes an interesting web of projects, programs, and publications that fit into the ongoing saga of Texas history. First however, it is time to explain many of the rhetorical techniques and the various mediums for those words.

CHAPTER 4

WORDS, WORDS, WORDS

Post–Civil War white Texans believed in using words to move people, both figuratively and literally. Texans assumed that if they gave time and energy to the development of written enticement literature, they could influence the flow of migration to their state. Many were not willing to allow supposedly natural forces to bring settlers automatically to Texas. Instead, a large number of Texans grabbed at the power they believed rested in the written word to influence those outside Texas. They often tackled their work with an unbounded optimism.

A TASTE OF TEXAS RHETORIC

The combined efforts by countless people living in Texas between 1865 and 1915 produced page upon page of persuasive words. These labors were not in any real sense coordinated or chronologically dependent one on the other. They coexisted within the swirling activity of a busy, growing state. A wide-ranging, diverse group of writers with eclectic reasons spent untold hours writing. Motives ranged from conservative Democrats wanting to end Republican rule in postwar times to communities seeking an increase in the size of their towns to brothers encouraging sisters to settle in the west where land and men were plentiful. The intentions that propelled their writings were many—sometimes obvious and clear, but other times more hidden in the general routine of individual choices. The rhetoric underlying this enticement material was meant to change people's lives.

Those already settled in Texas literally opened their arms to newcomers, continually producing a stream of literature meant to invite "all industrious and law-abiding people" to come cast their lot where they would be cordially welcomed. "Come to Texas" reads the title of a poem published in 1888. "Come to Texas" heads an advertisement for the International and Great Northern Railroad in 1904. "Come to Texas—come quickly" encourages the final line of an 1869 article in the *Houston Telegraph*. Repeatedly Texans, amidst the hustle and bustle of their own life-sustaining activities, committed their time and their physical energy in a personal effort at encouraging others to move.[1]

Texas in the late nineteenth century experienced phenomenal growth. There was land for the taking—expansive acres waiting to be tapped for agricultural opportunities. There were Texans who knew that more people on those Texas lands meant greater prosperity for the state as a whole and for each little community sprinkled throughout the state. Their mindset also simply assumed spatial mobility in the American society. Concepts of easy "migration and movement, mobility and motion"[2] undergirded intense labors at making sure people came to the state. These Texans, both native and adopted, told the "Texas story" to whomever would read. One goal in documenting this effort is an attempt to feel the weight and importance of those words on the written page—especially the weight given to those words by their users.

The formal term applied to persuasive language is rhetoric. The art of debate in the seventeenth and eighteenth centuries utilized eloquent rhetoric to make a point or to change opinions. In a similar fashion Texans of the late nineteenth century tried to make their own point: "Come to Texas." They aspired to redirect a population flow to their extensive lands. This was a newer kind of rhetoric aimed at the common citizen. Not meant to be classic documents for the ages, these rhetorical pages were meant to be a temporary venue because quick change was the assumption. While not eloquent or lean prose or necessarily well edited, this persuasive language was not second-rate either, since it seems to have accomplished its goal to change impressions about Texas and bring large numbers of people to the state. This Texas rhetoric could be called elongated advertising—it lured, enticed, persuaded, promoted, and publicized. It advertised. Its aim was to market Texas.[3]

Texans' success or failure of persuasion is not the direct purview of this book, although connections appear obvious. Records tell us, for example, that a young recently arrived immigrant from England, John Leonard, left Rhode Island because an uncle in Beaumont wrote and suggested to him, "Come to Texas."[4] Others read similar words and moved, but scholars don't have the documentation in hand for each and every new arrival. The key focus here is the faith of the writers. Faith in their own ability to shape population movement into a Texas current energized their endeavors. Their presumption that if you merely tell people about Texas they will come, lay behind the onslaught of efforts to attract newcomers.

Private letters carried this message of encouragement, often in simple expressions of care and concern. One Galveston tea merchant, himself a recent arrival from England, wrote home to his sister in March 1878, "I am glad

Willie has not given up the idea of coming out here, we can always find a store for a good man and at a good salary." Fred Bergman wrote to his sisters in Sweden, "Texas is a place for the poor to work their way up by means of work and thrift. Poor Swedes come here practically all the time, and in a few years they are independent." Another European wrote to family in 1879, "The men of Texas are gentlemen in every sense of the word. One is as safe from Indians here as in Wales. There are few snakes." A woman recently from Mississippi but living in East Texas in 1866 wrote back home, "You will be pleased with Texas. I know you will. It is certainly a glorious country, destined to take the lead among the Southern States, certainly the best adapted for the recuperation of our worn energies and wasted fortunes." Each of these letters contained a kernel of hope held out to entice others to consider migrating.[5]

Letters often sparked people to journey to Texas. But many others also heard the call put forth in newspapers, almanacs, and various pamphlets published by Texans. Under the title "A Cordial Welcome," *Bryant's Texas Almanac* of 1882 exclaimed, "And, now, to the immigrant, we say, come and see this goodly land, midway between temperate and torrid heats, where brave men fought and died, and whose descendants will offer all men coming with honest intents a ready and cordial welcome." This warm, though wordy, handshake reflects and repeats an earlier call made by Lieutenant Governor Richard B. Hubbard in 1876 when he addressed the Philadelphia Exposition. "Come among us, to our churches, to our homes, to our firesides, in the busy fields, on our exposed frontiers—anywhere, everywhere, from the palace to the cabin—and you will return to your own gallant people, telling them that we have a civilization, a hospitality, and a respect for law, alike the pride and the glory of a commonwealth." Quickly published and distributed widely, Hubbard's plea was his way of encouraging everyone to see Texas for themselves and in the process observe a place with doors open for all newcomers—a desirable place to live.[6]

Hubbard's speech aimed to overcome negative publicity that had been circulating about Texas. Similar efforts to reassure readers exist in many examples of enticement literature and they reflect an interest in drawing in a wide diversity of people. One almanac contained the following communication:

> Another encouragement to immigration, and a powerful one, too, will be found in low taxes, a faithful administration of the laws, the suppression of crime, and the protection of individual rights, regardless of race, creed, color or nationality. To that end the best talent of the State is now directed, and the immigrant from

Denmark or Sweden, as much as one from Virginia or Massachusetts, will be pro-
tected alike with the native.

Texas extends the right hand of fellowship to all the States and invites within her
borders the good and true from earth's remotest bounds.[7]

In 1869 the *Houston Telegraph* made a similar statement and then added, "We
have plenty of room and large hearts to welcome you." A couple years later the
same paper included copy that read, "Come to Texas. . . . This is a new country and an improving country. Are you thinking of changing your location?
We say again come to our beautiful prairie State and you shall have a cordial
welcome." The same message continued in enticement literature throughout
the late-nineteenth and early-twentieth century. A 1908 brochure for Smith
County, Texas, and its city of Tyler proclaimed, "WHETHER You are a farmer,
artisan, laborer, professional man, merchant, manufacturer, homeseeker or
investor, YOU ARE WELCOME HERE."[8]

UNIQUENESS OF TEXAS

One frustration in relating the activities of so many Texans remains placing
their work within the broader framework of United States history. In trying
to demonstrate continuity or diversity, Texas ends up in the "unique" category
yet again. Definitely a southern state, due to its inclusion in the Confederacy,
maintenance of slavery, and common cash crop of cotton, Texas was unlike
other southern states in its less intense experience of Civil War battles, its international border with the resultant Hispanic population, and the line of
forts with settlement on the western frontier. Clearly a western state, due to
its geographical location in relation to the Mississippi River, Indian population, and immense acreage, it had issues of race and intense political divisions
that mark it as different from the majority of western states. Thus its story of
immigration holds unique elements with a dynamic difficult to pinpoint
crisply. Its effort to entice newcomers to the state is an amalgam of both typically western approaches and southern concerns. It shares with western states
the importance of railroad development and huge tracts of land. Yet it di-
verges from the typical western story in which the federal government controlled and dispersed the vast lands of the West. Texas had communal lands
at its own disposal. State government alone could parcel out the vast public
domain of Texas. On the other hand, Texas shared with the remainder of the
southern states issues such as mild climate influencing agricultural decisions
and the presence of a large black labor force. The "leavings" of Reconstruction
with attendant violence and attitudes toward those different from the major-

ity white population influenced much of Texans' thought patterns. In addition Texas shared with other southern "redeemer" governments the turmoil of the era.

Distinctly southern? western? or southwestern? There is actually a melding of traditions, cultures, and outlooks that places most of the Texas story of enticement efforts into a unique category. Complicating this analysis is the mythology that the South was not a place for immigrants, i.e. not a place for people who were different from the predominant white Anglo stock. A look at statistics alone will show that a wide variety of population movements existed among the many southern states. For example, between 1860 and 1920 North Carolina's population increased by 158 percent, while Mississippi registered an increase of 126 percent. Yet during the same time frame, Florida increased in population by 590 percent and Texas increased a remarkable 672 percent.[9] Migration into each state along with its natural increase in population thus suggests a wide variety of experiences for those southern states and would discount any general label saying the South did not and would not attract immigrants. Negative statements about immigration southward tend to gloss over the influence on their receiving states and on the regions where migrants settled. Such dismissive approaches also fail to take into account the efforts by southerners to entice newcomers to the South.

PUSH/PULL FACTORS IN MIGRATION

Liz Carpenter, a twentieth-century Texan, wrote about her family, saying, "a recurrent pattern in American history, and in our family's history, has been the quest for a new Canaan. The pushes and pulls generating such quests have, for some families, led to, not only one, but a series of moves. America moves incessantly today." She went on to note that "a hundred years ago the Sutherland family from Jackson County was pulled by the availability of cheaper land and pushed by the 'fevers,' as they called malaria."[10] The decision to migrate from one place to another is a complex mix of multiple push/pull factors. But in focusing on the energy of the people and their production of written materials, the emphasis here is solely on the pull factor of such endeavors. Immigration is not a simple, monolithic movement, nor one carried out by an indistinguishable mass of people. Hundreds, then thousands, and eventually hundreds of thousands of human beings made the decision to move to Texas. Each person's move is a unique story in its own right. As more and more of these single stories are told, the wider picture of migration and mobility will be enriched.

ANTEBELLUM RHETORIC

Texas has always been an immigrant state. Much of its population has arrived after their birth elsewhere. This was certainly true of the early settlers in the 1820s, 30s, and 40s. It was also true of the population in the period of early statehood, Confederacy, and postbellum eras, too. Migration represents a continuous thread of activity often underestimated by historians of the state.[11] The momentum for this activity began extremely early, with both Moses Austin and Stephen F. Austin's energetic involvement in opening Texas to Anglo settlement. Letters initially carried the written word praising the land and the potential for agriculturalists. As more people came, words of attraction evolved into a number of published guidebooks that described Texas and gave information to the potential settler.[12] Antebellum rhetoric in this enticement literature set the pattern followed by most writers in the later half of the nineteenth century. The techniques and approaches of the earlier writers were copied and adapted to late-nineteenth-century efforts at attracting immigrants. For example, the dangers and problems of travel are "largely wanting in the guidebook." Disease, accidents, Indian depravations, and white banditry are rarely if ever presented in either antebellum or late-nineteenth-century enticement literature. Emphasis on settlement by families was a major theme in these guidebooks. There were clear statements discouraging "the vagabond or soldier of fortune" and the assumption was evident that good law-abiding settlers would provide the sturdy stock needed for the area's development. One guidebook noted "that more children are born in Texas, in proportion to the population, than elsewhere, and more in proportion are raised to adolescence." In proclaiming a low infant mortality rate, the writer spoke directly to the hearts of parents who often lost children early in life. In another pull at the heartstrings, this same publicist talked about cheap lands soon to become more valuable. Then he tacked on, "if not for yourselves, for your children, come to Texas." This same guidebook then suggested that schooling "will be in the reach of every child in the State."[13]

This last statement not only appealed to the emotions of parents, it also addressed those looking to the future. Immigrants have almost always been future-oriented. Perhaps this explains why such pronouncements about school systems not yet in existence were announced as present realities for the readers of such pamphlets, news articles, or booklets. In most written material the rhetorical technique of blurring the line between what existed in reality and what existed in the mind's eye of the developer or businessperson was common. This fuzziness of presentation left windows open for dreaming immigrants to project their own vision of life in the new land.

Listings of potential land holdings around the state often appeared in the columns next to advice for immigrants. The importance of specific, helpful information shines throughout the pages. For example, one Texas document of this era encouraged travel to Texas in October. This simple nugget of information was critical for Texas immigrants. Soil needed preparation in January and February for planting in March. Timing an arrival before that, in order to build a cabin and clear some land, made strong economic sense. Most writers inserted what they called absolute "facts." Jacob de Cordova, an early land developer, utilized a colorful image to reinforce his message. He wrote, "One fact may be stated, which, however wonderful it may appear, is susceptible of every proof: A COW CAN BE RAISED IN TEXAS AT LESS COST THAN A CHICKEN in any other place in the United States."[14]

Themes of reassurance abound in antebellum literature. A common approach is to state the fact and add a "but." One author wrote in his 1860 work *Western Texas, The Australia of America: Or the Place to Live,* "Snakes and poisonous insects are quite plentiful in parts of western Texas; but where cattle and hogs or stock of any kind are kept they soon disappear." Since he had not known anyone attacked by such pests, the writer assumed that people were seldom bitten. To continue the message of reassurance, he then presented a personal observation. "I suppose the awful reports sent abroad from Texas about them are from new-comers, and women principally, who no doubt have a perfect horror for and loath the snake or poisonous insect, as they picture them by accident under their hoops or in some way in their imagination over and around their heads."[15]

Enticement literature already existed in the pre-1865 era of Texas's settlement. While the Civil War marks a sharp break in sustained attraction efforts by Texans, the flow of people from elsewhere to Texas continued, partially based on earlier enticement efforts. Immigration and immigrant-attracting efforts after the close of the Civil War therefore represent continuity with Texas's history before 1860. Texans wanted more people to come to their state. Their interest in immigration began with the first Anglo-American efforts at settlement of the region and have continued into the twenty-first century.

DEFINITIONS

Words are the centerpiece for this analysis of migration to Texas. Therefore, it is essential to clarify one word in particular, since in some cases the mean-

ing of a word can change over time. The term "immigrant" illustrates this perfectly. To the early-twenty-first-century reader the term immediately conjures
up images of a person originally born across the oceans. There is a "foreign-
ness" associated with other continents and other cultures subsumed within
the use of the term today. This was not the case for the person living in 1860,
1880, or even 1900 in Texas or in the United States. To the politician in Austin,
the businessman in San Antonio, the cotton factor in Galveston, or the land
developer in Fort Worth in the 1870s and 1880s, "immigrant" meant anyone coming to the state. In the documents of the day, many words were used
interchangeably: homeseeker, colonizer, immigrant, emigrant, northerner,
westerner, southerner on the move.

The term "immigrant" also was not defined typically by ethnicity, but
rather by mobility. Yes, some immigrants were Norwegian, German, English,
Irish, Italian, or Chinese. But, many "immigrants" were Mississippians, Ken-
tuckians, Georgians, Ohioans, and Californians. Some Texans came originally from New York, Alabama, North Dakota, and Minnesota. Sometimes
the written material would specify the kind of immigrant of which they
spoke: the foreign-born immigrant, the immigrant from Georgia, the immigrants from Dewitt County, Illinois, or the German immigrants off the ships
in Galveston. But just as often the term was not modified by any adjective and
thus took on a "generic" sense inclusive of any person who moved. It also
helps to read "immigrant" as a person of either gender and of any chronological age.

TACTICS, TOOLS, TECHNIQUES

Not typically trained in formal rhetoric, most Texas writers probably could
not have identified their tactics or techniques. But as we today review their
written words, several common rhetorical devices emerge.

Reassurance was one common technique used no matter what the subject
of discussion. Making a negative into a positive, dispelling rumors commonly
held in other locales, and pointing to stabilizing features of the new home all
served to provide reassurance to the questioning immigrant. Another common tactic employed by writers of this genre included noting the importance
of family and kinship. The central experience of most immigrants remained
a familial one. The brochures and pamphlets of the time knew this and
catered to that audience. In addition, immigrants by nature tend to look optimistically to the future. They relate to the "will" and "shall" of the future,
often confusing it with the "now" expressed in statements using "is" and "are."
While this hope may be impossible to delineate, Texas business leaders, poli-

ticians, and common folk knew intimately that sense of hope and played to it as they used their rhetoric to bring new people, new faces, and new money to the state.

In the tool kit of those producing powerful persuasive enticement literature, a major technique was the blurring of the present with the future. One study of rhetoric suggests that if this approach is done well, it "transports us momentarily at least, across the boundaries of time."[16] The future and present become enmeshed. Reading this material in the light of the twenty-first century makes us want to cry out to the late-nineteenth-century reader with a clear "Watch out!" "Think twice about what they are saying!" "Question their motives!" "Read with a critical eye!" Our emotional response today is based partly on the knowledge that the dreams of the immigrants who came to the United States and to Texas did not always materialize and partly on our more skeptical age.

A careless reader could miss the subtle blending of the present and the future and might assume that conditions projected into the future were in fact already in place. Phrases like "will be," "soon," and "in the near future" were common and slipped in next to descriptions of the land and the towns along the way. In July, 1872, George Sweet, publisher of the *Texas New Yorker,* printed a letter from a farmer in Gatesville, Texas. It read in part, "This is the first letter I ever tried to write to a newspaper in my life. . . . Crops are good. As for wheat, it is better than good. Corn is also good. In fact, better than I ever saw it." His enthusiasm continued as he linked this good fortune to future developments in Coryell County by saying that a courthouse was going up and a bridge would be built "soon."[17]

As writers described their hometowns or their farms or their city's growth, pride in their locale obviously spilled over into their descriptions. But when the rhetoric inflated the present into the future, it took pride and enthusiasm one step further. Sometimes it reflected an innocent blending of information as in the letter from the Gatesville man; sometimes it was deliberate. Often writers assumed they were not so much describing scenery as expressing a vision meant to be read as a reality. Railroads commonly used this tactic in their promotional literature. Past and present statements often existed side by side. The Missouri, Kansas and Texas Railroad (MK&T RR) published a pamphlet proclaiming: "Lands, in this division of the State range from fifty cents to ten dollars per acre" and "The pecan here finds its favorite home; it becomes the giant of the forest, and every year throws its rich oily nuts to the ground." Then comes the future intertwined: "And when this beautiful and health-restoring section shall become better settled and known, there cannot be a doubt of its becoming the great resort of the thousands of invalids who an-nualy [*sic*] seek a change of climate to prolong their lives." In a later paragraph, the same pamphlet itemized the advantages to life in Texas and then trum-peted the belief that, "all these and more are in the near future, each day and year are marching her [i.e. Texas] onward and upward."[18]

Even the fairly conservative Texas Bureau of Immigration material suc-cumbed to the tactic of fusing present with future. In a section on the west-ern, more arid portion of the state, a Bureau pamphlet reported that, "Farms have already been started, and are now being cultivated with the assistance of irrigation, from which the yield of crops sounds fabulous." But then the pro-jection into the future began: "when its vineyards shall have been planted, the wines from which will rival in quality and quantity those of France, and greatly add to the wealth of this region, it will be the finest portion of the American continent." One scholar suggests that the success inherent in such an approach meant "listeners lingered in the future and felt better because of it."[19]

Immigrants too blended the present and the future in their written mate-rial to others. In one letter Thomas Blackshear of Navasota County wrote about what he personally saw and what he heard, thus mixing the close-up ob-servation with the hopes that such activity would continue elsewhere. He wrote, "Movers are passing by my house nearly every day, going West, and I hear of large numbers of immigrants from the old States, coming into every part of our State." A Norwegian immigrant living in Galveston wrote home praising Texas, saying, "Texas is generally acknowledged to be one of the most healthful and fertile states in the Union." Then he moved stealthily into the future, "it only lacks people and capital, railroads, and canals to become in time one of the greatest grain- and cotton-producing areas in the world." His personal hopes for the future in his adopted state colored his present percep-tion of Texas.[20]

City boosters dreamed of the future, too. Their blending of present and fu-ture spoke to their hopes for improvement. Sometimes the city spokesperson overdrew its projected future. Overstatement was yet one more rhetorical de-vice. In one promotional pamphlet entitled *Texas: Its Climate, Soil, Produc-tions, Trade, Commerce, and Inducements for Emigration,* the anonymous au-thor wrote about the present and future of the city of Jefferson. He placed Jefferson in 1870 as Texas's fourth largest city with a total population "num-bering more than 15000 inhabitants." Census records would indicate the as-sertion was a slight exaggeration, but the writer continued with the following statement: "As *this portion* of Texas is well watered, very rich and productive,

"FREE!" This 1877 pamphlet produced by the Missouri, Kansas & Texas Railroad offered its information "FREE!" encouraging newcomers to use their transportation lines. Courtesy Texas State Library and Archives Commission.

increasing rapidly in population and trade, in all probability Jefferson, in a few years, aided by the construction of the International and Transcontinental Railroads, will be the second if not the first city in the Lone Star State."[21] The reality of fertile soil and good location allowed this writer to see the addition of the railroad as the spur to making Jefferson supreme among the cities in Texas.[22]

Typically the present and the future were so closely aligned on the pages of multiple pamphlets that the hopeful immigrant failed to distinguish the difference and saw the future already in his or her present. Writers routinely placed statements about the future next to concrete descriptions of the present. They wrote to the hopes of their audience. This spark of hope to which individuals tenaciously clung exerted a strong current of power. No matter what the ethnic background, class, gender, or race, many people held to a hope that a better place and a better time awaited them just around the corner or at the beginning of a new year. Most difficult to dissect or explain, this intangible hope propelled many to make at least one move, often to make several moves.[23]

Another strategy employed by enticement literature was the assumption that families were the norm. In his classic work on immigration, John Bodnar writes of the centrality of the family to the immigration experience. Taking issue with Oscar Handlin's image of "uprooted" people, Bodnar prefers the gardener's view of "transplanted" life. While disorientation and some chaos surround the immigrant's experience, Bodnar sees the connection to family as a stabilizing and crucial part in the whole journey from citizen in one nation to productive member of another country.[24] It is extremely doubtful that authors of enticement literature of the late-nineteenth century spent time debating this theoretical framework. Their efforts, however, illustrate their awareness of immigration as a familial event. Written material that was meant to attract new people to the United States, and specifically to Texas, addressed its message to men and women, wives and husbands, and mothers and fathers as parents of children. In other words, the promotional literature spoke to families of all shapes, sizes, and ethnic background.

The *Texas State Register* of 1876 aimed to inform and inspire: "Texas is a new country; large areas of her domain have never seen the plow or been tickled with the hoe. She desires to receive a large amount of immigration. . . . She asks men and women in all parts of the world . . . to come to her territory." An advertisement in *Bryant's Railroad Guide* began with the boldface heading "A HOME IN TEXAS!" and went on to tout its "excellent schools & churches" as a lure to settlement. A pamphlet proclaiming the virtues of life in Austin and Travis County addressed the same kinds of issues as the ad in the railroad guide. It included columns on such topics as the churches, by number and denomination, and the numerous schools for white and colored students. The pamphlet also noted ethnic associations like the Turn-verein for the German population and the Hibernians for the Irish. Masonic lodges and the Grange association were listed as well. The enticement literature seemed to be sending a message that addressed the whole family's activities, not just discussing the work of the farmer in the field.[25]

Family is a word that conveys more than its mere six letters—family is higher on the hierarchy of values than other issues and so much of the rhetoric "talked" about families. Some promotional pieces took an additional step in their efforts to attract new citizens. They subtly, and sometimes not so subtly, tried to motivate by reference to family duty. The *Houston Telegraph* in an 1869 article asked, "Why stay in countries where you and your children must be hewers of wood and drawers of water, when you can come to Texas and carve out for yourselves an independence?" H. C. Mack in his booklet *Texas. Information for Emigrants* said it more boldly: "It is your duty to avail yourself of all the advantages of country and climate that you possibly can—by emigration if necessary, not alone for your own comfort and convenience but that your offspring with you and after you may be relieved of many of the hardships and much of the burthens of life." Yet another exhortation to migrate to Texas put the message to the family in this way:

> Should fathers and mothers in the older States, who have children, wish to go to a new country where they can raise them up and accustom them to the flowery and joyous paths of honor and virtue, so that they may in after life be the pride, delight, and support of their parents, my advice to them is:
>
> Go to Texas! where the land is cheap and rich—where labor and capital are in great demand—where the poor man by honest labor may become rich—where no such things as hunger and starvation are known.

These writers perceived family obligations and family interest as primary motivating factors in the final decision to migrate. Believing that change would be better for everyone in the family, parents often bought into the message.[26]

The typical assumption of most enticement literature was that immigrant families would engage in farming. They would move onto the land and grow crops for export utilizing the growing rail system around the state to deliver their goods to market. Many of the booklets and pamphlets also mentioned other agricultural alternatives. One almanac stated, "Boys take readily to the stock-raising business, and their interest can be easily stimulated by making them the owners of a few head." The encouraging words continued: "The occupation is healthful, and if the parents are moral and intelligent, they can train their sons after their own image and likeness just as easy in following this as any other business." The tug at parental duty to "train" and prepare the family members for a livelihood is obvious.[27]

Sheep raising was also something encouraged by enticement pamphlets. The Texas Bureau of Immigration in printing information on sheep raising in West Texas gave slightly discouraging advice, but still suggestions oriented toward family considerations. The recommendation read:

> To conclude, I will say that wool-growers, using several thousand acres of land each . . . are not likely to have many neighbors. Therefore, men having families, used to society, must have a residence in a village as near to his business as he can find a suitable location. Otherwise, the females in the family are lonesome, being often left alone, while the men are attending to the flocks.
>
> The business suits single men better at the present time—but upon the general occupation of the country, that difficulty will be less felt.[28]

Such a somber admonition seems detrimental to the attraction of families. Yet seen in another way, the advice expresses the reality of a special type of agricultural business. The writer assumed migration by a family unit and gave information that would make the move successful for all. His advice would be the kind that families would want to consider as they pondered moving from their homeland.

Enticement literature provided a whole host of information that would comfort anxious families. One railroad publication made the comment, "as a hand-book for the immigrant, this work would be incomplete did it not contain some allusion to the homestead, marital and other laws of the State." Most pamphlets, whether issued by the state government, railroads, real estate agencies, or other business endeavors, included some material excerpting state laws as they applied to families. Texas's unique heritage built on earlier Mexican and Spanish law needed to be explained to potential newcomers. The chance to obtain a homestead and keep it free from bankruptcy proceedings served as a concrete lure. The assurance that widowhood would not automatically result in loss of one's home soothed fears for prospective migrants. Reproduction of constitutional provisions or state laws thus served to inform the family unit of its central role in settling the state.[29]

Pleasant and positive promotional material took direct aim at the immigrant as part of a family on the move. The Missouri, Kansas and Texas Railroad (MK&T RR) produced a flier entitled, *Free Guide to Texas*. Aware of the concern for travel costs to new lands, the railway offered reduced rates for children. The railroad proudly advertised that children under five were entitled to free passage, while those between the ages of five and twelve rode at half fare. The MK&T RR even promised to entertain the children during their travels. One mother's testimonial was prominently displayed in an MK&T RR brochure:

> All the Children kept well on our trip to Texas. . . . The only trouble we had was with the children after we reached the "Indian Territory." They were fairly crazy with delight, and their little heads were out of the window all day long. First they would see a drove of deer; then thousands of prairie chickens; then a tree full of parrots and mocking birds; then the hill sides and valleys just one mass of verbenas . . . then great towering rocks, looking like glaciers of ice with grand cascades pouring over them.[30]

Her enthusiastic portrayal of the children and their excitement over the scenery from the train was meant to reach the parenting concerns of other immigrant travelers.

A third rhetorical tactic widely used in enticement literature was that of reassurance for it helped the reader become comfortable with new ideas. The publisher or author assumed the existence of a specific, usually negative message previously received by the reader and worked to change that idea. Often the source of misinformation remained a nebulous "they have said" or "rumor has it." Rarely did Texas promotional literature identify specifically an institution or person or business that had spoken negatively about the state. The unknown assailant of Texas's reputation remained foggily generic. For example, one railway pamphlet stated, "the erroneous opinion prevailed that a Northern or Western man, and in fact the immigrant from every where, was not safe here."[31] A pattern developed within enticement literature. First, the existence of the negative message was often proclaimed. Then that message was forcefully refuted. Writers hoped that by tackling the rumor or negative publicity head-on, they could lay it to rest forever. Most gave no evidence for their counter claims but simply assumed that their assertions would be accepted.

A number of different rumors provided fodder for defensive statements by those writing enticement pamphlets and books. To the assumption that workers were not needed in a state with a substantial black population, one newspaper proclaimed, "Labor is in great demand, and prices now rule high. . . .

In no State in the Union is labor so well paid as in Texas. While labor is high, living is astonishingly cheap." One letter writer to the *Texas New Yorker* denied that Texas was only a cotton-growing state, asserting that wheat too was grown there. In June of 1872, he claimed he had gathered some heads of wheat from his fields, shelled them, and counted the grains—he bragged that they had "averaged 55 grains to the head!" To the argument that cities in Texas were not healthy places to live, the *Texas State Register* stated authoritatively, "Galveston is a healthy city, being entirely free from any prevailing sickness. . . . There has not been a case of yellow fever in the city for the last year." Then in a classic example of the blending of the future and the present the author added, "There is no reason why this fever should exist in Galveston at all, and it is believed that sanitary improvements, made and in progress, will effectually protect the city from any future visitations of the yellow fever."[32]

Negative impressions of Texas were numerous. Some of the most common reflected the state's western and southern heritage and its weather—already fabled, even at such an early date. One persistent story about Texas grew partly out of its position on the western frontier, its proximity to Indian territories, and participation in the Civil War hostilities: that Texas was a lawless, violent place. Enticement literature, especially those works published during the decade from 1865 to 1876, had to address that concern. Almost every document of this early era had a statement relating to perceptions of violence in Texas. One said, "Law and order are as rigidly maintained, and crime as promptly punished as in any of the States. Every neighborhood is supplied with church privileges, and the cause of the Bible is well maintained." Another pamphlet stated: "There is a great prejudice existing abroad against Texas on account of its reputed lawlessness. Those wild reports so often circulated about the outlawry of Texans are greatly exaggerated." The issue of lawlessness was brought up time and again by writers who paradoxically were trying to lay the discussion to rest.[33]

As writers tried to minimize the rumors about Texas and its western-style lawlessness, they also had to work to counter the perception that Texas, a southern state, did not want northerners. As with other rumors, this one had some basis in fact. In the immediate postwar period, some northern soldiers, educators, and government representatives arrived in southern territory seeking to participate in efforts at "reconstruction" of the southern states and their reunification with the north. Perceived as outsiders and meddlers by many old-timers, these carpetbaggers provoked angry responses on the part of some southerners, and their hostility was sometimes reported in the northern press. Occasionally anti-northern sentiment was exaggerated, giving rise to a strong reluctance among some potential settlers to move south. Efforts to dispel this rumor as it applied to Texas varied from the very flowery to the very direct. One writer speaking of "The New Era" in Texas wrote, "The people of Texas, do most sincerely desire, and still labor for an accession to their numbers of all such, without reference to their nativity, or to their religious or political opinions—who may come in *good faith* and *honesty of purpose*." Another promotional pamphlet noted the past experience of men who "came from Massachusetts, Vermont, New York, Connecticut, and even the State of New Jersey," thus supplying Galveston with "several very good citizens." Its writer noted that the population of Texas had people "from all parts of Christendom" and then added, "Texans born and reared in Vermont, Massachusetts, and Connecticut, are often seen associating on terms of intimacy and friendship with the fire-eating natives of South Carolina." Taking his argument one step further and perhaps stretching his own credibility, the author added, "In fact, many of the richest and most influential citizens of Texas were born, reared and educated in the Northern States, and no class of emigrants are more warmly desired in Texas than the sharp, ingenious, labor-saving Yankee."[34]

Texans also tried presenting a national message. Lieutenant Governor Richard B. Hubbard spoke at the 1876 Centennial Exposition in Philadelphia, a big celebration of the birth of the United States of America. This event offered each state at least one opportunity to improve or develop its public image by asking each governor to address assembled guests at the Exposition. Hubbard utilized that chance to describe his beloved state and all its resources. He also used the speech to denounce the negative publicity abroad about Texas. After rehearsing the obligatory history of the settlement of Texas, its development as a Republic, and then its inclusion in the United States of America, he boastfully listed its natural resources. He mentioned the "fabulous growth" of the state's population and then directly began to refute what he called the "carping critics and willful maligners of our good name."[35]

Specifically addressing the issue of emigration and toleration, Hubbard addressed the Philadelphia crowd on a warm September day:

Texas invites the emigrant to come hither, and from whatever land, he will be met at the threshold by genial and honest welcome. . . . What care we for your political opinions, or under what flag you have fought? Texas wants men, honest men, with hearts and strong arms, to populate her wilderness and prairies, with freedom to vote or to speak as if "native and to the manor born.". . . Why, sirs when you are told that we dislike for our Northern brethren to immigrate hither, it is a base slander on a brave and generous people.[36]

Hubbard's speech, made in the North to a predominately northern audience, had an initial impact on the populace and later through newspaper accounts of the time. In addition, W. G. Kingsbury, an employee of the Galveston, Harrisburg, and San Antonio Railroad Company, reprinted it in its entirety. On the directive of the railroad's officers, Kingsbury had the speech printed with the idea of distributing it throughout England as a means of overcoming negative publicity. In his preface to the printed speech, Kingsbury said in reference to Texas that "certain anonymous writers in newspapers, and Agents of Colonial Schemes have undertaken to blacken her fair name, and dispute her many advantages." With that as the incentive, Kingsbury felt the weight of authority ascribed to a state executive officer would lend exceptional credence to the message so "that no man worthy of notice would dare dispute them." The lieutenant governor's speech reached a much wider audience than just those who stood before him in Philadelphia.[37]

Hubbard's speech serves to make two points. One, since it is clearly addressing the impression that foreigners or northerners were not welcome in Texas in 1876, it suggests that the question of who was welcome in Texas had been an issue for all of the ten years since the close of the Civil War. The rumor obviously still had great strength throughout the country. Two, the speech hints at the linkages among promotional literature of this time period. Material was freely used, re-used, edited, and re-edited by the many different pamphlets, booklets, and brochures published. The example of a Texas politician's speech made in Pennsylvania being appropriated in its entirety by a railroad for distribution in Europe illustrates such overlap and re-use. It hints at just one thread of the network cast everywhere to attract the potential settler to Texas.

Weather posed another hurdle for people considering immigration from Europe or northern or western states: the state was infamous for its "Texas northers." The approaches taken to dispelling the stories surrounding this severe weather were as numerous as the many pamphlets published. One approach was to minimize one aspect of the climate to the glorification of all the other weather. The Texas Colonization, Land and Trust Company in its short pamphlet said simply, "The only disagreeable feature of our climate is the 'northers.'" By implication none of the rest of the year's weather could be maligned. A writer for the 1872 *Texas Almanac* attacked the issue directly in a piece excerpted for re-use in the *Texas State Register* of 1876: "Texas northers have not only become famous abroad, but they deserve notoriety for the suddeness [sic] and violence of their winds, but not, generally, for the severity of the cold which attends them." An 1872 document also tried minimizing the severity of northers: "Some complain of our Texas northers, and others of the severe heat of summer. Our northers are of short duration. They conduce to health and give the farmer fine opportunities to kill his pork." This argument took a common approach by admitting that northers existed but presenting the flip side or advantage to such a change in weather.[38]

After traveling the South, Edward King published a lengthy book of observations on each state. For Texas, he described the "flood of emigration" as "formidable." The sketches that accompanied his accounts demonstrate how an outsider saw Texas and the impact of migration in the late 1870s. From Edward King, *The Great South: A Record of Journeys* (Hartford, Conn.: American Publishing Co., 1879), courtesy Louisiana State University Press.

Some writers simply could not deny the harshness of the winters but tried to impugn the motives of the climate's critics. One, after devoting over a page to the subject, blamed the negative impression of Texas's northers on disgruntled migrants. He wrote, "The effect of these Northers is most prodigiously magnified, and especially by those who becoming dissatisfied with the country, are disposed to retromigrate, and naturally attempt to justify their course by berating the country." And then he added, "There is no denying the unpleasantness of these Northers, even by those entertaining feelings of the greatest partiality for Texas, but this unpleasantness is greatly magnified by those who acquire a dislike for the country."[39]

The Texas Bureau of Immigration even tackled the subject of northers in a section several paragraphs long in its promotional brochure. The bureau took a simple, practical approach to adapting to the weather. The brochure described the sudden wind and the quick change in temperature but noted that "the man recently from the North or West, does not mind them, while the Texan puts on his warmest clothing, or keeps in doors." Then as in other descriptions of these winter storms, the writer pointed to their positive side: "These winds are highly charged with electricity, and there is no doubt of their purifying effect of the atmosphere and beneficial effect on the health of the people."[40]

Over and over the pattern repeats itself. Identify the negative; explain the reality. Sometimes point to the beneficial aspects in the midst of the seeming negative. Then move on to another subject, assuming that the rumor has been neatly laid to rest. The very forcefulness of the approach reflects the belief in their own rhetorical efforts. To these Texans the written word had power. They believed that information published for the potential immigrant carried a great deal of weight in helping the immigrant make decisions.

Some have called these written efforts at encouraging migration—the "literature of beguilement."[41] Others may discount these various efforts as mere hucksterism. In one way this analysis of various Texans' words might be considered a study in rhetoric—"the art of using language so as to persuade or influence others" (Oxford English Dictionary). But it is not a study of the words so much as a study of the effort; not a detailed picking apart of the techniques of persuasion or manipulative wording as it is a journaling effort to record the intangible overarching energy of the people of Texas. What methods or mediums did they use to broadcast their message? It is to that description that we now turn.

CHAPTER 5

A TANTALIZING ARRAY OF INVITATIONS

A tantalizing array of promotional literature existed between 1865 and 1915. Public, private, corporate, and political outpourings became multiple strands in a loosely connected Texas network sending information outside the state. Promoters were not a heterogeneous constituency for immigration, but they all shared respect for the value of the written word. Component parts of this network included newspapers published within and outside the state. Many papers with visionary editors contributed columns and columns of booster material. Journalists also published almanacs or almanac-like books meant for a wide audience. Land agencies and real estate agents published pamphlets extolling the values of their specific holdings, but in the process also wrote pages and pages of information on Texas in general. Railroads, as they built across the Texas interior, through the panhandle, and over the western plains, produced an unending flow of short fliers identifying possible settlement along their train routes. These businesses used words and, as the technology advanced, added photographs to supplement sketches and tables and graphs.

Newspapers, almanacs, and company publications helped weave a communication web that spun out across the United States and even overseas. Almost all this written material held a dual purpose. A definite connection existed between the business interest that paid for the publication and the ultimate goal of attracting immigrants. This double motive proved central to such works and was interwoven on almost every page. Newspapers conveyed information destined to be of help to the immigrant. But they also needed to sell their paper through the advertisements and make enough money to print the local and foreign news for its readers. The almanacs served as advertising mediums at the same time they shared information designed to help the immigrant decide when and where to settle in the state. The land broker spoke of the potential lying dormant in the soil, needing only an "industrious farmer" to unlock it. The railroad company wrote of great expanses of land at cheap prices ready for investment of time and money by the hardworking family from elsewhere. The town-booster pamphlet shouted the benefits of a community to any good and upright citizen willing to come and settle down.

Whether the newspaper publisher, the land broker, the railroad, or the small Texas town published the material of allurement, the message met two needs: the business interests of the publisher and the informational desires of the potential immigrant. Letters from individuals also entered this network for they were often published in one way or another after reception by the intended addressee. And finally, letters sent personally from one individual to another fit into this expansive network of various instrumentalities enticing people to Texas. While personal letters may not have resulted in huge numbers of people moving, their written words influenced smaller rivulets of movement that added to the overall stream.

NEWSPAPERS

Newspapers met several needs for the burgeoning immigration movement. First, they reported the news around the country relating to immigration efforts by other southern and western states. They would tell, for example, of efforts in Virginia and North Carolina to obtain a portion of the immigration heading toward the United States. Second, they wrote about the movement of immigrants into their area and responded as cheerleaders in this population shift. For example, in 1871 the *Gonzales Inquirer* took notice of several wagonloads of German immigrants destined ultimately for New Braunfels. "They were as fine looking a set of men, women and children as we could wish to see. They are the very people to build up our State." And third, they advertised themselves as the best source of local information for the potential resident. In performing all these roles, the newspapers formed a substantial part of the network attracting people to Texas.[1]

Sometimes a calamity of one sort or another would spur efforts on the part of Texans. In October, 1871, the event was a major fire in Chicago. The Scandinavian Club of Houston initiated the response, while a Houston newspaper reported the efforts. Under the heading "Immigrants! Immigrants!" an announcement of "50,000 Germans and 30,000 Scandinavians (Swedes, Norwegians and Danes) homeless and desolate" served to bring to the attention of Houstonians a great need. The Scandinavian Club went on to state, "in behalf of these, our unfortunate countrymen, we now appeal to the inhabitants of Texas, soliciting their aid in enabling as many of them as possible to emigrate to this State." The Club agreed to serve as a temporary employment agency, matching requests for specific workers with potential disaster victims, and helping to facilitate transportation. Another article in the same day's paper alleged that Superintendent Loeffler of the Texas Bureau of Immigration had assurances that the Illinois Central Railroad was ready to deliver "the unfortunates" free to New Orleans in lots of twenty-five. If Loeffler could raise the $6.00 per person needed to move them from New Orleans to Galveston via the Morgan steamers, Texas would be able to help the victims, and Texas. Then in an editorial statement, the journalist praised Loeffler and criticized the government by saying, "Thus with this small outlay, hundreds of industrious immigrants could be brought here, and yet the Legislature gobbles up the money as fast as it goes into the Treasury, and Mr. Loeffler can obtain none of it." While obviously discouraged with the Texas Legislature, the newspaper tried to whip up interest in its readership. How many fire victims actually made it to Texas is unknown. The newspaper, however, saw itself as an arm in the efforts of Texans to influence people to move to Texas.[2]

Many articles supported immigration, however attitudes about inclusiveness varied. An editorial in the *Houston Telegraph* glowingly spoke of the advantages of Texas, stating the need for millions of new citizens. "Let the people come. . . . We are a tolerant people. We will welcome the Yankee, the Radical, the Republican, the native, the foreigner, and men and women of all faiths and creeds. Therefore come to Texas, the land of promise. Heaven made it for you." Not all felt as inclusive in their call. For example, one observer for the *Houston Telegraph* noted in 1869 that some recent German immigrants were "stout, intelligent looking people, and more to be desired a hundred fold than the much talked of Chinese." One Austin County group demonstrated a similar narrow vision. We want "emigrants congenial with us in social habits and education, and in political sentiments. . . . Resolved, That we most cordially invite emigrants from our sister Southern States to come and settle here."[3]

Periodicals outside of Texas contributed to an evolving news network. The premier example of such activity was the publication, the *Texas New Yorker.* The editor was George H. Sweet, a one-time resident of San Antonio, who enthusiastically supported the development of Texas. In New York he utilized his Texas journalistic experience to publish a monthly paper of twenty-six pages describing Texas and praising its possibilities. New York, at the time, was the center of most immigrant activity in the country and dominated the financial business of the entire United States. The *Texas New Yorker* published its first issue in September, 1870, and continued publication through March, 1878. The bold masthead portrayed a single star with clasped hands shaking in welcome. Around the star were scenes of life in Texas, including ships loading and unloading at a wharf, a farmer walking behind a plow, and livestock grazing in the field. Just under the woodcut was the proclamation, "Devoted to making known to the Capitalist, Merchant, Mechanic, and Emigrant the

Texas New Yorker. Published in New York between 1870 and 1878, the *Texas New Yorker* presented the state as a teeming commercial location supportive of the farmer. Note the masthead's use of the Lone Star of Texas and the hands connecting across the continent. Courtesy Center for American History, University of Texas at Austin.

Agricultural, Horticultural, Stock-raising, Manufacturing, Railroading, and other Latent Wealth of Texas."[4]

A wide variety of material filled the pages of the *Texas New Yorker.* A standard inclusion was a "Travelers' Railroad Map" printed large across the back of four pages of news articles. Internal advertisements for the *Texas New Yorker* spoke directly to the main goal of the periodical. "50,000 New Subscribers wanted for the Texas New Yorker!!! . . . Every Live Texan should take it, and send a Copy to his relatives and friends in the Old States. If you want People, Back your State, and make her Resources known." Sweet's scheme aimed to put 288 pages a year before the New York reading public for the subscription rate of $1.50 per annum. And obviously he anticipated that Texans at home would read and subscribe as well. George Sweet's office in New York served as a magnet for material and information on Texas. The postal service provided the link between contributors and the publisher, and again from the publisher back into the hands of the readers.[5]

A running column in the *Texas New Yorker* was entitled "The Texas Press." Its main purpose was to provide space for laudatory letters and comments from newspapers around the state of Texas as they observed the work of the New York paper. A typical statement was one from the *Sherman Courier* suggesting that the *New Yorker* "is doing a great deal for Texas, and deserves our patronage,—$1.50 per annum." The listing also allowed the *Texas New Yorker* to stroke the Texas papers. By using their name in print, Sweet publicized their existence and efforts. Newspapers such as the *Victoria Advocate,* the *Navasota Tablet,* the *Waco Register,* and the *South-Western Index* received such publicity from Sweet's columns.[6]

Letters from subscribers and letters of inquiry repeatedly appeared in the columns of Sweet's periodical. The editor reveled in letters like one from Dr. M. D. Raiford of Smith County, Tennessee, who wrote he was "bound for Texas" and needed information, particularly information on the community near Marshall. Sweet boasted in another issue: "We have on our table, letters from Doyleston, Bucks Co., Pennsylvania; Otsego, Allegan Co., Michigan; Level Land, Abbeville Co., South Carolina; Hopkinsville, Christian Co., Kentucky; Southport, Connecticut, and numerous other points" all requesting information on Texas. It is easy to imagine him just rubbing his hands together gleefully and thinking what great news for the growing state of Texas.[7]

Notes from papers in the home state and letters of inquiry were reproduced verbatim and helped Sweet make his persuasive message. Contributions by Texas newspapers were another common approach to the enticement journalism practiced by Sweet. Whether these came as a direct gift of the respective Texas papers to the editor's office or were lifted, a la typical nineteenth-century journalism, is not always clear, but examples abound. The November 1871 issue included the following, "The *Austin Democratic Statesman* says: In spite of the huge taxes the administration has levied upon us, the immigration is likely to be larger this Fall than ever." The next month's issue included an observation from the *Brenham Enquirer* stating, "Yesterday's morning Gulf train brought up about 200 immigrants, mostly Germans and Bohemians. There were a good many women and children, and the immigrants look to be of the better class."[8]

Editorializing also gave Sweet the opportunity to praise his home state. In a front-page lead article in May 1872, Sweet noted the existence of pauperism in New York and went on to compare the lack of same in Texas. For the *Texas New Yorker* the opportunities inherent in Texas for industrious young workers precluded any expectation that some people might not find the state to be their Garden of Eden. Concerning Texas's participation in the upcoming Philadelphia Centennial Exhibition of 1876, Sweet said in 1872 that the state must have an exhibit for "Nothing will so command attention and attract capital and immigrants, as a proper interest in this thing by Texas."[9]

In addition, Sweet's *Texas New Yorker* contained numerous columns about the activity of the Texas Bureau of Immigration from 1870 to 1875. The *Texas*

New Yorker was in peak production during those years and used the bureau, and information provided by it, to feather its own publication's efforts to attract immigrants. Sweet refers to letters he has received and then notes that he will turn them over to the Bureau of Immigration for further responses. The Texas Bureau of Immigration was a small agency and the *Texas New Yorker* was a fledgling journal. Together they increased the influence of each.[10]

Entrepreneurs in St. Louis initiated their own version of enticement literature, using the heartland of America's transportation and food growing area as their base of operations. James L. Rock and W. I. Smith attempted the publication of the *St. Louis Texan* in 1878, claiming it to be an "independent, vigorous, weekly newspaper, devoted to a more intimate relationship between the North and East and the great Southwest, especially the State of Texas." They asserted absolute truthfulness to their work and promised "a full and reliable description of the country in which more than a quarter of a million are annually finding new homes."[11]

In February the *St. Louis Texan* wrote, "It is enough to make one's mouth water to know that at Galveston, Houston and San Antonio, they are luxuriating on fresh strawberries. Let's immigrate." The weekly four-page newspaper had a fair sampling of diverse articles. They noted the establishment of a Land Emigration office by the St. Louis, Iron Mountain, and Southern Railroad. This office reportedly would assist immigrants in selecting homes and had samples "of all kinds of grain, fruit, cotton, grasses, vegetables and woods" obtained from land along the rail's route. Another article identified San Antonio as an "oriental city" set down in the expanses of southwest Texas and then proceeded to identify some of the unique aspects of that community. They quoted in full the Homestead Laws of Texas, obviously believing them to be a distinct attraction for the potential immigration; and they did this in subsequent issues as well. In an interesting column entitled "Answers to Correspondents" the *St. Louis Texan* included the following: "F. W. writes from eastern New York, wanting to know the best way to go to Texas, and if it is a good place for a person without money. In answer to the first inquiry we send him a specimen copy of the TEXAN, and refer him to our railroad time tables. To his second inquiry we would say no. If you have not means to help yourself with, stay at home." We can only wonder how such straightforwardness was accepted by the readership of the paper, whether in Texas, Missouri, or New York.[12]

"We are sending several thousand copies of the TEXAN into the State of Texas each week" claimed the editors, Rock and Smith. They asked each reader who received one of those copies to correspond with them and provide truthful information for possible settlers. What we want, said the editors, are "all of the bad characteristics of the state as well as the good, and no fancy pictures either way." Their positioning on the issue of veracity continued. By announcing their mailings "each week to every County Clerk in the State of Texas," asking for reliable descriptions, they unmistakably pointed to their efforts at getting reliable information. How did they support their journalistic undertaking? No clear statement exists, but apparently the newspaper depended heavily on the railroads, because a full page of each four-page issue contained time schedules and rate tables from at least ten different rail lines. St. Louis, Missouri, was unquestionably a railroad hub in the Midwest. The Texas editors may have hoped their connections to the various railroads would sustain their publication until it blossomed in size and distribution. Many things factor into the success or failure of any journalistic endeavor. Reasons for the demise of the *St. Louis Texan* after only a short run remain clouded in the past. Considering the railroad support of their endeavors, it is surprising that the paper did not have a longer life.[13]

Most enticement literature of whatever persuasion often directly addressed negative publicity circulating about Texas. The *St. Louis Texan* was no exception to this approach. It decried such negativism forcefully with such advice as the following: "The readers of the TEXAN should take the criminal reports from Texas, which are being written up and telegraphed over the country, with a large amount of salt. It is only a system of 'artful dodging' in the interest of immigration. Not that Texas is free from crime but because every incident of that character is magnified into an hundred." Obviously angry at what they labeled "truth-killers," the editors claimed such negative publicists were manufacturing "falsehoods enough each week to construct a double track railway four times around the globe." A week later the paper defended Texas by saying, "'A terrible tragedy in Texas,' is now the standing headline of several papers which would divert immigration from that state. Every casualty upon the frontier and along the border of the Rio Grande is sufficiently magnified to cover the whole [of] the state. No state in the Union has more wholesome laws and more vigorously executed than Texas." Their editors' intense loyalty to Texas's interests was woven into and throughout their regular as well as editorial columns.[14]

Another technique often used by enticement literature was the pull on family heartstrings and sense of parental responsibility. One rather long article in the March 16, 1878, edition of the *St. Louis Texan* utilized this approach to the fullest. The writer of the article noted the large numbers of "old farmers from the east and north" who are considering their options in order to provide future homes for their children. Praising such concern, he related the recent visit to the newspaper offices of an Ohioan. This "gentleman" seeking information about lands in southwestern Texas had lived in Ohio all his life and had a "fine farm of 220 acres." Asked for his motivation in traveling to Texas, he responded that he was going to buy land to eventually divide among his six children. "You see . . . I have four sons and two daughters, and they have arrived at that age when they should commence to 'shift' for themselves." He went on to say, "The old homestead ain't big enough for us, so I am going to do by my children as my father done for me—give each of them 200 acres of as good farming lands as I can buy in Texas, and let them make for themselves and children, as I have made for myself and them—a home." With great praise for such a caring father, the journalist called him "sound to the core" and encouraged other fathers to follow this perfect model. Give them their inheritance and then say, "There is your natural mother embrace her, and obey her demands, and her ever fruitful breast will always sustain and nourish you." The article ended with a rousing call, "'Go west' old man and buy that son of yours a farm."[15]

Such enthusiasm often came from newspaper editors. One critic of western newspapers said they were "shrill, intense, promotional, and numerous."[16] That assessment of journalism in the West could just as easily be applied to the newspapers dealing with Texas. The out-of-state versions, such as the *St. Louis Texan* and the *Texas New Yorker,* shared with in-state papers the intense promotional nature of boosters for their subject.

ALMANACS

Almanacs also served to entice newcomers to Texas. They carried a host of information packed into one neat composite reference work. For the agriculturally oriented families of the nineteenth century, possession of an almanac was frequently as common as ownership of a Bible. Astronomical and meteorological tables, included in such documents, served as guides for planting and harvesting. In addition these sources might include lists of governmental officials, post office locations, descriptions of counties or cities, advertisements, reports by various authorities on a wide variety of subjects, as well as anecdotes and entertaining stories. The most widely distributed and read of the Texas volumes was the *Texas Almanac* published by Willard Richardson of Galveston.

Richardson published his first edition in 1857 and continued to do so through 1865, although the editions during the war years were more pamphlet size than earlier efforts. Possibly the confusion and chaos at the end of the

Civil War caused a short hiatus in publication, but in 1867 Richardson again was in full production, remaining so through 1873. The 1869 almanac changed its title from earlier issues. It became the *Texas Almanac and Emigrants' Guide to Texas.* The specific use of this title reflects accurately an essential element of the publisher's purpose. It reflects, too, the widespread acceptance by Richardson and his readers that Texas needed people and those people needed information to entice them to consider Texas as their home. While the name change only began in 1869, earlier issues also addressed the information needs of immigrants. The new title in 1869 merely put up-front one primary use of the volume.[17]

A close connection existed between the *Galveston Daily News* and the *Texas Almanac.* Willard Richardson was the publisher of both and his office at the newspaper served as a communication hub for obtaining any and all information about the state. Richardson knew the people to contact for information and encouraged their participation in his publications. He offered *News* readers "a copy of the Almanac and Map will be sent free to each contributor." The resulting compilation of information thus had multiple authors. One historian suggests that this fact embellishes for the twenty-first-century reader the value of the *Almanacs* because "these contributors lived in all parts of the state. They contributed grass roots data accompanied usually by opinion of the straight-from-the-shoulder variety." The *Almanac* was truly a collated volume of information. A reading of its pages suggests that many around the state loved their homes and in turn wanted other people to see the potential available in settling nearby. Valuing his own participation in the immigration movement, Richardson claimed, "we confidently believe it [the *Almanac*] has done more to bring immigration to the State than all our legislation during the same time, and in this opinion we think most [of] our intelligent readers will agree with us."[18]

Another dimension of the *Texas Almanac* was its role in describing political conditions. In his 1870 edition Richardson chose to reproduce the newly adopted constitution in full. Instrumental in the process providing for Texas's readmission to the Union following the disruption of the post–Civil War years, adoption of this 1869 constitution marked a milestone event in the eyes of most Texans. In the *Almanac* of the next year Richardson followed with an extensive overview of the laws passed by the Twelfth Legislature. In justification for such coverage, he wrote, "All our laws have been entirely changed and are now very imperfectly understood by a large majority of our people." His decision seems directed both to a concern for current residents and for the knowledge of future immigrants.

Richardson, however, shared publicly his very personal disappointment with the Texas politicians. He wrote in the 1872 *Texas Almanac:*

> We had hoped that the devotion of so large a part of this work to the great cause of immigration, would have induced our Legislature to order a few thousand copies for distribution in those countries where such information could not fail to add many thousands to the number of immigrants now seeking a home in Texas. But all such hopes have thus far been disappointed. It is true, we have now an Immigration Bureau, and we believe a very competent man placed at the head of it. But no adequate means have been placed in his hands to enable him to give aid or even information and encouragement to immigrants. While other new States are distributing books and pamphlets gratuitously all over Europe, by means of which they secure thousands of immigrants annually, our State has practically done nothing as yet.[19]

Richardson's disheartening assessment of the Texas legislature shows first his dashed hopes for the distribution of his special publication, the *Almanac.* But it also demonstrates the struggle in Texas during this time over taxes and expenditures for newly established state agencies. Richardson's lament, included in the preface to the 1872 edition, does not identify Gustav Loeffler by name. However, he does label the superintendent of the Bureau of Immigration a "very competent man" and includes an article about the bureau. Loeffler became part of the communication web centered at the *Galveston Daily News* office. Richardson's reference to Loeffler having "kindly placed at our disposal the answers he has received from sixty-five counties to his circulars asking for information" demonstrates how Richardson incorporated such information in his newspaper and his *Almanac.* But he also bemoaned the fact that the state agency was "left almost totally helpless, for the want of an adequate appropriation to enable him [Loeffler] to send abroad the valuable information at his command."[20]

Richardson continued his booster activities. "All that is necessary to secure thousands of immigrants annually, is to give them correct information of the advantages offered by this highly favored State." The various boosters were saying in effect: "Get it published for the reader far and wide." That seems to be the message of journalists, superintendents of governmental agencies, and writers of many persuasions. Faith in their own rhetoric and faith in their readers' subsequent decision-making skills propelled their unending insistence on publishing solid, clear information. It is easy to see the *Texas Almanac* throughout the period from the Civil War to 1873 as one kind of this entice-ment literature. Other almanacs or almanac-like books also fit comfortably into this genre. Albert Hanford wrote of his efforts in the *Texas State Register for the Year of our Lord 1872* as "the means of inducing more good men to visit the State than any other private individual." *Hanford's Register* maintained a sustained interest through 1879 in providing information for the potential im-migrant. The 1876 issue claimed that the "demand for Our Register has in-creased so much outside of Texas, that we have dropped many of the adver-tisements, and enlarged the work to make it THE EMIGRANTS' GUIDE TO TEXAS, and offer it for sale at a very moderate charge."[21]

Yet another almanac first published in 1875 seems more like an undisguised 161-page advertisement booklet. It was poorly edited in terms of providing concrete information, but since Richardson's *Texas Almanac* had suspended publication by this time (his last issue had been 1873), it seemed to fill a need. The title page identifies it as the *Texas Rural Register and Immigrants' Hand-Book, for 1875* and states it was "Compiled from Various Sources by J. Burke, Jr." A later edition carried the title *Burke's Texas Almanac and Immigrant's Hand Book, for 1879*. There were breaks in publication in the years 1877 and 1884 with the last edition published in 1885.[22]

This *Almanac* illustrates several points of the enticement literature of the day. The author lists himself, along with his associate E. H. Vasmer, as "Pub-lishers of Texas Maps and Immigration Pamphlets." While this by its very ex-istence is an advertising statement, it also points to the extensive use of maps to help describe and define the state. Their 1876 issue of the *Texas Rural Al-manac* included the map work of R. Roessler, a noted geologist who had par-ticipated in the 1871 U.S. Geological Survey of Texas. The reference also sug-gests a multiplicity of immigration pamphlets already on the market, for the reader would need some reference point to understand the meaning of the pronouncement—"Immigration Pamphlets."[23]

Burke, as well as Richardson and Hanford before him, viewed his work as crucial to the population growth of the state, and all of them were willing to take such credit, even if it meant self-promotion. Burke wrote about the in-creased population of Texas in his 1876 issue saying that, "Fully two hundred thousand people from other States have found houses among us during this year. They have come from every quarter of the Union, and from Europe." Referring then to his *Almanac,* he wrote in a slightly immodest tone, "we feel as-sured that it has been instrumental in bringing some, at least, of the thousands who have found homes with us during the past year." Such announcements served to plug the importance of the book so that potential advertisers would come on board in subsequent editions, but it also spoke to the inner sense of what the compiler felt he was doing through all his energetic work.[24]

These almanacs were clearly documents intended to reach farmers. The subject matter dealing with rural concerns points to this, as does the editorializing evident in some of the short articles included in the books. An especially light-hearted appeal for farmers can be found in the 1876 edition of *Burke's Almanac* under the heading "The Class of People Most Wanted in Texas." After suggesting that the country has more doctors than it needs, the author then attacked other professionals. "We have nine times too many lawyers. The State could well afford to make a "big swap," and trade off seven-eighths of her lawyers for Northern farmers, at the rate of forty lawyers for one farmer, and make "big money" by the exchange." It went on to say "We have all the clerks, counter hoppers, book-keepers, lawyers, doctors and deadheads the country can well support, and we can not advise any more to come. But we do want, and must have, farmers. We have plenty of room, and will gladly welcome within our borders *five million good farmers.*" The effort to entice people to settle in Texas may have concentrated in the cities of Houston and Galveston where these various almanacs were published, but their message was ultimately directed to the common farmer from everywhere to come and settle on the lands throughout the state.[25]

Almanacs in general, because of their expected yearly publication dates, suggest the belief that information must be updated regularly in order to keep the reader current. They can be seen as one type of written material, fitting on the continuum somewhere between the daily or weekly pages of a booster newspaper and the typically one-time pamphlet published by a land agency or railroad company. Almanacs in their more journalistic pattern consisted of odds and ends loosely tied together by a slender thread. They shared with newspapers a time-related intensity typical of strong rhetorical material. There is an inherent urgency best expressed by the phrase: Do it now. Texas enticement literature had that quality. Paragraphs of information and statistics in the almanacs and newspapers had "a forceful, staccato quality"[26] that gave it power—the power of persuasion.

GENERAL BUSINESS PUBLICATIONS

While almanacs had a standard format and typically included the same subject matter regardless of the publisher, a multitude of other documents of the era served as enticement literature but do not fit into any such clear pattern. As these documents are read by contemporary scholars the primary question remains, "Who wrote this document? and why was it published?" If we make the assumption that the material was published to entice people into moving to Texas, the question then goes a level deeper to ask what other motive did the person or organization have? Sometimes this is easily identified. For example, John W. Forney was the author of a ninety-two-page book entitled *What I Saw in Texas*. Published in Philadelphia in 1872 it would seem on first appearances to be typical of the travel literature of the day where a northerner goes south, observes activities around him, and reports for a newspaper or journal in the North. However, as one delves deeper into the pages, it becomes apparent that Forney is traveling as a companion to Thomas Scott, president of the Texas and Pacific Railroad. Scott's goal in visiting Louisiana and Texas was to consolidate business with urban communities along the designated future roadway of the railroad. Forney's task then became publicist for the trip and recorder of events for later publication to interest business investors in the work of the Texas and Pacific Railroad.[27]

Other documents do not so easily explain themselves when read by the contemporary scholar. *Texas: Its Climate, Soil, Productions, Trade, Commerce, and Inducements for Emigration* states the title of a thirty-four-page pamphlet with no identifiable author. Published in New York by Martin & Fulkerson Stationers in 1870, the title page includes the image of an official-looking state seal with its single star and laurel leaves and the notation "Fifth Edition." The inside copy has a light journalistic tone and begins under the subheading "The Paradise of the South." On continued reading it becomes clear that the pamphlet is a poorly put-together group of letters from a "correspondent" to the *New York Sun*. The newspaper simply served as a collection point receiving and publishing the letters of J. M. Morphis. This format thus allowed a dialogue via letters with a number of people asking questions that Morphis answered. Texas comes out the winner in this interchange as Morphis relates a multitude of positives to be experienced for those living in Texas.[28]

Titles of various enticement literature varied, but the inside material had a repetitive ring to it. William Brady, a Houston real estate broker, published *Glimpses of Texas: Its Divisions, Resources, Development and Prospects*. Over seventy pages of text describing Texas, agriculturally and commercially, preceded another thirty-plus pages of advertisements as well as land listings for Brady's firm. A smaller document of only twenty-seven pages presented the alluring features of Texas and then simply referred the reader to Catlin, McCarty & Co., located at 71 Broadway, New York. Entitled *A Few Practical Remarks About Texas,* this book ends with a ringing "Appeal":

Flee ye hither ye oppressed and homeless of other lands, here you receive a welcome
from all, with land enough and homes for all who seek them, on our broad and
rolling prairies. Here the virgin soil lies basking in the rays of Sol, inviting the hus-
bandman, the fore-runner of civilization, to occupy the lands so lately vacated by
the "Comanche," the Buffalo and Antelope, to plant the seeds of other lands and
reap his reward of wealth which will spring as if by magic from her lap.

Such effusive language, in high rhetorical style, was also admittedly presented
with the motive "of bringing our rich and desirable lands in this section before the world, offering the emigrant and wanderer a good home and at a low
price." McCarty was a real estate developer singing the praises of Texas and its
available lands.[29]

Texas. Information for Emigrants, published in Tennessee and authored by
H. C. Mack, is more of a mystery document. There is no concrete sense from
a reading of the full 207 pages (a document that its author calls "our pamphlet") as to the ulterior motive of those paying for the publication. The work
is very supportive of railroad development in the state, but this was typical in
1869. While there is no sure sense of the motivation of its author, the document has a fascinating approach in its first fifteen pages. The writer addressed
the potential immigrant on a very personal level, sharing concerns and considerations in moving as if talking with a friend or neighbor. Mack suggested
a sort of mid-life assessment for each person. "Your labor supplies the wants
and necessities of a rising family, but . . . your children are rapidly pushing
forward to assume their positions upon the arena of life." In reality said Mack,
"the rigid exactions of society and the consuming taxations of fashion, well-
nigh or may be entirely cancel your income, and the twilight of age is rapidly
paleing [*sic*] your countenance, and the question presents itself as to what you
had better do to improve the circumstances and amend the condition of your
family in life." Such inward soul-searching suggested by the author led him ultimately to the rest of his book in which he detailed the advantages of selecting Texas as a future home. Texas becomes the ultimate place to put one's
hopes for those later years of life. Mack's approach incorporated a detailed balance sheet of reasons for migrating anywhere. It then laid out all the information to help the immigrant make a decision to the advantage of Texas.[30]

Railroads spread their tracks across Texas in the years after the Civil War.
Sometimes haltingly, sometimes with the speed of their own locomotives, the
bands of iron and steel moved across the vast territory of Texas. Railroads
both stimulated immigration and were stimulated by this influx of people. An

excellent example of the relationship of railroad development and immigration can be seen in a small pamphlet issued by the New Orleans, Mobile and Texas Railroad Company. In their brochure advertising mortgage bonds, they praised Texas saying, "A constant stream of thrifty German industry, mingled with steady accessions from the Northern and Atlantic States, is flowing in and spreading over the Texas country; but there is room for millions more." Seeing themselves as the force that could help the South develop its resources, the railroad company tied the growth of the population in the gulf states to the potential for the railroad's growth. This 1871 document successfully used immigration itself as the rationale to sell bonds.[31]

LETTERS, PRINTED AND PERSONAL

Vast numbers of letters written by individuals also left the state and at least in part served to entice migration. Each letter made some impact upon another human being, most typically influencing the recipient to think about or rethink their decision to remain where they were or to move to Texas. By their very nature letters suggest personal interaction. An individual sits down and puts his or her thoughts, reflections, and opinions on paper. The letter travels across space, eventually reaching the recipient. When opened by the addressee, the letter immediately establishes a connection as the reader takes in those written words and strives to understand the feelings underlying the message. Letters link a writer to a reader. This is true whether the letter is kept as a personal experience or is published in some formal way. The letter format conveys the sense of an interpersonal experience. Knowing the influence such letters muster, editors frequently turned their columns over to long letters or extended excerpts. The editor used the letter format to enhance the impact of the information being presented.

The enticement literature concerning settlement in Texas is replete with examples of the letter format, printed for a public forum to digest. Horace Greeley, a New York newspaperman, traveled to Texas and the states bordering the lower Mississippi River in 1871. Whatever his ultimate motive, and many would suggest the trip served partly to fuel Greeley's political aspirations, the journalist came to Texas. He proceeded to travel mostly by railroad, sending dispatches back to the news office. Later the *New York Tribune* collected these columns into a small volume and published *Mr. Greeley's Letters from Texas and the Lower Mississippi*. The *Tribune* assumed a large audience existed for such information. The letter format allowed the journalist to speak casually and directly to the reader and in the process convey in a personal way impressions about his travels. Greeley remarked on a wide variety of subjects. Texans latched on to some of his observations with pride, as in the one that read: "Whether it be a recommendation or not, I judge that it has required less effort to live in Texas than in any other State of the Union. The common saying, "It costs no more to rear a cow here than a hen at the North," is literally true. . . . Many a man has thus grown rich without effort and almost without thought." Greeley's visit and subsequent "letters" back to New York served to place Texas in the minds of readers across the country.[32]

Sometimes Texas letters even appeared in publications overseas. Newspapers with connections around the globe reported on activities far from the homeland. Information about the United States, including its many states and territories, arrived in Europe through many mediums. The letter format provided one method for such information to be shared in a way that hinted of a little more intimacy and personal connection than other approaches. Witness portions of one letter written from Texas on April 19, 1867, and printed in *Morgenbladet* two months later:

> You may well believe that we are often surprised by the dispatches in Morgenbladet and your reports from America, colored as they all are by radical views. And we are amused to see the warnings against the many dangers that threaten those who emigrate to the southern states! Probably there can be no greater error. At present there is no place in America where capable Norwegian emigrants would be able to do so well for themselves as in Texas and some of the other southern states, now that the Negroes no longer can be depended upon. For those of your readers who might be interested I shall give a little description of Texas and its glories.

The letter then proceeded to speak of new construction in Texas and specifically the many houses going up in Galveston. The writer wrote glowingly of this Texas city, recounting the fact that residents called it the "Queen of the Gulf."[33]

Letters often traveled much closer to home. Norwood Stansbury was a sugar planter looking for work in the early months of 1875. He traveled from Louisiana to the Texas coast and during the year wrote back to his friend J. Y. Gilmore, editor of the *Louisiana Sugar-Bowl*, published in New Iberia. The letters give today's reader a glimpse of life in Texas in 1875 just as they did for Louisiana readers of the *Sugar-Bowl*. Stansbury had visited Galveston previously, so he had a convenient reference point with which to compare Galveston's recent development. He wrote to Gilmore, "The growth of the city has been wonderful. The population exceeds forty thousand, and has more than doubled in fourteen years." Continuing the comparisons, he wrote, "There is an air of life and thrift here not visible in any of our towns at home."[34]

The letter format assumes a sharing of both good and bad experiences, positive and negative responses. Stansbury's letters bear out this pattern, for while he praises some things, he frankly complains of others. Weather, politics, and health concerns pepper his letters.[35] Stansbury's letters also point to the fact that while he is working in Texas he is reading the Louisiana papers. This gives him both the appearance and the reality of keeping up with the happenings at home, and so when he writes with intimate knowledge of the problems back home, his letters continue to carry that very personal touch that Gilmore admired and utilized in the pages of his weekly paper. The fact that the *Louisiana Sugar-Bowl* was printed both in English and in French increased its readership and may have influenced a wider spectrum of people to begin thinking about Texas.

Straightforward description could also convey secondary messages that had the potential to attract immigrants. Stansbury's September 15, 1875, letter referred to the Morgan Company's efforts to dredge a channel in the Galveston Bay area. "Hundreds of men find employment during these hard times at liberal wages, and the cash at the end of every month is as sure as the rising of the morning sun." Such a statement served as its own lure to men struggling with making ends meet back in Louisiana. Stansbury did not have to say "Come to Texas, Jobs abound!" He conveyed the same message with his simpler (and because it was in letter format possibly more believable) statement about the activity of workers on a local transportation project. In a February letter this workingman explained, "The great mass of immigrants and excursionists come by the railroad direct to the interior, with little expenditure of time and money." His reassurance conveyed the ease with which that move could take place. Readers took note and then rethought their own commitment to remain in Louisiana or move on.[36]

Letters in newspapers often beget more letters in an ongoing process of shared confidences. J. H. Lippard served as an agent of the Texas Bureau of Immigration stationed in New Orleans. In November, 1871, he sent a letter brimming with enthusiastic news to his employer Gustav Loeffler. The editor of the *Houston Telegraph* obtained a copy and used this agency report/letter as part of his personal campaign for immigration into Texas. "I am happy to say that I found the people fully aroused, as to the futurue [sic] prospect of Texas; many hundreds are on their way and many more prepareing [sic] to follow their friends to our State," wrote Lippard. Then this agency representative said, "let me state that I had a notice inserted in the *New Orleans Republican* stating my mission, locality, etc., which notice brought more correspondence than any one clerk could answer, and was still increasing when the notice was discontinued." If we assume Lippard is truthful in his statement, the response he received seems to indicate an interest in one-on-one contact with someone who is knowledgeable about Texas. People were willing to write letters to a non-acquaintance in order to obtain the information they sought.[37]

Immigrants in Texas, like the Norwegian who sent an 1867 letter overseas from Galveston to Norway, sought to maintain contacts with people back in Europe and to share information with them about migrating. Closer to home, a farmer originally from Perry County, Alabama, wrote a short letter to the editor of the *Mobile Alabama Daily Register.* Dated September 19, 1870, from Columbus, Texas, the letter read in part, "Last fall, in the general drift to Texas, I followed in 'the course of human events.' Landing at Galveston, I went up the Central railroad, in the current of immigration, not knowing where best to go in this vast empire of territory." Then he explained his experiences, ending the letter with the statement, "I merely wish to state these facts that those coming this fall will not have to run around so much to find cheap lands, and where best to go to find a place. I shall be back in Perry county soon after my family. Crops good." Signed, W. Bradley.[38]

This letter by an Alabama farmer conveys the personal nature of letter writing even though he is addressing the letter with the intent of its publication for countywide consumption. Others reading the letter as they perused their local paper must surely have begun to wonder about migrating elsewhere and specifically about whether Texas really had anything to offer people from Alabama. The fact that Bradley came from a county that in 1880 had 7,150 white citizens and 23,591 blacks is reflected in the body of his letter as well. He hints at partial motivation for considering such a move. "The State allows 160 acres to every family, and 80 acres to single men. There is enough here, it is said, for 500 families. I found west the health better and the lands equally as rich, and by odds less negroes. In fact, they are comparatively few." Obviously racial concerns entered into the reasons why Bradley was moving to Texas, and he felt his information on that subject would influence others.[39]

Letters back home, via the local newspaper, provided one vehicle to convey personal interest and concrete information. George Sweet in his *Texas New Yorker* columns also utilized personal letters to convey his promotional efforts. He went a step further by encouraging Texans to capitalize on the interest expressed in letters by writing directly to these potential immigrants. The June, 1872, issue of the *Texas New Yorker* included a letter from a New Englander requesting a copy of the New York paper and stating:

A friend and myself (and our family of course,) have intended locating in Iowa or Nebraska, next season, in fact had made up our minds to do so—when I happened to see a copy of your paper (May, 1871). We now feel as if we would like Texas best and wish all the information you can give through your paper or otherwise. We are poor in pocket, but have pluck and character.

E. C. Ryer

Box 549 Burlington, Vt.

Sweet followed this printed letter with the suggestion that Texans correspond with these "Green Mountain" people, saying "Perhaps a number of families might be induced to join with him and all settle in some good neighborhood in Texas." Sweet valued the drawing power of a letter, as well as the influence of chain migration on the development of a new territory.[40]

"To migrating families, letters were a tenuous link between the known and the unknown." With this sensitive statement, Lois Myers introduces the edited letters of Anna Louisa Wellington Stoner. What was true for the Wellington-Stoner family was true for most families on the move in the late nineteenth century. Letters tethered their writers to the seemingly stable world left behind and to other people. They provided a needed "connection" when the experiences of day-to-day life were full of breaks and changes in routine and environment. These same letters met other needs as well, especially the conveyance of information about the territory being traversed. In those descriptions and extended explanations of these migrations, letters influenced the flow of people. They definitely influenced the movement of people into Texas.[41]

Connections remained the rationale for letter writing. Mitchell Daniel moved to Texas in 1877 and wrote back to his uncle in Virginia. He shared that his main motive for the move was his interest in his children's future. He explained his own willingness to make a change from Virginia to Texas in order to secure their happiness. He then launched into a description of his new homeland. He viewed the influx of people to the state as indication of its improvement. He had the advantage of being able to compare this area of Texas with the same place he had seen eight years earlier. The comparison lent credibility to his observations. We can only wonder how much his enthusiasm peaked the interest of others back in Virginia when they read, "Immigrants are pouring into this state from all sections of the world, and the progress & improvement of the county rapid. The State has doubled its population within five years and will double it again in five more. This town when I left here in 1869 was only 1500 people now has 8,000 and is still rapidly improving, though property is very cheap, and has not advanced in price within the eight years I speak of."[42]

Not everyone in correspondence with a Texan made the decision to move. The important point for analysis of enticement literature is to be aware of the part such letters played in the process of thinking and rethinking the potential of such a move. Family ties influenced decision-making. One woman with the given name of America lived in Pattersonville, Louisiana in 1872. She wrote a letter tinged with desperation. In part it read, "There are but three of us left of a large family—all passing rapidly away. I am so anxious to be in Texas among my relations, and would have gone long ago if our circumstances had allowed, but we are now left homeless and very poor by the war, and have never been able to make anything more than support since." America felt confident she could support herself by running a boarding house, and so she asked, "Please tell me where is best place for me in your town and what you would advise me to do. I will await an answer from you, as I have a month to remain here. . . . Any arrangements you and Charles make will please me." Reliance on family and friends to help in the migration process was a common circumstance back then, as it is to this day.[43]

Women seldom traveled alone to new places in the postbellum South. But obviously America was willing to do so. Another adventurous woman was Martha Ann Otey. Letters written in 1866 by Martha Ann to her parents and sister in Holmes County, Mississippi reveal a widowed woman of courage seeking a new life in Texas. With a heavy sense of responsibility for the maintenance of her parents, Martha left two young children with them and traveled westward to seek a position as teacher in east Texas. From the beginning her "mission," as she saw it, was to find a job as head teacher of a school and then help her mother, father, sister, brother, and her own two children move to Texas for what she herself called, "a new people, a new element, a new home." Success depended on her shouldering these heavy familial duties, but her future also lay at the hands of fate, weather, and the economy. From March through November of 1866 she kept up a continuing correspondence with family in Mississippi, constantly describing her activities and experiences in Texas. As she chronicled those events, her Mississippi family began to imagine Texas in their own minds and slowly grew accustomed to understanding Martha's world as it came closer to being their world. Martha wrote both about the negative and the positive. She chronicled the bad weather, the impassable roads, the lack of rail transportation, and the bugs. But she also wrote with great hope in her letters:

Galveston is a beautiful place. I like its appearance better than any town I ever saw. Had I the means I should settle here for life. I went down on the beach this evening. The sight was worth all I have seen since leaving home. . . . I am perfectly charmed with this country [Texas], and hourly wish that we were all here in a good home, all fixed to mind. I think we can do much better in Texas than East of the Mississippi. . . . I see nothing yet to make me despond of success. Of course, not being wealthy, I shall have much to contend with in establishing myself in Texas, but, if we can get all here with "whole bones," we can live.[44]

Letters she received from friends who had earlier made the decision to emigrate may have fueled Martha's positive attitude.

While she was residing in Washington County, Martha received a letter from a woman named Genie living in Gonzales County farther to the west. Genie wrote, "A hearty welcome to this lovely land. I trust you will become as much infatuated with its beauties as myself, and here amid the broad and luxuriant prairies, long flowing moss, and bright sparkling streamlets, take up your abode and be one of our number." Martha wrote home about the people she met during her travels and her work experience in Huntsville. "The kindness of the people in this State only makes me more anxious to live among them," she wrote. In another letter she reiterated similar sentiments saying, "Such kindness as the people of this State have shown me, I never dreamed of." She perceptively looked at the wider world picture, noting the migrations going on around her. With her typical mixture of hope and realism, she wrote on July 15, 1866, "I think this State will fast fill with people from all parts of the South. It certainly presents greater facilities for the unbounded energies than any other."[45]

Letters conveyed the full spectrum of news and hopes. Sometimes the letters were not from family members, but friends striving to serve as family members in similar situations. An Englishwoman wrote to her European friends in 1871, reporting on her work to help settle immigrants in Washington County, in or near the town of Brenham. The letter writer noted the arrival in Galveston of the immigrants via New Orleans by ship from Liverpool and then recounted their trip inland. She wrote, "I am thankful to report that all have been placed in good homes where the prospects before them are favorable. They came trusting in the Lord and we have never seen His hand more conspicuously displayed in any temporal matters than it has been on their behalf in closing doors which needed to be closed, as well as in opening in new and unexpected quarters." The newcomers had spent six weeks traveling by ship. In Galveston they were cared for by Mr. C. M. Hurley, "a Christian Merchant" who helped them settle in boarding houses overnight. Short worship sessions were held in Galveston, where thanksgiving was rendered and "the Lord's goodness was recounted as we meditated on Psa. CVII. 'He brings them to their desired haven.'"[46]

The real motive for the letter appears in the single line: "Friends at home who helped will be glad to know how the various members of our company have been placed." Those assisting first-time immigrants wanted to ease the discomfort of travel and the safety worries that change entailed. The care demonstrated by this Englishwoman reflects the deep religious commitment of her group, as well as their collective joy in the success of settlement. The immigrants had come in family units. Many obtained positions as servants, for "in every case the wife works in the house, & and the husband outside in the care of horses, cattle, garden, & farm; the husbands have all been accustomed to farm work." The letter mixed the more positive news of high wages and good employment positions with the downside story of transportation difficulties, the low price of cotton this season, and the changeable weather. Yet in all the information conveyed by the letter, the outstanding message was one of connections among caring people as they worked to facilitate immigration to Texas.[47]

How many people came to Texas based on a letter written in their local newspaper or a personal letter sent by a friend of a friend? While an intriguing question, it is doubtful that such information can really be known. In the same way it is impossible to identify the numbers who came in response to railroad literature or to a pamphlet issued by the state government. In the unstructured network of interest at attracting people to the state, letters helped fuel the movement. Letters carried hopes, dreams, reality, and struggle. Those reading the letters and responding to them heard those frustrations and those visions, and many ultimately made the decision to be caught by this movement to Texas. The vast net cast for people by Texans depended heavily on the belief that the written word was a mainstay of the effort. Many clearly read letters and made a decision to move. Others used the newspaper accounts for their information hoping their move would be an easy one. Still others read almanacs, business pamphlets, and railroad informational sheets and dreamed of moving to Texas.

CHAPTER 6

GOVERNMENT GETS THE MESSAGE OUT

The population of Texas shot upward from 604,215 in 1860 to 818,579 in 1870 and then onward to 1,591,749 by 1880, a 163 percent increase in two decades.[1] Whether people came to Texas because of the written words or not, citizens in Texas believed that such publications were essential in peopling the state. Lines, paragraphs, pamphlets, and books sent out the message and were issued prolifically at the time. Volumes and volumes described Texas. The variety was endless and the approaches taken were numerous. These publications by private individuals, various business enterprises, or governmental agencies supported a common goal. They all announced that Texas had something to offer that no other state in the Union could provide.

People did not stop moving to Texas after the death of the Bureau of Immigration or because of the 1876 constitutional prohibition. Foreign-born and American-born migrants continued to arrive in Texas. This influx sustained interest in publishing information to speed up that process of population growth. There was interest by state agencies *in spite of* the state prohibition and interest by private enterprises *because of* the prohibition. Two major avenues existed for Texans working toward the ultimate goal of increased population in Texas. Private business efforts moved down one pathway in a complex but ongoing parade of multiple endeavors. Another avenue involved surreptitious efforts within the state bureaucracy to accomplish the very goals to which Section 56 of the Constitution expressly forbid the spending of Texas's tax dollars.

What was the public perception of the Section 56 constitutional prohibition? One of the more casual, contemporary accounts comes from the pen of Alexander Sweet. In his 1883 book entitled *On a Mexican Mustang, Through Texas, From the Gulf to the Rio Grande,* Sweet included a full quotation from Section 56 and then he wrote:

It is currently believed that the framers of the Texas constitution had moss two feet in length growing on their backs.

That such a provision as that quoted is to be found in the constitution of the

State, is a disgrace to the people of Texas, and a painful commentary on their intelligence. I was gratified to learn that fifty-six thousand voters cast their votes against the adoption of the constitution containing the anti-immigration clause.

Texas needs immigration,—there can be no question about that,—and the kind of immigrants Texas wants are men who will produce something.

Sweet then launched into multiple paragraphs describing Texas's resources and the industrious people needed to develop that potential.[2]

Hubert Howe Bancroft published a more formal history of the state in 1889. Covering Texas government during the Reconstruction era, Bancroft pointed to what he called "defects in [the] constitution." He continued, "provision was made that separate schools should be provided for the white and colored children; and foreign immigration was discountenanced." This statement was footnoted and the author quoted verbatim Article 16, Section 56 of the state constitution.[3]

These written accounts by Sweet and Bancroft were typical of the time. People inside Texas's borders, in addition to those looking at Texas from the outside, ascribed a heavy influence to that short constitutional provision. George Sweet in his March 1876 edition of the *Texas New Yorker* headlined an article "Immigration still pouring into Texas" and then quoted material excerpted from the *Houston Telegraph* that said, "Although the new Constitution is silent on the subject of immigration, and is calculated to retard it, yet some will come to our State." The use of the term "silent" is an intriguing way for a booster medium such as the *Houston Telegraph* to downplay the absolute prohibition stated in the constitution itself. Yet the newspaper is clearly aware of the impact this constitution could have on immigration.[4]

A sense of general wonderment about any government refusal to help finance the immigration movement appears in the correspondence of B. J. Gautier, the Spanish Consulate in Galveston. On May 17, 1889, Gautier wrote to the Commissioner of the Department of Agriculture, Insurance, Statistics, and History (D.A.I.S.H.) with a personal as well as a public request. Gautier was planning a trip to Europe and wrote that "while there [I] would like to do something for our State, my native home." Aware of the upcoming Paris Exposition he expected the state legislature would be providing a display representing the state. When he discovered that no such exhibition was planned, he wrote to his senator "making inquiry and suggesting such actions." Reporting the senator's response, Gautier wrote, "but he informed me that it was inhibited by the constitution (?)" Gautier's use of a question mark in parentheses seems to indicate his disbelief that such a prohibition existed. It is almost as if he is asking, "Can this be true?" But he didn't dwell on that point and proceeded to suggest a course of action on the assumption that the senator's information or interpretation was accurate. A real "go-getter," Gautier sadly wrote, "I am only sorry that Texas should be behind the times." Then adding in a more positive vein, "But we need not remain completely obliterated and out of sight. If we are not there with a display of our national and industrial products, we yet may draw the attention of the World and open the eyes of capitalists with a display of maps, charts, statistical tables, etc. accompanied with reports, circulars and other printed matter, so displayed that, he who passes may read." Gautier's suggestion, involving written materials, reflects an enthusiastic Texan's interest in "thus inviting immigration and foreign capital to our shores." He assumed the D.A.I.S.H. had a similar interest and requested help from the state agency. No response is recorded in the files of the department, so we can only wonder if Gautier was left hanging with a great idea but no help in carrying it out, or if the agency did provide some pamphlets, brochures, and maps.[5]

Sweet's informal history, Bancroft's more voluminous history, the *Houston Telegraph* via the *Texas New Yorker,* and at least one state senator, all suggest some general knowledge of Section 56. Those aware of the prohibition often saw it as a detrimental clause hurting state efforts. They highlight in written form what seemed to be a pervasive sense around the entire state: this constitutional prohibition would influence development in Texas and the way that Texans participated in that development. In light of Article 16, Section 56, the deliberate actions and persuasive writing of the continuing enticement effort shine even more brightly. Gautier's letter with its reference to a state politician would lead us to believe that people within the state government knew about the constitutional prohibition and interpreted it as a total interdiction against using state money to encourage newcomers. But, governmental agencies within Texas participated in the immigration enticement effort *both* before *and* after 1876.

The Texas Bureau of Immigration during its entire existence had placed primary emphasis on producing written material for distribution. It proudly published its major document, *Texas: The Home for the Emigrant, From Everywhere.* The title page of the 1875 English edition clearly states: "Published by the authority of the Legislature and Under the Auspices of the Superintendent of Immigration of the State of Texas."[6] *Texas: The Home for the Emigrant, From Everywhere* used government statistics and information to make its plea for newcomers. It encouraged the immigrant to consider the possibilities and then make choices based on the best advice that she or he could obtain. The assumption in the brochure was that the state agency was providing just that specific, concrete, and trustworthy advice.

The 1876 state constitution brought funding for such endeavors to an abrupt end. In light of that knowledge, it is fascinating to look at a published document entitled *The Home for the Emigrant. Texas: Her Vast Extent of Territory, Fertility of Soil, Diversity of Productions, Geniality of Climate, and the Facilities She Affords Emigrants for Acquiring Homes.* While it has a publication date of 1877, it is almost an exact duplicate of the 1875 edition of *Texas: The Home for the Emigrant, From Everywhere.* Statistical tables have been removed from the earlier publication or updated into a more compact style. One table dealing with the public free schools was completely reworked in the later publication into paragraph form, using June, 1877, as its reference date.[7]

In the Bureau of Immigration's pamphlet, Superintendent Robertson included multiple letters written to him by knowledgeable people around the state. This use of the letter format led the reader to see the state agency as fostering communication between the bureau and leading authorities around the state. In this way, Robertson reinforced the image of an interactive state agency getting the most up-to-date information available. The earlier 1875 pamphlet also included specific references to services of the Texas bureau. For example it stated, "the best efforts of this Bureau and its agents will be given to aid the immigrant, by giving him information by which can be procured the lowest rates of passage possible . . . [the bureau] has nothing to do with buying and selling lands, nor with any other private enterprise."[8] All references to any such state bureau of immigration were exorcised from the later 1877 pamphlet. Yet, overall, the same information is presented in essentially the same style with presumably the same audience in mind.

So questions arise as to this mysterious pamphlet of thirty-six pages. Who paid for its publication? How was it distributed? How many copies were published? And was it, like the 1873 to 1875 bureau documents, also translated into other languages? Two clues exist from which it has been impossible to draw any conclusions. First, in the 1877 document the last two pages include an article entitled "A Model Sheep Ranch" with the byline "From the Corpus Christi Times." It describes with an observer's eye the sheep ranch of a Mr. Reynolds, but draws no concluding statement either about the ranch or about the pamphlet as a whole. Second, the title page of the later document provides the following publication information: "Austin: Institution The For [*sic*] Deaf and Dumb, 1877."[9] Archival information points to programs designed to help inmates of this and similar institutions develop a marketable skill, thus turning them into productive citizens. Did the Institution for the

Deaf and Dumb house printing equipment? Could the publication of this work have been used as part of the learning process for these handicapped students? If so, was not state tax money used to produce a piece of enticement literature in strict defiance of the 1876 constitutional prohibitions? This intriguing document remains a mystery. It does, however, verify the continued presence of enticement literature published in some way with assistance from a state agency.

Actions of the Texas legislature demonstrate complicity in creating immigrant-recruiting tools. A chain of events reveals a suggestive narrative in the formation of state agencies to service the needs of the developing state. In 1879, the Sixteenth Legislature passed enabling laws establishing a Commissioner of Insurance, Statistics, and History to oversee an executive department with the stated task, "to obtain from every available source all reliable information and statistics relating to the population, wealth and general resources of the state, and particularly in regard to agriculture, stock raising, manufactures, mining and other industries." The state agency was also to compile information "relating to commerce, exports and imports; also relating to internal improvements of all kinds, public and private, and such other objects as may be of general interest or benefit to the state." Provision existed for the commissioner to call on other state officers for such information and then to make available such information "in tabulated or other convenient form, and report the same to the governor, annually." Not only was the commissioner to keep in touch with government officers statewide, he was also charged to "keep in constant communication with the department of agriculture of the United States."[10] The emphasis on communication within and without the state is a key to seeing this particular executive bureau (Department of Insurance, Statistics, and History, or D.I.S.H.) as an avenue for discreet, if not actually undercover efforts to attract immigrants.

Various reports were sent out from this agency, but an 1882 document best illustrates the information-gathering tasks of this state commission. Entitled *The Resources, Soil, and Climate of Texas,* the work includes the phrase "Report of A. W. Spaight, Commissioner of Statistics, Etc." on the title page. Pages one through 360 provide an alphabetical listing for each county, with paragraph descriptions of population totals, assessed value of taxable property, and county activities. Spaight included information on railroads, churches, animals, soil, crops, schools, and manufacturing facilities, as applicable to each county. An "official map" prepared expressly for this report and printed by the Chicago-based Rand McNally & Company provided additional data. The only other explanation for the report exists in a four-page letter of transmittal from Commissioner Spaight to Governor O. M. Roberts in the preface.[11]

The letter is essentially an explanation of how Spaight collected the information, in spite of the fact that the legislature failed to appropriate the money necessary to do so. "Left to my unaided individual efforts, I began the work of collecting, as best as I could, the multifarious statistics" from around the state. He labored for twenty months on the task, first sending out blank forms and a circular letter to each of the federal congressmen representing Texas as well as each member of the state legislature. Additional requests for information went to various judges around the state, "to each county judge of the one hundred and seventy organized counties, and to one or more citizens in each of the fifty-six unorganized counties." As "a month or more had elapsed without bringing forward the looked-for statistical returns," Spaight took further action. He sent out more copies of the "blanks" and cover letter to "a number of citizens of known competence and character in each of the organized counties" as well as county judges and officials. In this second round of requests Spaight admitted his efforts at spurring action by appealing "to their county pride." Hinting at the bad image that would result from a blank page under a county's name, Spaight worked to coerce from these officials information he could not obtain in any other way.[12]

The commissioner edited the many contributions into paragraphs, written by himself or by one of his assistants, so that everything was "carefully revised and shaped by myself to conform to what I believed to be the actual facts and the proper manner of stating them." He felt the need to minimize any account that had been "colored by the pen of some ready writer inspired by self-interest or local attachment." Concerned that the report be perceived as the most truthful account obtainable, Spaight wrote, "I have endeavored to adhere to the rule, adopted at the outset, of systematic understatement of all the advantages and of explicit mention of whatever of drawbacks might attach to the particular localities outlined."[13]

Commissioner Spaight made reference to numerous letters received by his department from overseas and from other states requesting information "from official sources, and strongly implying a want of full faith in the accuracy of representations emanating from private and presumably interested parties." The existence of such letters indicates that an interest in Texas as a place of relocation was already widespread. It also reinforces the accepted belief that information from whatever "official" source was perceived as carrying more influence than information obtained in any other manner. Finally, the letters also hint at the potential use that Spaight and others in the state government made of the final report: *The Resources, Soil, and Climate of Texas.* As out-of-state inquiries arrived, this document probably served as a primary source—both a reference work used by private agencies attempting to attract immigrants as well as the "official" government document on resources in Texas for use by state employees.[14]

The map enclosed in the 1882 D.I.S.H. report provides indirect information regarding the motivation of Spaight's work. Geographers drew a detailed representation of the state with counties and cities listed. Railroad lines, both those "in operation" and those "projected," crisscrossed the map. All of this would be expected on any map of the time period. But in addition Spaight squeezed onto the corners of the map sheet supplementary information not typically incorporated on a map. One corner table listed the railroad lines in operation, their company mileage, and the state's total 4,926 miles of track. In the upper left hand corner a square was marked off with the heading, "The Area, Population and Assessed Value of Taxable Property of the State, By Counties." Then 226 counties were listed including data for each. Yet another corner gave information about the annual and monthly rainfall, state finances, and quotations explaining homestead provisions for all settlers.[15]

Spaight was clearly a state bureaucrat interested in facilitating immigration. For whatever personal or professional reasons, he used his position and his appointed task as a vehicle to disseminate information not only helpful to potential immigrants, but aimed in their direction. The map, with its effort at concise information and reference to homestead laws, could speak to potential newcomers in addition to meeting the legislative mandate to provide the state with updated statistics.

In Texas politics battle lines have often been drawn between those who value fiscal conservatism and those who strive for progressive reform. However, uniforms for those engaged in this struggle have never been distinct. Outward colors, crisp labels, or distinct groupings have not always evolved since one party, the Democratic Party has long dominated state politics. But concerns over perceived high taxes, government expenditures, and governmental organizations have dominated many an election year debate and many a legislative proposal.[16]

Often labeled "progressives" by the historical community, some Texans maintained a less restrictive approach to state financing and state budgets. These liberal-leaning citizens were willing to spend government time and money to accomplish commercial and social changes that would be beneficial statewide. For example, they saw increased money for schools as a boon to the future of Texas and they supported expenditure of state money to provide internal improvements. These same "progressives" saw efforts at encouraging the peopling of Texas's vast lands as essential for long range development.

The dynamics of this struggle can be seen in efforts by state political leaders from 1877 to 1914 to either discourage or encourage the use of governmental agencies to entice immigration. Since the state constitution expressly forbid use of state money directly to help immigration, those citizens supporting government involvement in luring immigrants were forced into a quasi-undercover effort. How did state agencies or officials support or not support government efforts at enticing immigrants? Statements by political figures of the time provide one window into public perceptions of state involvement.

In 1879 Oran Milo Roberts became governor of Texas, having run on a platform of conservative state spending and efficient government. In his inaugural address on January 21, he warned:

> Gradually, and much more in the last ten years, the State has been assuming other and extraneous burdens beyond the capacity of the productive wealth of the country to sustain. . . . Some of these burdens are due to our frontier position in the Union and our extensive territory, and others of them are taken on to an extent not common in young and intrinsically feeble states. Reference is here made to the protection of our frontier and our police force; to the penitentiary and its enlargement; to our free common school system . . . to our pensions to Texas veterans and to our immigration bureau, formerly.

Roberts obviously felt the state had overextended itself fiscally and urged more circumspect use of state funds. He called for efforts "to retrench expenses from top to bottom," noting that some believe "this policy will stop immigration." "Not so," he went on, "for the railroad companies owning millions of acres are the best immigration agents we ever had, and those that buy the lands who are not settlers will help them." Roberts clearly thought private enterprise was the best energy source in attracting newcomers. Two years later he seemed to hold much the same position, as he praised the influx of over one-and-a-half million people to the state which he said, "give promise of three millions [sic] of people in the next ten or fifteen years."[17]

Others in his political party did not share such a conservative fiscal view, urging a more aggressive stance on the part of the government. The Democratic lieutenant governor at the time was Joseph D. Sayers.[18] Sayers and Roberts squared off as opponents for the gubernatorial nominations in the subsequent election. Sayers's concept of government action is best illustrated in his January 11, 1881, address to the state senate as the Seventeenth Legislature convened. Sayers pointed to the great territory and fertile lands within the state's borders, claiming this natural wealth needed only to be developed to make Texas great. Then he said:

> Already, our great railroad companies have taken the matter in hand, and with commendable enterprise have united their efforts to attract the immigrant to our borders.
>
> Will not the Senate of Texas also recognize our present great need of labor, and exert itself to secure such legislation as will relieve the State government of the inactivity into which it has been forced by the Constitution?

Sayers did not suggest exactly what measures should be taken in order to amend the constitution or work within its perimeters, but he continued praising the potential resources within the state. In glowing political rhetoric he announced, "Truly, the harvest is great and ready to be reaped, but the laborers are few; not particularly because immigration is disinclined to come hither, but rather because our rich, varied and more than imperial domain is almost a *tierra incognita* to the thrifty and energetic peoples of the earth." If the land and its potential are unknown, then the solution, Sayers seemed to be suggesting, was to tell the world just what Texas had to offer.[19]

The political wrangling between Roberts and Sayers also erupted at the 1880 State Democratic Convention in Dallas. On the issue of immigration, a minority report seeking "the most liberal and active policy to encourage and increase immigration" was voted down in favor of the less aggressive approach reflected in a final plank of the party's platform:

> We repudiate as false the charge that the Democratic party of Texas has been opposed to immigration, and, while the constitution prohibits the use of public money for the support of a bureau of immigration, we urge the next legislature to make ample provision for the collection and dissemination of statistics pertaining to our agricultural and other resources, to the end that all seeking new homes, knowing our great advantages, may settle in our midst, extending to them a most cordial welcome.[20]

Obviously there existed full knowledge and awareness of the prohibitions in the 1876 constitution. However, many Democrats saw the compilation of statistics, if even for the purpose of attracting new settlers, acceptable within those constitutional restraints.

During Roberts's second term as governor, L. J. Storey served as lieutenant governor. In his inaugural address, he expressed sympathies more in keeping with those of Roberts. His conservative message claimed "a mighty tide of immigration [is] pouring into our State from every land and country" but then pointedly noted, "these immigrants are not brought here at the expense of the State." He said that Texas welcomed them "with outstretched hands" and encouraged them to "enter the race of life upon equal footing with our own people." These newcomers are pushing back the frontier, claimed Storey, and adding to the state's stability and prosperity. He then echoed Governor Roberts's belief in private initiative as the best force to entice immigrants: "Would you increase the volume of this mighty tide without corrupting the purity of its waters, then, let the reading world, through channels opened up by private enterprise and capital, be furnished with correct official information concerning the condition, resources and prosperity of the country." Storey's confidence in written material coincided with many others, both in and out of his party. His opinion, shared by Roberts—that this material should not come from government sources—was not as universally accepted.[21]

The Democratic Party dominated Texas politics during this era, but other political parties reflecting a wide spectrum of political opinion assumed stances supporting immigration. The 1880 State Republican Convention adopted a resolution stating, "We also hold it to be the duty of the State government to invite and encourage immigration to our State." Later in 1882 Republicans asserted, "We believe that the State ought to promote and foster immigration by all practicable methods." In 1878 a small but vocal group, the Greenback Labor Party, met in Waco. While they denounced "the importation of servile labor from Asiatic countries," they wrote "that the emigration of the liberty loving from other lands should be encouraged." Two years later, the Greenbackers placed a statement in their platform encouraging more government involvement. Seeing an increase in population as a way to insure prosperity, they suggested, "inducements should be offered to all honest and intelligent immigrants to come and assist in the development of the great State of Texas." They failed to identify the specifics of these "inducements" but their pro-immigration stance surely sent a message to the more powerful Democratic Party.[22]

Political leaders and political party platforms come and go. Executive bureaucracy tends to persevere throughout those leadership changes. The Department of Insurance, Statistics, and History continued to function throughout the early 1880s as an executive agency. Commissioner Spaight's 1882 report illustrates the character of work done by this department. In addition, the legislature charged the commissioner with collecting all kinds of historical material and papers and then serving as a repository for such works. The present Texas State Archive owes some of its holdings to the efforts by this agency to obtain or at least to encourage the retention of historical documents for future generations. During this same time period, there evolved a growing interest in developing a state department of agriculture. This was not a new idea. Support for such work had been growing gradually at the federal level. The national government organized a Department of Agriculture in 1862 and elevated it to Cabinet-level status in 1889. Various states organized their own departments of agriculture, although their size, connection to other state agencies, and date of organization varied.[23]

In Texas the Patrons of Husbandry took an early interest in establishing state agencies to support agriculture. They campaigned for the establishment of a state school to teach farmers the newest and best agricultural techniques and as early as 1877 passed a resolution "memorializing the legislature to establish an agricultural department in our State government." The Grange was not the only such voice, but it was a strong and loud voice. And ultimately the state legislature heard the message and attached a wing to the older Department of Insurance, Statistics, and History (D.I.S.H.). The enabling legislation, approved April 1, 1887, set in motion the department's reorganization. Interestingly, the name change may reflect state priorities since they placed agriculture at the head of the list, creating the Department of Agriculture, Insurance, Statistics, and History (D.A.I.S.H.).[24]

How did this reorganization come about? The political story begins when the Twentieth Legislature convened in early January 1887 during the last few days of Governor John Ireland's second administration. In his executive address, Ireland noted that "much good has been accomplished to the people" through the D.I.S.H. and pointed to the suggestion by its current commissioner, H. P. Bee, that the agency expand to include the field of agriculture. Ireland said, "I believe this would redound to the great good of the country, and I join in the recommendation."[25]

Ireland's successor, Lawrence Sullivan Ross, addressed the same legislature just nine days later on the same topic making a more forceful argument. First, Governor Ross praised the work of the D.I.S.H., saying that while many regard it "as a useless and merely ornamental adjunct" to state government, he valued its existence. He especially noted the importance of its purpose toward historical preservation and even encouraged the establishment of "an exhibition" of the state's "wonderful and unparalleled growth. . . . Thus inviting the industrious emigrant to settle among us, while, at the same time, we encourage a pride of country in our citizens." It would seem that Ross saw clearly the connection between the agency, its current mission, and the peopling of the state.[26]

He then went on to recount the current mandate of D.I.S.H. as well as the failure of successive legislatures to fund its work to appropriate levels. Looking to the future, Governor Ross suggested "a more thorough development of the agricultural feature" of the existing department. Utilizing an old "push" technique, he appealed to state pride and state competition when he said, "An agricultural bureau on a liberal and comprehensive scale has been organized in nearly every State except Texas." Similar statements have often served to spur Texans into action. And in this case, Ross seemed to accomplish his ends.[27]

Bowing to pressure from farmers and from the governor, the Twentieth Legislature in its closing days passed a bill establishing a new government agency to be designated the Department of Agriculture, Insurance, Statistics, and History. As with the earlier D.I.S.H., the commissioner was encouraged to maintain communication with the federal agriculture department as well as those in other states and in the territories and "at his option, with those of foreign countries." One plainly stated goal was "the promotion of agriculture in any of its branches." Section Five of the enabling statute assigned the department's primary task, requiring the commissioner "to arrange and adopt some plan for collecting and publishing agricultural and farm statistics, in connection with his annual report, in such form and numbers as he may deem best or the condition of the department will permit." The law then proscribed explicitly the process to be followed. Before January 1 of each year, the commissioner was to give to each county tax assessor "the necessary blanks" and instructions on the procedure to be followed. Tax assessors as part of their job in listing taxable property were charged with questioning each taxpayer "for necessary facts and information for filling out the blanks." Provision existed for paying each tax assessor for his service, an amount equally shared by the county and the state.[28] Thus, the less-than-efficient manner of collecting information utilized by Spaight in his 1882 report for the D.I.S.H. was dumped in favor of greater structure and accountability.

Steps leading up to the formation of D.A.I.S.H. illustrate growing political support for an agency concerned with agriculture. The legislative wrangling over this agricultural addition to D.I.S.H. is yet another example of the battle between fiscal conservatives and those with a broader vision. In this case, the decision to spend taxpayers' money represented the eventual willingness of politicians to accept expenditure of money because farmers were their primary constituency. The acceptance by enough fiscal conservatives of a need for an agriculture department allowed them to vote for higher appropriations and greater government expenditure. They had not been willing to make a similar commitment when the issue was facilitating immigration.

The *First Annual Report of the Agricultural Bureau* of the D.A.I.S.H. (1887–88) deserves an in-depth analysis. Such an attempt will clearly bolster the contention that this document was in reality and at least in part, a government-subsidized effort at producing written information to attract immigrants to Texas. The most outstanding proof exists in the letter of transmittal to Governor Ross from Lafayette Lumpkin Foster, Commissioner of the D.A.I.S.H. Under the heading "Scope of the Report," Foster said he wanted "to offer a word of explanation to any who may not understand why matter unusual in agricultural reports has been incorporated in this [report]." To his way of thinking, the enlarged number of questions on the informational "blanks" added "but little, if anything, to the cost" of the endeavor. He noted the continuing stream of letters received by his department asking for just exactly the kinds of information he solicited through the survey by county tax assessors. Finally, he showed his full hand of cards when he wrote:

There is no official literature descriptive of the advantages of Texas and the inducements offered to immigrants, for distribution in reply to these requests, and the greater portion of them are thrown into the waste basket. In attempting to briefly call attention of the overcrowded population of the East, who are eking out a living on the high-priced soils, exhausted by the skill of their forefathers, to our millions of acres of rich virgin soil, which can be had almost for the asking; to direct the attention of the seeker after profitable investments to our splendid industrial achievements and vast undeveloped mineral and other resources yet in reserve, and to convey to the outside world an idea of the character of our State and county governments, our public institutions and the cost of maintaining them, this work has been enlarged beyond the original intention.

His transmittal letter covered seven pages. Then followed a forty-three-page summary and overview of the information as collated by Foster and his clerks. And finally, with counties listed in alphabetical order, 250 pages recorded the statistics acquired for each of the counties in the state.[29]

Other evidence exists to support the assertion that undercover motives animated this particular agricultural canvas of the state that became the *First Annual Report of the Agricultural Bureau.* Governor Ross admitted as much when he said, "In addition to the special information relating to agriculture, the reports contain a vast deal of miscellaneous information in regard to the soil, climate, and resources of the State, presenting its superior advantages to those seeking homes or profitable investments." This acknowledgment of peripheral information fired a backlash response. Legislation passed by the Twenty-first Legislature clarified the future boundaries of D.A.I.S.H. tasks. It limited the contents of future "blanks" to be provided yearly to county tax assessors by saying, "such blanks shall contain only such questions as relate to agriculture, horticulture, and stockraising."[30]

The document also betrays itself upon a perusal of information requested and tabulated for the reader. Yes, counties provided information on the number and value of livestock and the acreage of various field crops for the year 1887. Stands of bees, pounds of honey, tons of cotton seed, eggs sold and used, butter produced—all became part of the statistical count. But also included in each county tally were the number of schools and teachers; the presence of mineral wells, springs, or natural resorts; the population by ethnicity; the number of newspapers; and the average wages for farm laborers.[31]

Files for the D.A.I.S.H. also reveal the impact and extent of distribution for this *First Annual Report of the Agricultural Bureau.* Letter upon letter requested a copy of the document or thanked the department for sending the volume while praising its contents. The North Texas National Bank asked for "several copies to send to parties outside the state" and upon receipt of the report sent back a thank-you note. The Fidelity Trust Company of Kansas City, Missouri, requested a copy. The library of an agricultural college in Michigan thanked the D.A.I.S.H. for a copy of the report. Requests came from such people as a real estate broker in Des Moines, Iowa; a Texas man in Kentucky Town, Texas, who wanted "them [the D.A.I.S.H. Reports] to send to acquaintances in Indiana"; the Massachusetts Agricultural College in Amherst, Massachusetts, requested a copy as did a farmer from Cherrycreek in White County, Tennessee. The correspondence in D.A.I.S.H. files is extensive and clearly shows interest inside and outside the state for trustworthy, concrete information. Specific reference in these letters to the *Annual Report* is frequent. And much of that correspondence relates to people or agencies involved in relocating to Texas.[32]

The undercover use of this agency to help facilitate immigration was but one skirmish in the ongoing conflict between fiscal conservatives and progressive reformers. In this case those working for change financed through government money won a victory, albeit a small one. The *First Annual Report of the Agricultural Bureau,* or what Terry Jordan, the noted geographer, calls

the "forgotten" 1887 state census, was the ultimate expression of this undercover effort in the 1880s. It provides yet one more strand in the complete story
of efforts by Texas and Texans to attract immigrants during the last half of the
nineteenth century.[33]

Finally, in reference to official government work at attracting immigrants
in spite of Section 56 in the constitution, the ongoing work of the D.A.I.S.H.
must be noted. This bureaucracy supported continuing immigration efforts
in two specific ways: They facilitated geological surveys of the state and,
once survey work began, pushed for continuing appropriations to perform
that task.[34]

Another way the D.A.I.S.H. assisted immigration efforts was through its
function of providing information—a task typical of any and all governmental agencies. While this could be termed a passive function dependent
upon incoming mail, the performance of this work suggests a state agency interested in actively dispensing information to help potential immigrants.
How this agency used the resources at hand to respond to these letters tells us
much about the unspoken, yet implicit motivation of its leadership.

The extant files of the D.A.I.S.H., between the years of 1889 and 1891 while
L. L. Foster held the administrative reins of the agency, suggest an extensive
correspondence. This agency responded to letters from everywhere—overseas, other states, and within its own borders. Of course each letter was
unique, meeting the needs of specific individuals who took pen in hand and
were motivated to obtain more information. However, a representative letter
will allow an overview analysis of the D.A.I.S.H.'s work.

Clawson Ohio 1/22, 1889
Mr. Gov. Sir.
    Hoping that I will not be intruding on you I wish to ask concerning your state
as *I like* many other young men here can't think of getting a home here where land
is $100 & 150 per acre. And I prefer a warmer climate as the winters are to [*sic*] se-
vere here & and the farming season is to [*sic*] short & and the stock feeding season
too long. I have been through Ga. but don't like soil & water in the part where I
stopped. On what terms can I get government land. What does settled & improved
lands sell for? Where is your best land for farming. How about society water Indians & other advantages & disadvantages in general. What are the general products.
How many bu[shels] of corn wheat & oats potatoes are considered an averaged crop
& what are the average prices for same. They say "go west young man & grow up
with the country.["] But should I make a change I want to get in a milder climate

as I dread the cold winters & there is many more here that will agree with me & have been talking about Texas. If a few from here was to settle in your state and prosper they would have many friends & friends that would follow. but they have no leader. Fearing that I may be intruding on your time I will close hoping to hear from you soon. I remain yours

Hiram Clawson
Clawson Ohio.[35]

Multiple observations come to mind for today's reader. Clawson's letter shows an uncertainty in addressing his letter to the governor of the state and "intruding" on his time. Other letters that ended up in the D.A.I.S.H. files were addressed to the Secretary of State or to the land commissioner, or as in this case, to a governor. People did not know who to write to, but they were still writing letters to people in authority looking for specific, believable information. It is intriguing that Hiram Clawson asks for and thus expects the governor to share both advantages and disadvantages with him. Is this merely his naiveté? Or is it his strong assumption that government officials would be the most truthful source of information?

This representative letter notes the northerner's concern with climate, his interest in farming, and his knowledge of northern farming practices. Another typical letter dealing with the cold weather as a push factor came from Conrad Doering of Dakota who wrote, "Many families intend to go away from here because the Winter is too long and too cold."[36] The fact that almost all enticement literature emanating from Texas repeatedly praised the mild climate suggests that southern writers knew the lure such information had on the snowbound farmer struggling with a harsher climate in the north.

Hiram is also a well-read individual, if we take his reference to the well-publicized injunction to "Go West Young Man" as any indication. Most potential immigrants had experienced a relative bombardment of articles in newspapers, journals, and magazines informing readers of opportunities in the southern or western states. Many of these articles resulted from journalists traveling through the West and sometimes into the South, collecting observations, and then filling columns for their editors in the North. Letters to the D.A.I.S.H. usually reflect some previous experience with written or verbal information. Enticement writers typically tried to sow in a curious mind the proverbial seed that grows into a full-blown idea and sometimes results in physically moving to a new place. In addition to referring to Greeley's oft-repeated injunction, Clawson wrote of a previous visit to Georgia and his dissatisfaction with what he observed there. It was not unusual for immigrants to "scout out" territory using visits to friends or business trips as a way of seeing new lands for themselves. Others had no such opportunity and depended on the written letter to do such reconnoitering for them. For example, a Missouri man wrote in October, 1889, saying, "I wish to settle in Texas. How can I finde out which cos [counties] have State Lands to Homestead or School lands for sale on long time can you give me any information on the subject It is so expensive to travel and hunt up such places it is not like knowing what counties to go to pleas answer and much oblige."[37] While Clawson had the means, at least to some extent, to see for himself, others were not as financially able. They depended on postage stamps.

Yet another aspect of Clawson's letter to the Texas governor was his mention of friends of friends following in the wake of one leader who makes the initial plunge to settle in Texas. The current term for such a population movement is "chain migration." Hiram clearly understood the process and in mentioning the same to the governor must have touched that Texan's desire to fill up the state with industrious, hard-working farmers. When Hiram speaks of "many more here . . . that have been talking about Texas," surely Governor Ross saw the value of fueling such "talk" with good information that would help pull those potential migrants to Texas.

Each letter to the D.A.I.S.H. begs for interpretation. Trying to imagine more about each writer from the few lines on a letter is an intriguing exercise. It also reminds us that immigration as a movement consists of the journey of just one person or family group, followed by yet another, and then yet another. The cumulative immigration movement reflects individual choices and decisions made one person at a time. The D.A.I.S.H. clerks and commissioner who opened these letters and responded to them must have had a sense of this very individualized process, even though the information they sent out could be very standardized and commonplace to them.

An intriguing fact gleaned from the letters in the D.A.I.S.H. files is the extremely quick turnaround time on incoming and outgoing mail. In bureaucratic fashion each filed letter has a dated reference to an agent's action in relation to the correspondence. Sometimes the letters, such as Hiram Clawson's letter, were detoured a few extra days once they arrived in Austin. His letter addressed to the governor had to be rerouted to the D.A.I.S.H. and was officially re-addressed to L. L. Foster. This happened frequently, since letter writers often were not knowledgeable about state bureaucracy, something that varied from state to state. But once the letter was at Foster's office, a response usually went out within a day or two. A Fort Worth request dated March 23, 1899, was answered on March 25. A Philadelphia letter dated April 26, 1889, got a response on May 1. A Eureka, Kansas, man sent a letter dated January 15, 1890. Today this letter sits in the D.A.I.S.H. files with the handwritten note, "attended to Jan. 17, 1890."[38] This prompt attention to letter writing could indicate many things: a good appropriation for stationery and postage; clerks with few other tasks to divert their attention; the importance of the postal system in the late nineteenth century and its efficiency; an industrious office complement of busy state employees; an agency head who valued the importance of his office to immigration interest; or many other possibilities. The latter— a bureaucrat with the means and the interest to foster immigration—seems a distinct possibility.

D.A.I.S.H. files show letters going overseas to such places as Naples, Italy (1889), Manchester, England (1890), and Hamburg, Germany (1889). Stateside requests were common as well. One newly arrived Texan from South Carolina asked for a copy of the report, saying, "I have letters from friends in the old state asking for information all of which I could get from said report." The potential for yet another chain of migration exists in this one letter and in this one person's request to a state agency.[39]

As the Department of Agriculture, Insurance, Statistics, and History remained active, it continued to provide the state with concrete statistical information for home use and for dispensing information elsewhere.[40] While the work of this agency and its predecessor D.I.S.H. was neither flashy in presentation nor as extensive as attempts by private enterprise, its efforts demonstrate official governmental involvement in the immigration movement during the last quarter of the nineteenth century.

CHAPTER 7

ADVERTISING TEXAS

Tucked away in Article 16 of Texas's 1876 constitution was a statement prohibiting the use of government money to encourage immigration to the state. Realizing the full impact of such a restriction on the state's potential growth, a multitude of separate business enterprises moved aggressively into the perceived vacuum. They initiated new endeavors or re-energized earlier enticement efforts with the ultimate goal of peopling the vast lands within the state's borders. Private enterprise decided to do what it appeared government would not do.

Many Texans, both the newly arrived and the pre–Civil War variety, participated in this immigration movement that loosely filled the years from 1876 to 1915. Motivation varied widely for these private citizens. People held different goals: to make money from the sale of land as a realtor or as a lawyer handling the legal paperwork; to earn a salary as an employee of a company such as a dry goods store or a railroad; to encourage the development of one's town so that more businesses would be available for the consumer and more people would be there to contribute to schools, churches, and social life; to share in the loyalty and pride that comes from identification as a Texan or a Southerner; to bring other people of their own ethnic origins or religious background to participate in the growth of their community. Such lists can be endless and often tend to overlook the fact that motives overlap as well. No matter what the incentive, the handiwork of individuals and various associations left an imprint on the state's development.

Central to all this activity was a continuing belief in the efficacy of the written word. Those sending out the message "Come to Texas!" believed in the need for written publications. Those interested in relocating also believed in and desired written materials. The words put on paper met the needs of both those wanting to proclaim the resources of Texas as well as those wanting to know more about the state. The following narrative focuses on the production of the written material and by implication, the energy, interaction, and diversity of the immigration enticement effort. Throughout the period 1876–1915 Texans sustained a belief in the need to encourage immigration, and the written word was seen as central to that goal.

One very aggressive private agency in Texas was the South Western Immigration Company. Their 1881 publication boldly asserted their rationale for existence. They directed their readership back to the 1876 state constitution quoting Section 56 verbatim. Claiming that this provision "has been construed abroad as an evidence of hostility on the part of the people of Texas to those coming among us seeking homes," the company felt compelled to redress this perception. The group, incorporated under the laws of Texas, stated "it is the purpose of this company to supply the needs of a State Bureau of Immigration" and they would accomplish this by "collecting, collating and disseminating correct information." To that end they "earnestly solicited" help "from all corporations, enterprises and individuals who desire to hasten the development of our country." One of their first publications was a 253-page document entitled *Texas: Her Resources and Capabilities.* Its opening eight pages were a cheerleading effort at encouraging participation in their work. The rest covered a broad spectrum of information gleaned from multiple, often previously published, sources.[1]

As with most enticement literature, this book included statements referring to its trustworthiness and veracity. Loud and clear, it said, "This company has no lands and will acquire none. It has nothing to sell; nothing to buy. It has no interest, directly or indirectly with the land department of any railroad, nor with any private land agency, nor other business or speculative enterprise." It went on to say "our only object is to aid immigrants in every possible way to acquire trustworthy and intelligent information about the country we represent." One would naturally ask then, "Where did they get the money to publish such material?" Quite openly they explained, "Certain railroads have gratuitously placed a large sum of money at the company's disposal, to be expended in the accomplishment of this object."[2]

The material presented by the South Western Immigration Company demonstrates clearly the interconnectedness of most immigration efforts. The company overtly sought help from everyone interested, plus openly admitted to having already accepted financial assistance from some railroad systems. The president of the company was William W. Lang, a most powerful and influential farmer, and late Master of the Texas State Grange. The front page of *Texas: Her Resources and Capabilities* bears a rough facsimile of the Texas state seal, yet the document was definitely not a government one. This lengthy publication presented a double goal: to encourage Texans to take up the challenge of becoming involved in the immigration movement and to provide concrete trustworthy information for "those seeking homes in a new country." This South Western Immigration Company even suggested the erection by counties of homes or way stations at convenient railroad connections to be used by immigrants in their travel to new destinations within the state. A reflection of the company's practical bent was the way it encouraged awareness of how manners and kindness influence people. "A civil word, a little politeness, or an act of kindness, costing nothing, may be the means of favorably impressing a stranger, who, in turn, may be the cause of turning hundreds of immigrants in this direction. On the other hand, a short, uncivil answer and gruff manners will, in a measure, confirm the unfavorable reports given him by the enemies of Texas, and he returns or goes, disgusted, to other portions of the country and uses his influence against us." Such observations interwoven into the informational aspects of the book demonstrate unmistakably the two-prong approach of this particular publication.[3]

The book presented extensive knowledge about the state. One portion gives a brief overview of the railroads and then lingers through almost eighty pages of county sketches for those areas through which the trains traveled. Climate, newspapers, crops typically grown, city names, and population statistics, were just some of the subjects included. More typically throughout the book were multiple, short sections with intriguing headings: "Is Texas a Land of Lawlessness?" "What Can an Immigrant Do In Texas?" "What Conditions Immigrant Farmers from Great Britain May Find in Texas," "Healthfulness," and "When to Go to Texas." For enticement literature of this era, many publishing agencies would cut and paste a volume together. *Texas: Her Resources and Capabilities* fits within this genre of writing. For example, in boasting about Texas's healthfulness the authors quoted excerpts from a speech by Jerome Bonaparte Robertson, an earlier superintendent for the Texas Bureau of Immigration and later a railroad agent. The publishers thus drew inexpensively on some of the best talent in the state.[4]

Another early endeavor at stimulating immigration was actually the continuation of a previous journalistic effort. The *Texas New Yorker* had opened their New York offices in 1870, printing their first edition in September of that year. They continued publicizing Texas well into 1878—past the period of the 1875 constitutional convention. The pages of their paper suggest a subdued response to the constitutional prohibition, for while they followed the debates and reported on them, they made only minor comments about the convention in their pages. In effect, their response to the passage of Section 56 was to ignore it. Such an approach can be seen as their way of minimizing the impact of the debates. Before 1876 the *Texas New Yorker,* under the leadership of

George Sweet, called itself the "Official Organ of the Texas Bureau of Immigration, Without Pay" and routinely included information about the bureau's activities. After 1876, the paper more typically broadcast news from organizations such as the Lone Star State Immigration Labor Bureau and Real Estate Trust Company or the Immigration Aid Association of Limestone County.[5]

As an editor Sweet was at his best when proclaiming the value of his own work at encouraging immigration. In April 1876 (two months after ratification of the Texas constitution) an extensive self-advertisement included reason after reason for a subscriber to "Take the Texas New Yorker!"

— It is the spiciest, jolliest, and newsiest monthly in America.
— The "Texas Farmer, Gardener and House-wife's Page," and the "Historical, Education, and Scientific Department," are alone features of the paper worth more than its subscription price.
— The map is printed fresh every month . . . and kept corrected right up to date with regard to railroad extensions and the organization of new counties. The best immigrant's guide to Texas ever published.
— It is non-partisan, unsectarian, independent, frank and outspoken on all the live questions of the time.

Sweet identified a Texas branch office to his New York newspaper as Montgomery County and encouraged communication with one and all. In boisterous journalistic rhetoric he also crowed, "Take the Texas New Yorker!— if a toiling Granger, and aid me in proclaiming the advantages of Texas, and thus attracting to your farms more intelligent laborers, men of muscle and mind, who are not afraid to pull off their coats and sweat for good pay."[6]

One of the first requirements, it seems, of any progressive growing town in Texas was the presence of a newspaper. Such a business signified the town had "arrived" and the editors of these papers typically evolved into their city's primary booster. A systematic study of newspapers statewide would be both enlightening and fascinating, since boosterism was prominent in their pages and inducements meant to lure people to the community fit that schema perfectly. The topic deserves more research. One teasing hint of newspaper activism for immigration exists in the concise, positive report of the *Fort Griffin Echo* for February 3, 1881. They reported, "The woods are full of immigrants." Similar statements peppered newspaper columns across the state.[7]

A more focused effort to entice newcomers evolved in the 1880s and culminated in what one writer of the time called the "Immigration Movement."

Interest developed statewide in a cooperative agency to coordinate efforts at bringing homesteaders to settle. The enthusiasm driving this activity is marvelously conveyed in a textbook written by Anna J. Hardwicke Pennybacker for the state's school children. Published at Tyler, Texas, in 1888, the text recounted the events of each governor's administration and then inserted under material dealing with the then-current Governor L. S. Ross, the following:

> Immigration Movement.
> Strong efforts are now being made (August, 1888) to bring more immigrants into Texas. Clubs are being organized all over the State, whose duty it is to arouse public interest, to scatter abroad literature showing the advantages of Texas, to send out speakers to other States; in short, to do every thing to make the movement a success. The railroads have promised to give reduced rates, and to extensively advertise "Texas Excursions." The probabilities are that 1888 will bring to our State more people than any previous year.[8]

The enthusiasm jumps off the pages of this textbook. This excitement is all the more compelling since it is not the boosterism typically directed at the potential immigrant, but is instead a teaching paragraph for young Texans. The textbook quote suggests the pervasiveness of the feeling in Texas during the 1880s that immigrants were wanted and needed. It also suggests the belief that deliberate efforts were required to accomplish those ends. Many people believed personal activism could influence in a decisive way the history of their own state and neighborhood.

Many factors animated the so-called Immigration Movement of 1888. One experience of many Texas counties during 1886 and 1887 was a terrible drought. News of the hardships endured by Texas farmers traveled throughout the state leaping into national headlines as well. This negative publicity intensified booster fears that immigration would come to a halt or at the very best only trickle into the state. Countering this negative publicity was the growth of railroad lines penetrating farther and farther into west, west-central, far southern, and panhandle counties. As the overall mileage of railroads increased, the ease of transporting people became more and more obvious, and in turn the need for people to settle as residents and utilize those railroads became a more pronounced concern. Still yet another factor was the knowledge, through the expanding news structure in the United States, of competing interests around the country all seeking in their own way to attract immigration to their state or their territory. In this climate of competition some Texans took it upon themselves to call a statewide convention with the goal of uniting people "to encourage immigration and capital to come to our State."[9]

Over 850 people served as delegates to that convention, testifying to the wide interest in doing something. A group of seven Dallas business leaders met on December 3, 1887, and issued an invitation to interested people across the state to meet in Dallas later that month. The newspapers took up the call, spreading the idea throughout the state. Communities selected representatives and the newspapers duly noted the interest and activity. Large and small communities responded.[10]

A rousing address by J. S. Daugherty, Dallas businessman and chair of the convention, opened the proceedings on December 20 and set the tone for the two-day event. Pleased with the "hearty response" from around the state, Daugherty then said there were three questions for their consideration: "1. Is an increased flow of law-abiding, industrious immigration and capital to our State desirable? 2. Can we, as citizens, bring it about? 3. How best to do it?" The first two questions were obviously rhetorical and led naturally to the chair's extensive remarks on his own vision for the future. Calling the assembled group "a committee of the whole on the condition of our State," Daugherty acknowledged the state's prosperity but questioned "whether it is [in] the best possible condition that we as citizens can, by our united efforts, make it."[11]

The phrase "united efforts" reveals much about Daugherty's vision and the feeling in the hall that cooperation could yield results. This was to be a "citizen's meeting," a voluntary collaboration destined to stimulate people all over the state to take action. The convention created an egalitarian structure calling for a committee of thirty-one with one delegate from each senatorial district. Administrative decisions would be facilitated by a smaller executive committee.[12] Leaders told the convention that "the success of the movement would rest with local organizations." With that in mind, the committee members encouraged formation of city and county immigration committees whose purpose would be two-fold. First, they were to collect and prepare data about their locale for publication. In addition, they were to raise money locally so that each senatorial district would have $500 to contribute to the collective work of the statewide committee. Dollars and information were seen as the essentials to accomplishing the stated goals.[13]

Little is known about the continuing viability of this specific organization. What can be ascertained about the accomplishments of this specific 1887 convention? Documentation is scarce. Negotiations with the railroads did result in the institution of special excursion fares or tickets. These tickets would allow a potential settler a round-trip fare to Texas for the price of a one-way ticket with the option of staying in the state for sixty days maximum. Another note of cooperation with the railroads was the offer by rail representatives to help in distributing any printed material developed by the State Immigration Committee. Support for a state geological survey blossomed at this 1887 convention. Farmers and business people around the state had earlier lobbied the state government to conduct such a survey. Enough of those attending the immigration conference spoke up for such a survey and obtained from the assembled delegates unanimous adoption of a resolution addressed to the next state legislature.[14]

What happened in Texas after the December, 1887, meeting in Dallas? Enthusiasm grew in a way that had not existed for many years. The Pennybacker textbook article on the "Immigration Movement" illustrates the sense of wholehearted cooperation that either existed in reality or stood as a goal to be reached. Statistics, numerical graphs, and population estimates cannot, even if they did exist, provide an understanding of the spirit of the times. Activity took many forms. Some of these efforts were already in place before the 1887 conference but received a bold stimulus to re-energize their work. Other organizational structures began anew.

Of these many collective projects, city and county booster clubs began to form and develop written material as the main way in which to make their community known to others. The 1887 conference spurred several communities into immediate activity. By March 1, 1888, twenty of the thirty-one state districts had established within their boundaries some organ for coordinating that area's immigration work.[15]

Several of the counties took up the challenge without delay. In February, 1888, a group of citizens in Navarro County earned an official seal of approval to their document entitled, *Texas. Description of Navarro County. Her Resources, and Inducements Offered to Immigrants.* The clear connection of this document to the State Immigration Committee is demonstrated by the printed note on page twenty-nine signed by the state committee's secretary, Frank B. Chilton, stating that the publication was "hereby approved." Information for immigrants as well as advertisements fill R. W. Haltom's 1888 *History and Description of Angelina County, Texas,* which boldly met all the qualifications of a local enticement brochure. Yet another example was the joint effort by a city and a county. *Facts for Immigrants* illustrates the possibilities that could come from such cooperation. This thirty-two-page brochure was evenly divided between "truthful" descriptions of Palestine and of Anderson County.

These boosters proudly stated on their title page, "Homes for Thousands in one of the Best Counties in Texas" while they beckoned the pamphlet holder, "Read and Hand to your Neighbor."[16]

How many of these pamphlets were printed, how they were distributed, or who read them are questions for which there are no clear answers. That they were published at all reflects widespread involvement in the immigration movement of the 1880s. It also reflects the way in which some portions of the state jumped on the bandwagon of opportunity presented by a statewide organization. In the absence of subsequent reports and files for the State Immigration Committee, it is also impossible to know how many county or city or local organizations existed. One insight comes from the Missouri Pacific Railway Company's complimentary brochure entitled *Statistics and Information Concerning the State of Texas.* Under the heading "County Organizations of the State Bureau of Immigration," sixty-three counties were listed with post office location and leadership names for each of those counties. They proudly wrote, "The State Bureau of Immigration of Texas is thoroughly organized, and has officials appointed in every county of the State. These can be addressed relative to lands and any other information valuable to the settler."[17]

County brochures were not unique to this 1888 movement. However, they served distinctly to carry within their promotional format the message of welcome to newcomers. In 1891 the New Birmingham Development Company published a fifty-six-page booklet claiming, "large and valuable iron ore deposits" in the area. Located close to Rusk, Texas, in Cherokee County, New Birmingham developed a reputation later as one of Texas's ghost cities. But the promotional literature of the boom time expressed only optimism for newcomers to the area.[18]

In December, 1887, Cooke County had reportedly formed a society in support of the immigration movement statewide. Whether that organization continued to exist throughout the century has not been ascertained. But in 1898 a nineteen-page pamphlet entitled *Cooke County: Its People, Productions and Resources* appeared and stated it was "now the fashion" for areas to proclaim their advantages and "invite immigration." Their introductory statement suggests the recent formation of an "Immigration Society" with the goal of setting forth "its claims to a portion of the immigration that seems to be ready to pour into the Lone Star State."[19] Whatever the immediate spur for this particular document, it too fits comfortably in the long line of typical booster literature by counties and cities.

The Cooke County pamphlet demonstrates a unique flair in producing enticement literature. Common to other booster efforts, this booklet laid claim to complete truthfulness. Then the authors took a slightly different tack and referred to their pamphlet, saying, "We know that it will be considered very tame when compared with many of the immigration documents that are flooding the country. But Cooke county is no such paradise as is described in many of these publications, hence we cannot put forth such gorgeous descriptions as some of them do." Their approach suggested a more folksy or homey face. All enticement literature tried to explain the mildness of the climate in Texas. Cooke County put it this way: "While the climate does not equal that of Italy, still it is far ahead of many favored parts of our own country." Their seemingly negative comparison thus emerges in a positive light. Knowing potential settlers care about their future neighbors, this subject was addressed as well: "Our population is made up of people from all parts of the world, but the greater part of the people are native Americans . . . the proud southerner, the polished and shrewd Yankee and the sturdy western man, all mingle and blend into a society unlike that to which either was accustomed before coming here."[20]

The many topics covered in this pamphlet reflect the multiple interests of potential settlers. Nine of the nineteen pages were filled with illustrations of buildings and people in Gainesville, Cooke County's largest community. A disclaimer in the section entitled "The Kind of People We Want," read, "We do not need population badly enough to invite anybody who may want to come, but every decent, law-abiding man is welcome to Cooke county . . . we have no place for tramps and sharpers." The town must have been in great need of a tannery, for they spent a full paragraph describing the potential for such a business. They claimed that, "a rich reward awaits the man who will inaugurate such an enterprise." Once all the information and statistics were presented, the brochure ended with the following statement: "Now, reader, if you think from what we have said you would like to come to Cooke county, we shall be glad to give you a hearty welcome and have you share in the good things which its future has in store." The down-home flavor of this short brochure represents just one of many approaches used to attract immigrants.[21]

Some writers of booster literature put their intent in their title, such as the Waco Immigration Society's *Immigrant's Guide*. Other publications made more oblique statements, rather hinting at their desire for more population. One title page read, *Smith County, Texas: The Land of Diversified Farms and the* ♥ [in symbol form] *of the Great Fruit and Truck Belt*. At the top of the page was the statement in quotes, "Quit Growing $20 Crops on $100 Land—Grow $100 Crops on $20 Land."[22]

Another document that by its title would not give notice of its intention to attract immigrants was the *Grimes County Directory.* Yet on the preface page, it claimed that its object was to tell "the outside world" about the county and do it in a truthful way. Then the authors added, "It is to be hoped that many of these books will find their way to people who are seeking homes in some good, healthy, fertile country; also that Immigration and Land agents will use it as a medium of developing one of the best counties in the state." The *Grimes County Record,* a local newspaper, was assigned the task of distributing the proposed five thousand copies "in a judicious manner" to all requesting a copy.[23]

County brochures, including those with a heavy emphasis on the urban communities within their spheres, presented an attractive picture of Texas to the outside world. Their descriptive approach encouraged people to come to their county and settle on the land. Although Texas remained predominately an agricultural state, cities gradually grew in size and population during the late nineteenth century. Frequently these cities felt the need to advertise themselves. In doing this they produced a fair amount of enticement literature that must have influenced capital investment and the movement of people. Since urbanization happened rather slowly, most of the city brochures date from the tail end of the nineteenth century or early years of the twentieth century. One interesting example of early-twentieth-century city boosterism is a sixteen-page pamphlet entitled, *Kerrville. U.S.A.* It was written by the editor of the local newspaper, J. E. Grinstead, who claimed to be "Artistic Illustrator, Advertising Architect, and Builder for Publicity." Knowing change was difficult and striving to reassure his readers as to the quality of Kerrville's citizens, he wrote, "The people of Kerrville are Texans and their adopted brothers. There is a broad-minded air of tolerance among the people that smacks of the 'old west.'" Continuing its description the editor wrote, "Coming from all parts of the continent, the people of this city form, if such a thing may be said of a people who were chiefly born in the same nation, a cosmopolitan population. Each one brought some new and good idea and upon arriving imparted it to others. The result is we have a wide-awake, progressive, enterprising and highly prosperous people." Each city brochure, whether published by a booster club, an individual, or an immigration society, presented its own unique perspective, typically using down-home rhetoric to convey their message.[24]

City enticement literature often emphasized the need for capital investment and pointed to industrial growth. Galveston had an active city booster group and typically praised their port facilities in published material advertising their town. Boosters of San Antonio, with its thriving mix of Hispanics, Germans, and Anglos, frequently spoke of their community as a resort area

for invalids. In written material they capitalized on the transportation connections that made possible ease of travel for those seeking health cures. A
unique effort by a U.S. Army Lieutenant to promote south Texas was entitled
The Twin Cities of the Border and the Country of the Lower Rio Grande. Published in 1893 as a booster brochure for Brownsville, Texas, and Matamoros,
Mexico, the compiler used collated newspaper articles to present the opportunities of this far southern region of the state. Some cities either joined with
railroads to produce city enticement literature or benefited from brochures
put together by railroad companies looking to increase freight and passenger
service to certain urban locations. San Antonio and El Paso are at least two
places that were publicized in this way.[25]

The 1887 Immigration Convention, held in Dallas, served as a stimulus for
some of this activity. It clearly spurred some cities and counties into publishing written material promoting their location. According to the *Galveston
Daily News,* a second immigration convention was in the planning stages for
December 3, 1888. They reported on November 2, 1888, that, "This convention promises to give a renewed impetus to the Texas immigration movement,
which, for a time has appeared to be dormant." It would seem the enthusiasm
generated the previous year had fizzled somewhat, at least in the eyes of the
Galveston editor. For whatever reasons, the convention project was scaled
down to merely a meeting of the State Immigration Committee in Austin. As
the Galveston paper reported that ultimate event, they noted the "limited results—limited owing to apathy in many counties." They also announced to
their readers that they would "file the proceedings" for the moment and wait
for reports on the Southern Interstate Immigration Convention scheduled to
open December 13 in Montgomery, Alabama. The short shrift given the state
organization's meeting seems to indicate a judgment on the part of the Galveston editor as to the committee's success.[26]

The failure of that group to capitalize on the 1887 convention's energy and
enthusiasm seems obvious and is reflected in the way counties failed to send
in their assessed dollars for the financial maintenance of the endeavor. In spite
of such a bleak picture, the secretary of the State Immigration Committee
maintained a positive attitude. In unblushing overstatement he wrote that
"the state immigration movement has been a success beyond the hopes of the
most sanguine." He noted the inexperience that hampered the committee's
work, as well as the scarcity of financial support, but ended on a positive note
by saying, "The immigration outlook for Texas could not be better." While
the outlook might be bright for immigration, the future of the organization
meant to facilitate that movement seemed dismal.[27]

Almost hidden within the proceedings of that December third meeting is a tip-off as to the committee's inability to persevere. They resolved to set up a committee of twenty men with the intention of memorializing the state legislature to establish a "bureau of general information for the purpose of developing and making known the resources of the state of Texas." The resolution also requested that "at least $100,000 be appropriated" for such a bureau. Money was unmistakably one of the major problems in sustaining the drive behind the volunteer state immigration agency. Also, the memorial made no mention of immigration as a stated goal for this proposal. The committee definitely knew about the state constitutional prohibition against spending public money for "bringing immigrants to the State." Their request of the legislature appears to be a more underhanded approach to getting information about Texas out and about, since they did not list immigrants as their target group. In a very pragmatic way, they may have sensed the reality of the political situation and tried to accomplish their ultimate ends by developing a different path to the state pocketbook.[28]

One outgrowth of the State Immigration Committee's work was participation in the Southern Interstate Immigration Convention of 1888. When that convention met in Montgomery, Alabama, on December 12, Frank B. Chilton, a Texan and secretary of the State Immigration Committee of Texas, called the meeting to order and made the first address. When the convention closed, this same Texan had been selected as the General Manager of the Southern Interstate Immigration Bureau.[29]

Postbellum southern interest in immigration had always existed. Some of the states had held immigration conventions. In booster tradition newspapers across the South wrote of the value in bringing fresh settlers to the South's agricultural domain. Some states established government-sponsored immigration bureaus or agencies, like the 1870–76 Texas Bureau of Immigration. Even joint efforts across the entire south had been attempted. But the 1888 Montgomery Convention expressed region-wide southern interest in immigration better than anything that had gone before.[30]

The *Galveston Daily News* called it the "most important convention in many respects that has assembled in the south for many years." Frank B. Chilton as presiding officer expected it to be "the meeting of the largest and most influential Convention ever held in the South." The Alabama convention did not fulfill the dreams of such people as Chilton. But it did offer Texans in the late 1880s one more opportunity to work at developing a program of attracting immigration. By participating in this united effort of southern states, Texans hoped to benefit from help that comes from numbers.[31]

Journalistic estimates of the convention attendance ranged from the *Galveston Daily News'* statement that "about 600 delegates are present" to the much more conservative two hundred delegates reported by the Associated Press. Delegate names familiar to any Texan busy supporting the immigration impulse in Texas included those of J. S. Daugherty, Frank B. Chilton, and Robert A. Cameron. In typical booster tradition, the *Galveston Daily News* reported, "The Texas delegation is considered the brainiest and hardest workers in the convention, and really accomplished more for the great Lone Star state than any other state delegation."[32]

The kind of enthusiasm generated within this convention is best illustrated through an early speech given by General Robert A. Cameron, a Texan from the panhandle. He began with reference to the Civil War, saying, "We now present to the people of the North the olive branch of peace, and open wide our arms to welcome them to homes in our midst." He went on to say, "We want immigration, and to get it must organize in the States and towns and cities, and go to work for it. . . . The day will come when churches and school houses will rise on every hand and the people will thank God for the meeting of the Southern Immigration Convention at Montgomery."[33]

Many delegates saw their work as a religious mission to be accomplished. The opening prayer was printed in full in the published proceedings. And it too, like Cameron's later address, invoked God's blessings on the work of the conference. In part the convention attendants heard a preacher intone, "The plow stands still in the field of promise, and briars cumber the garden of beauty. We beseech thee to send us immigration."[34]

On a more earthbound level most delegates encouraged cooperation and discussion with the railroads, and transportation systems needed to facilitate the flow of people to southern areas. Castle Garden was mentioned more than once, for it was the immigration station located on the waterfront in the New York harbor. Castle Garden began operation in 1855 and was viewed as the main entry for immigrants to the United States until 1891 when Ellis Island in New York harbor became the federal detention point and immigration center. Envy for this northern immigrant port was expressed several times because southerners felt their region deserved better. Many of the delegates called for a southern port to service immigrants direct from Europe. In fact, a final resolution asked for the establishment of southern ports of entry at New Orleans and Savannah. Calls for a "Solid South" came from representative Chilton, as well as his injunction to be "up and doing."[35]

Chilton emphasized the opportunity for joint action by all southern states. The convention began on an individual note though, as each state was allowed time to express its own particular perspective. Most of these speeches also called for cooperation and spoke optimistically about the future. Cameron was able to address the convention a second time, as the representative from Texas, and when he did, state patriotism and eagerness were apparent. In part he spoke out, "we of Texas are enlisted for the war, and Texas proposes to do more in the future than we have done in the past. . . . Texas wants immigrants, and she is going to get them, no matter what the cost may be." The warfare imagery and the vigor of his address were obvious. He was carrying to Alabama much of the enthusiasm that had been generated back in Texas in 1887 and 1888.[36]

Little is known about the ultimate fate of the organization created and called the Southern Interstate Immigration Bureau (s.i.i.b.). Big beginnings sometimes fade into nothingness as months and years pass, and this bureau seems to fit that pattern. Some kind of relationship existed between the interstate bureau and agencies in Texas. At least once the s.i.i.b. requested material from the Texas Department of Agriculture, Insurance, Statistics, and History. However in order to succeed the Southern Interstate Immigration Bureau needed financial support on a regional basis. What this group of New South business leaders hoped to achieve—regional cooperation for the benefit of all—was a concept way ahead of its time. Voluntary efforts at unified activity across state lines have had a poor track record of success. In the twentieth century cooperation across state borders developed in some fields of endeavor. But a southern cooperative effort to attract immigrants was not to succeed or really influence to any great extent the flow of immigrants to the United States, either in the nineteenth or the twentieth century.[37]

This Southern Interstate Immigration Convention was heartily endorsed by Texas businessmen. The state was well represented in the deliberations. And the chosen leader of the ultimate bureau formed was a Texan—Frank B. Chilton. Many hoped his experience in trying to develop a volunteer bureau of immigration in Texas would carry over to the regional effort. While other southern states may have helped in an official capacity to support the Southern Interstate Immigration Bureau, such as through their departments of agriculture or immigration, the Texas government remained uninvolved. Why? The 1876 constitution and Section 56. Participation in the convention and then in the bureau demonstrates the energy and enthusiasm of private individuals, not Texas state government.

At least three other separate examples of determined private initiative to attract immigrants to Texas can be documented. A truly profound illustration of volunteer energy expended for the purpose of advertising Texas was the erection of the Texas building for the 1893 Columbian Exposition in Chicago. The state government spent no money on the building's erection. The legislative and executive branches of the state government interpreted Section 56 of Article 16 as prohibiting the use of any public money for participation at the fair. The news was out—statewide and across the country—that a constitutional prohibition would keep Texas from full involvement.

A building at a world's fair seems hardly to matter much in a discussion of efforts to attract immigrants to Texas. But to Texans in 1892 and 1893 this building provided a rallying point around which extensive activity took place. Efforts to encourage the state to financially support official Texas involvement in the Chicago extravaganza began early but failed in its goal. Finally, two private organizations—the Gentlemen's World Fair Association of Texas and the Texas Women's World's Fair Exhibit Association—took the lead and spearheaded a fund-raising venture that ultimately collected almost $30,000. The women's organization shouldered most of the responsibility and worked under the leadership of Mrs. Benedette B. Tobin. Tobin lived in Austin but developed a statewide organization, including a Board of Directors with nine members and an additional fourteen vice presidents-at-large around the state.[38]

The full story of this "women's work" has not yet been told, but they held teas, meetings, and local fundraising events in small and big communities around the state. The final building cost $28,000 and reportedly the Texas volunteer effort raised the $30,000 to cover expenses. A key point to all this expended energy on the part of citizens in Texas was that it was a direct response to the 1876 constitutional prohibition. Throughout the 1891–93 movement to fund Texas's participation in the Chicago Fair, Texans were clearly aware of the 1876 prohibition and referred to it often as instrumental in pushing private citizens to participate in this unique event at advertising Texas to the world and thus ultimately attracting new people to the state.

A different organizational drive began to develop strength in the last decade of the nineteenth century and on into the first ten years of the twentieth. Local business groups began to meet in order to develop business networks and to fund cooperative ventures. Known by various names, these commercial clubs depended on urban or community leadership. Much like the goals of state leaders in the immediate Civil War years, these business owners wanted capital and people to come to Texas. They wanted money to be invested in the state. They wanted workers, farmers, consumers, and craftspeople to settle in Texas and participate in the state's growth. Due to the ensuing urbanization in the later quarter of the nineteenth century, the emphasis on agriculture, however, diminished. Thus these business clubs published material referring to newcomers in a general way, rather than the earlier constant call for "farmers to till the land." They wrote about the potential for industrial development. And they drew a picture of transportation links across the state facilitating that development.

The largest and most comprehensive of these business clubs was the Texas Commercial Secretaries' Association. Their direct efforts to attract attention to the need for more immigration to the state can be seen in the numerous small pamphlets they produced. A thirty-two-page pamphlet entitled *Industrial Texas* was published in 1910. Another publication meant to encourage membership in the association was *The Master Builder.* This was a twenty-page pamphlet that outlined the work of the organization. By labeling themselves *The Master Builder,* the Texas Commercial Secretaries' Association saw themselves as instrumental in changing the face of their state. They emphasized two educational arms of the association: its available lecturers and its publications. Recognizing the value of people-to-people contact, they created visual aids, noting their inventory of "some fifty charts" to be used by those telling others about Texas. Then next to a page illustrating the covers of six of their pamphlets they talked plain marketing. Valuing the "printer's art" with its "charms and the skillful portraiture of opportunities," they called their work "high grade literature" to be furnished "at cost to any one desiring it." Seeing themselves as a central service agency for any group in Texas wanting to develop its own locale or region, they offered their services to one and all.[39]

In the Commercial Club approach, new imagery joined the campaign to entice newcomers. Pencil line sketches and circle graphs gave visual impact to the words. "Bigger Men Wanted" was one subtitle over a likeness of a farmer in jeans, boots, and scarf. The copy read in part,

> we must increase the size of the Texas farmer. We can't pass a law that will increase the production per acre; we can't pass a law that will increase the price of land; we can't pass a law that will increase the price of products. The increase must be made by the immigration agent bringing men and money into Texas; by the agricultural department increasing the production per acre, and by the Commercial Clubs bringing the factories to the farms.

Obviously "bigger men" meant more men who are productive. Another unique image was that of a spindly-legged bird in the marshes. The same pamphlet said, "The stork is a splendid bird, but too slow for Commercial Club work." Business people must turn with hope to the immigration agent,

"The Texas Barnyard." Produced by the Texas Commercial Secretaries Association in 1910, this pamphlet emphasized agricultural opportunities while incorporating a national image to suggest all were welcome. Courtesy Texas State Library and Archives Commission.

"The Door of Opportunity." An active promotional group, the Texas Commercial Secretaries Association often reached out to the larger world using Uncle Sam as a spokesperson. Notice the Lone Star of Texas on the door's welcome mat. Courtesy Texas State Library and Archives Commission.

said the club, for "we cannot populate Texas rapidly with home people." Still another of their pamphlets described the people and property sweeping "Texasward," stating, "Along this roadstead of nations there passes annually 69,000 homeseekers and \$123,000,000 of property. In this moving van of civilization can be heard the accents of every nation and the jostle of prosperity from every clime."[40]

The Texas Commercial Secretaries' Association served a coordinating function in the years at the turn of the century. The association envisioned a network of related business people addressing similar goals of encouraging population growth and developing industries. The club also saw itself as the source for tools to be used in such promotions; thus, their publications advertising their own publications were bent on getting the message out about Texas. This energy emanated from citizens throughout Texas. It was neither government subsidized nor explicitly encouraged by state government.

There were multiple organizations around the state doing similar work. Their names and activities varied over the years as well. Houston and Galveston each had a chamber of commerce in the 1860s. Austin in 1877 and Fort Worth in 1882 organized their commercial clubs and called them Boards of Trade. Gainesville established its City Commerce Club in 1888. The Waco Business Men's Club organized in 1899 and a chamber of commerce came into being in 1899 in El Paso. The 1912 *Texas Almanac* carried page after page advertising such organizations across the state. In the 1930s most of these prolific town clubs joined the national organization today known as the Chamber of Commerce. When many united earlier in 1906 under the umbrella label of Texas Commercial Secretaries' Association, they were inaugurating the first such permanent statewide association in the United States that one writer called the ultimate "quest for payrolls and population." Some communities maintained their independent status but followed in the same path as booster clubs seeking to improve their own prosperity and development.[41]

Such organizations by the business communities in Texas served to keep a focus on attracting new people to the state. The booster mentality and the "get-up-and-go" energy served to maintain an ongoing interest in enticement literature. One rather unusual project in this vein undertaken through private initiative was the Five Million Club. In this effort the stimulus was the upcoming 1910 federal census. The leaders defined their goal as a total population of five million people in Texas by 1910. The means to achieve such a goal involved publication of enticement literature emphasizing the advantages of Texas to all. The Five Million Club reflects a clear continuation in the belief that written material is extremely valuable, but this time with a specific end product: five million Texans. Removing the ambiguity of the "we want more people" phraseology, the club's leaders hoped to motivate the average citizen to get involved.

The idea was to focus on the census as a specific goal. One might ask, why seize the 1910 census as a focal point? The simple answer was political clout. The task of the census is to determine population totals in order to apportion congressional representatives in Washington, D.C. The obvious argument ran, if there are more people in Texas, there will be greater representation by Texas in the halls of Congress. Greater representation means a heavier in-fluence on national legislation. More people means the legislative voice of Texas will be proportionately louder.

While this argument sustained the basic energy of those working within the Five Million Club, it was only the symbolic end product of such efforts. Anything done along the way would enhance the economic growth and de-velopment of the state. Activists in the club talked of more production, more consumers, more taxpayers, and more neighbors. The Five Million Club ad-dressed its message to small and large communities alike. Hearkening back to post–Civil War cooperative efforts, the Five Million Club implored each citizen to join in working together. Everything from letter writing campaigns to donations of money for the publication of appropriate literature was sug-gested as means to support the club's work. Initial organization took place in 1906 and George H. Rockwell served as General Manager. With plans for a major convention to be held in El Paso, they developed a publicity bureau that used such rhetoric as, "It is time for Texas to quit being 'wild and wooly' and try being 'populous and busy.'" How to do this? Join the Five Million Club. "Don't KNOCK but HUSTLE," said one brochure.[42]

These brochures nourished the first aim of the Club, i.e. raise membership and interest. The next goal of the Five Million Club was addressed by the publication of enticement literature meant for the potential immigrant. One extraordinary advertising brochure was entitled *Texas from A to Z, A Com-pendium of Information*. Much like a children's alphabet book, this forty-three-page brochure utilized the structure of letters to introduce short sen-tences or paragraphs. "A" began with "Agriculture." This section included en-tries under apples, asparagus, and asphalt. "Z" had the lonely entry of zinc and claimed large but undeveloped quantities of the mineral in the state. A walk through the booklet suggests a Texas in which almost anything could be found or anything could grow. Bananas and pineapples were grown in the state, according to the booklet. Cattle, carrots, and cantaloupes were all raised there as well. Figs, horseradish, mangoes, and mulberries required entries also.

Under the letter "H" the entry "Holidays" told future Texans that two days unique to the state were Texas Independence Day on March 2, and "April 21, the anniversary of the battle of San Jacinto, when the final blow for Texas independence was struck." Although information on transportation, minerals, and manufacturing was also included, the emphasis on crops and animals reflects the continuing expectation that settlers in Texas would most commonly be rural and farm dwellers.[43]

In addition to pamphlets, the club used a new technique never before tried in the immigration movement. Red, white, and blue medallions stating, "I'm from Texas—Talk to me," were created for those traveling outside the state to conventions or taking business trips to other cities. Proudly, Rockwell reported the success of these medallions, which he said have "been called the finest piece of advertising Texas has had in years. We have barely been able to keep a supply of these on hand, so great has been the demand." Pamphlets with the same labeling as the medallions were being printed up for circulation, and mailings went out continually, according to this club administrator.[44]

The convention in El Paso was itself a publicity event of major magnitude. Media coverage helped make it one long rallying cry for the Five Million Club. The words of Mayor Will A. Miller, Jr., head of the fifty-member delegation from Amarillo, reflect the enthusiasm generated by the gathering. Miller said, "The Five Million club is doing great good for the state. It is advertising it and the population is on the increase. Get a man to stay in Texas six months and you can't drive him out."[45]

Boosterism was central to Five Million Club activity. Enthusiasm sparked with energy was necessary to keep the organization going. These qualities the club members seemed to have in abundance. As the delegates left the El Paso Convention their spirits were high. Financial resources are also a necessary ingredient for success. But this, the club did not have. As the nation's economy stumbled so did Texas, and in the process the Five Million Club faded out of existence. For a while, some of the communities around the state gave their local commercial associations names reflecting their population goal: the Childress 50,000 Club, the Abilene 25,000 Club, the Smithville 10,000 Club, and the Huntsville 100 Club were active groups. Goal setting and goal reaching involved an inward decision with a stated up-front object. The naming of their business associations put their label where their new perspective directed them. To what extent their message influenced population movement has not been documented, but the existence of thousands of leaflets and pamphlets surely indicates an educational interest on the part of many Texans at increasing state population.[46]

The composite whole of the immigration movement was made up of many single parts: One letter written here. Or one response to a letter there. A small meeting of interested citizens. Or a larger meeting of commercial businesses. The publication of a pamphlet extolling the virtues of a particular locale. The donation of money to see that the larger organization, be it Five Million Club or statewide commercial association, distributed the latest information about Texas. The contribution of pennies by women and children to erect a building in Chicago. Any one of these or any combination surely influenced people outside the state to think about Texas as possibly being their new home.

The activity in Texas between 1876 and 1915 to attract newcomers followed an up and down course of varying intensity. Once the 1876 constitution was ratified, official state financial support of immigration efforts ceased. But into that vacuum moved many individual and community efforts. Formal corporations developed. Land offices and real estate businesses advertised. Newspapers, inside and outside the state, acted as primary boosters. A statewide convention sparked renewed interest in bringing people within the borders. Discussions about participating in great expositions and fairs kept before Texans the idea that they needed to advertise their state's potential. Business clubs and commercial organizations also contributed energy and action. Once the assumption was in place—the assumption that private initiative would be necessary if Texas were to overcome the restrictions built into her constitution—Texans by the thousands took the challenge and worked actively to bring others to Texas.

CHAPTER 8

◆→◆←◆

RAILROADING PEOPLE IN

Railroads need people. They need people to construct the roadways, people to ride the rails, people to consume the products shipped, and people to produce the goods for transport. In settling the western and southern portions of the United States, the inter-relatedness between population movement and railroad growth is integral and obvious. Since farming seemed the best possible use of this territory, agricultural pursuits were touted by the railroads in their effort to lure people onto these lands. Texas, with its huge tracts of land and fertile soil, was a product to be sold. For the railroads Texas became an object to be advertised, both abroad and throughout the remaining states. Texas was the "Empire State," the "Winter Garden," the land of the Homestead Exemption, and the "Eldorado" for farmers, according to the railroad brochures produced in abundance.[1]

Such promotional activity by the railroads continued throughout the history of railroad development in the state. From the 1870s to the mid-twentieth century, advertising media by the railroads can be found exclaiming the benefits of going to Texas. Unlike such business-initiated efforts as the Commercial Secretaries' Clubs, town booster organizations, or immigration societies, which were literally energized by the official state pull-out from promotional work, the railroads merely continued previous efforts to produce written information that best met their needs as they grew in size and influence. These companies built track, platted new towns, sold railroad lands, and offered their services as "the" transportation link across the state.

Quite bold claims have been made about the railroads' impact on settlement and development. One American scholar called railroads "the most important single factor in the development of the Trans-Mississippi country." If we translate "development" as "enticement of people and capital," the observation rings true. Railroads—their construction and use—have tremendously influenced the history of the United States. The same assertion applies to Texas. The very size of the state and its lack of navigable waterways encouraged railroad development. In addition, the state's growth period coincided with the heyday of railroad construction. How much credit should go

"IMMIGRANTS HOME," PALESTINE, TEXAS.

TEXAS

"Homes in Texas." The International & Great Northern Railroad published a pamphlet in 1880 depicting Texas as the idyllic place for agriculture. A woodcut inside showed one of the immigrant homes built to help families during their search for land. Courtesy Texas State Library and Archives Commission.

to the railroads? A speaker at the 1893 Columbian Exposition in Chicago said in reference to his native state, "The truth is, Texas is what her railroads have made her." While this is much too comprehensive a statement, the rhetoric implies the symbiotic relationship that existed between the railroads and the many promotional efforts to entice newcomers. It also reflects the perception on the part of influential Texans that this connection was both positive and effective.[2]

Railroads must not be seen as a monolithic whole. The railroad industry was just that—an industry composed of multiple corporations individually out to make a profit. Various roadways in competition with each other aimed to take advantage of the state's natural resources and the human demand for good transportation. The complete saga of Texas railroads would include a study of appropriate legislation, corporate mergers, leadership styles, the engineering tales of construction, plus much more. The developing narrative would be a tangled web of small and large companies, rural and urban interests, competition resulting gradually in merged lines, as well as citizen complaints of monopolistic exploitation. Buried within that larger story is the special story of efforts by different railroad systems in Texas to entice immigrants to the land.[3]

There is a rhythm to railroad development—a rhythm that parallels population shifts. First came the surveying parties followed by larger construction crews. This initial stage involved pulling relatively small numbers of people into a location for a relatively short period of time. After these workers built a portion of the roadway they moved on, leaving small maintenance crews at convenient locations along the line. Railroads used a few depots at critical spots along their routes for repair supplies and boarding locations. The city of Palestine was a main terminal in this regard for the International & Great Northern line (I&GN RR). Denison served a similar purpose for the Missouri, Kansas, and Texas line (MK&T RR) moving into Texas from St. Louis. Once these ribbons of steel were in place, traffic increased and the rails facilitated a sustained flow of people. At various junctures small towns developed, often growing gradually as commerce increased. Depending on the location of the town, its possible position as a transportation hub for several rail lines, and the energy of its citizens, growth in population followed on the heels of the steel rails on wooden ties. Just as the construction crews continued laying steel, the process repeated itself as the roadbed moved across previously under-utilized land. The railroads thus served as a "pull factor" during the early settlement phase and continued as a magnet drawing later population to and through the area that the railroad crossed.[4]

Railroads never lost faith in the need to publicize Texas. All of the railroad companies produced various written documents meant to attract immigrants. They, like other enticement promoters around the state, assumed that if the best possible correct information about Texas was presented to the potential newcomer, then most would choose to buy land and settle in Texas. As late as 1911, one pamphlet by the Iron Mountain Route asked itself and its readers why would "intelligent" people living in the northern cold climates not move to Southwest Texas? In answer they excerpted material from a newspaper in Dimmit County: "The only feasible conclusion we can draw is ignorance, the lack of knowledge of what Southwest Texas has to offer them. So it behooves us to employ every honest and honorable agency at our disposal to convey this great knowledge to those who would seek homes in other climes."[5]

When telling people about Texas, railroad brochures freely appropriated written material from a multitude of sources. Similar to other enticement literature, railroads often produced volumes through the "cut and paste" method. This approach made publication faster and easier, since original copy takes more time to produce. In addition, the final document would thus appear to be a representation of diverse people not just a reflection of the desire by railroad administrators to market land or sell tickets. Well-worded testimonials were used extensively. Letters written to the company or elicited through circulars were frequently excerpted and thus gave a personal touch to the pamphlet or the brochure. Quotes from newspapers, which were usually a community's biggest booster voice, lent an aura of stability to the message, since a town newspaper meant a community with literate, energetic, and thoughtful people—and thus a desirable place for relocation. Speeches by government officials or messages from prominent citizens were also liberally appropriated.[6]

In addition to the standard rhetorical tactics of other people and agencies, railroads incorporated messages unique to their special operations and used them continually throughout the years. For example, the publication of excerpts from the Texas constitution highlighting homestead provisions continued to be a mainstay of almost all railroad enticement literature. These special laws assured that one's home could not be sold for debt. Each family could thus be given a sense of security not available everywhere. Whether published in 1876 or 1892 or 1911, these Texas laws were used by the publicity departments of the railroads as a lure and as an emphasis on the family nature of immigration to Texas.[7]

Consistency of approach can be seen through a number of other techniques. The cost of travel has always been a central concern for any person contemplating relocation. Aware of this factor, railroads made strenuous efforts to court the immigration business. Each railroad approached reduced fares in their own unique way. Some lines such as the Galveston, Harrisburg, and San Antonio Railroad (GH&SA RR) offered simple, reduced rates to immigrants. New settlers could travel for one and three-quarter cents per mile as compared to the regular rate of five cents a mile. Other railroads preferred what were called emigrant excursion tickets. These were meant to provide the potential settlers a chance to come to Texas and "look-see" for themselves. The I&GN RR called such enticing fares "Round Trip Prospector's Tickets," while the GH&SA RR used the label "Land Exploring Tickets." The ticket holder could stop at any station along the railroad's line to examine land. If a purchase of land was made within sixty days, the ticket cost would be applied to the first payment of the land. The MK&T RR also offered excursion fares, as well as advertised a rate break to children, in case the whole family came to scout out the possibilities or eventually settle. Children under five traveled free and those between the ages of five and twelve paid half fare. By the turn of the century the most frequent label was "homeseekers' fares."[8]

Frequently excursion fares were limited to certain days in the month, with the first and third Tuesdays typically designated as departure times. Commonly, newspaper articles copied or sent outside the state sparked interest in an area. Then potential settlers used the rail lines as the least expensive way of checking out the possibilities. For example, Dalhart in Dallam County recorded over four hundred homeseekers during just one week in December, 1910. They all arrived by excursion train, visited various local land companies, and many bought land with the plan of returning with their families.[9]

Real estate companies also worked directly in conjunction with the railroads servicing their areas, often providing excursion cars with special rates for their customers. The Standard Land Company, with headquarters in Kansas City, Missouri, owned land in Sherman County, along Texas's border with Oklahoma. Between 1904 and 1909 they regularly ran from one to three cars to Sherman County. Their advertising copy proclaimed, "Berths in these cars are free, both going and returning, for all Standard Land customers. Our customers also use these cars to sleep in while at Stratford, thus saving hotel bills." The Soash Company of the panhandle also used this technique to bring potential buyers to their land, often pulling together whole trains of seventy-five to 150 travelers. People from throughout the Midwest would congregate in such departure cities as Chicago, Detroit, and Minneapolis, and then travel to the Soash lands with a sales agent presenting an extensive sales pitch.[10]

Combining land and sea transportation was yet another way to deal with

"TEXAS." The simple title proclaims the message of this Houston & Central Railroad brochure, ca. 1880. Notice smoke trailing a train that is almost lost in the center of the woodcut—agricultural paradise is the main message. Courtesy Texas State Library and Archives Commission.

rates and fares. "As an inducement to immigration, for the purpose of settling up the State of Texas" the Houston & Texas Central (H&TC RR) offered "greatly reduced rates" and listed seven different steamship lines that made connections with Great Britain, Ireland, and continental Europe. Additionally the H&TC RR suggested the purchase of prepaid tickets to be sent to family and friends overseas thus helping to facilitate their travel to Texas. Envisioning a wider scope for their business, they tried to capitalize on that marketing technique.[11]

Moving expenses also involved costs of the final move as distinct from earlier charges in scouting out a new home. As late as 1926, the phrase "Emigrant movables" appeared in connection with land sales by the Atcheson, Topeka, and Santa Fe Railroad (AT&SF RR). The company defined this term as applying only "to property of an intending settler" and including "second-hand (used) household goods or personal effects such as clothing, furniture or furnishings for residences." The list allowed farming tools, fence posts, mechanical equipment, livestock "not to exceed ten head" and seeds. One person was usually permitted to ride in the boxcar in order to manage any livestock. Special rates would be applied to those fitting this category. The number of immigrants using this means to transport their family goods would be very difficult to determine. But an idea of the extensiveness of the practice is indicated by one Santa Fe Railroad report. In a three-month period of 1907, the company recorded arrangements for 1,340 cars, each shared by two families, traveling to Amarillo. One Texas settler recorded in his diary a 1918 entry describing his experience with an "immigrant car": "We shipped out of Roaring Springs about 3 o'clock, getting to Quanah 8 or 9 P.M. Unloaded stock. Cold as the devil. Hid the boys in the car. Saved $7.50 by doing so." His entry reflects the tight finances of most farming emigrants and the common practice of traveling during the winter off-season. One historian suggests that these trips "remained a nightmare in the mind of the farmer as long as he lived." The publication of special rates and fares in their enticement brochures served to act as an attraction, in and of itself, to the potential Texan, so the various railroads continued over the years to include such information in their advertising.[12]

Railroads consistently addressed their message to both foreign-born and native-born immigrants. While Europeans remained a small percentage of the total number of people moving to Texas, the railroads still spoke to that segment of society. One such example was entitled *Sud und Sudweft Texas* [South and Southwest Texas] and published by the passenger department of the Sunset Route. This 127-page booster brochure for Texas incorporated typical statistics as it provided city descriptions, county information, and articles on such topics as climate, dry farming, mining, and stock raising. The booklet included a map of the railroad line, a feature that was common in most train promotional literature. The only English in the document was a translation of the table of contents and one advertisement for the railroad itself. The message in German and English was the same: "Texas is Today the Best Field for the Rich Man, the Man of Moderate Means, and the Man who is anxious to acquire a Home and Future for Himself and Family."[13]

The H&TC RR noted in their English language booklet, *Texas,* that editions of their brochure were available in English, German, Swedish, and Norwegian. They encouraged interested parties to write to Robert M. Elgin, land commissioner of the road, to obtain a copy. A 1909 Southern Pacific timetable of sixty-two pages tried a new approach to easing newcomer stress by publishing the pictures of the passenger agents who would greet the traveler upon their arrival in New York or New Orleans. Paragraphs in French and in German were included and encouraged the foreigner to look for the Southern Pacific name. Another approach was to advertise in foreign language books or newspapers. One such example is the 1907 publication *Texas Voran! Handbuch von Texas.* This privately published book was completely in German. The back cover had a full-page advertisement for the Sunset Route, including names and addresses of railroad agents.[14]

Efforts to lure foreign-born immigrants were as varied as the railroads and their brochures. One approach was to bury their overtures within the more general statements of the state's growth and continuing prosperity. The H&TC RR tried to appeal to newcomers in this way as they described Texas:

> There are large areas of fertile districts upon which Colonies may be located— land of reasonable valuation, and well positioned as to water and timber. . . . There is ample room for an almost unlimited number of energetic people. . . . Although for a number of years there has been a steady emigration to Texas of people from the older States . . . the residents of foreign countries are apparently becoming better alive to, and more fully appreciative of, the innumerable advantages this State offers intending settlers . . . steadily increasing volume . . . from all ports of the Old Country. Germany, Poland, Scandinavia and other nations of Europe are furnishing their quotas.

Such general statements assumed assimilation of all groups of people. Using inclusive language they presented a positive image of Texas as the place for

Europeans to settle. Another pamphlet by the MK&T RR put it simply, "Texas is essentially cosmopolitan. Her inhabitants come from every country, State, and Clime."[15]

A minor theme in railroad promotional material was settlement by colonies. Railroads shared this approach with some of the real estate ventures that saw greater profits in large numbers. Railroads never overemphasized this idea but kept it routinely before the eye of the potential immigrant. One way of presenting the idea was to list the advantages of colonies. The agent might present a typical scenario saying that a group of people could select one representative person to travel to Texas. This person would examine the possibilities and select land for all—land that would receive a concession on price because of the large acreage sold. Once in Texas these colonists would be able to buy, through their agent, lumber and supplies at "car-load rates." They could make cooperative purchases of livestock in this way as well. Brochures encouraging colonies pointed also to the quick formation of schools and churches due to the number of people congregated in one area. Noting the influence of chain migration, one pamphlet pointed out that the group "will have a society of their own, and be the nucleus of population that will flock to them to enjoy the advantages they possess." This same brochure then listed some "prosperous" European settlements in Texas among the Polish, Germans, French, Swedish, Norwegians, and Scandinavians.[16]

Colonies were presented as a possibility for ethnic groups. But they were also encouraged as a way to stave off the loneliness that comes from leaving family and friends behind. The potential for one religious group to begin a town or plant a community became a vision for many. Colonies were thus an option for any group, whether set apart by religion, birthplace, family relations, or current residence in a previous state. Sometimes the colony might develop right on the railroad line, while others existed farther into the hinterlands. Historians have referred to some of the resulting communities as "folk islands." In one way, they provided all the positive aspects that ghettos in the northern cities provided for ethnic or religious groups. Some fifty different "folk islands" have been identified in the northwestern portion of Texas alone, including such diverse ethnic groups as German, Polish, Italian, Wends, Swedish, Norwegian, and Czech. Many of these communities began as a deliberate colonization plan that clearly prospered.[17]

Railroads were selling two items in the late 1800s and early 1900s: land and service. One service item was lodging for the immigrants. In the twenty-first century, hotels and motels are commonplace and easily accessible with a wide range of prices and accommodations for families. This was not the case in the nineteenth century well before the paved roadways that accompanied the proliferation of automobiles. In a few cases, railroads stepped into the breach offering help to the cost-conscious farmer. In Texas, at least three different railroad lines built immigrant homes for their passengers.

One such home existed on the Texas & Pacific (T&P RR) line in Baird, a city in Callahan County. The home was erected in the midst of the land that the company had for sale. Thus emigrants could travel along the roadway, settle into the home for a couple days, and then tour the area looking for land to purchase. The "Immigrant Home" coincided with the location of the railroad's branch office, so company personnel probably maintained the boarding facility. According to a T&P RR brochure of 1883, it was a "large and commodious two-story immigration house where families and baggage can be comfortably left while the head of the family is looking for a permanent home." A colony of Portuguese settlers from Fresno, California used the home in 1881 before selecting land nearby in Clyde, Texas. The same railroad reportedly built another such home in Midland. This home was described in booster literature of the time as "pleasant, neat and comfortable. Five or six families can reside therein at a time, each keeping house by itself. A thrifty and well kept garden is in connection, from which the occupants may purchase vegetables at very reasonable prices. A pump driven by a windmill affords an abundance of water."[18]

The GH&SA RR maintained several such immigrant homes along their route between Galveston and San Antonio. In the early years of the GH&SA RR, home locations included New Philadelphia, Converse, and Luling. Thomas Wilson, an immigration agent for the railroad, maintained the Luling home as part of his duties during his tenure from 1877 to 1883. Wilson's family, including his wife and ultimately twelve children, lived in the building and presumably helped maintain it.[19]

The I&GN RR with its north/south line through eastern Texas publicized its "Immigrant's Home" located in Palestine, the company's headquarters and the location of its Land and Immigration Department. The I&GN RR proudly proclaimed that the home "is under the exclusive control of the Railroad Company, is for the benefit of emigrants and their families only, and is under strict order and sanitary regulations." One I&GN RR map included the image of a home with the front verandahs of the two-story building filled with people, young and old, under the heading "Comfort, Free of Charge." If records were kept of the boarders in these many immigrant homes, they have not survived to provide us some indication of how many people used the free service or for how long the railroads offered the lodgings to travelers. These

AGRICULTURAL RESOURCES
IN THE

PAN HANDLE OF TEXAS

ON THE
LINE OF THE

MATTHEWS
NORTHRUP & CO
BUFFALO NY

·TEXAS PAN HANDLE ROUTE·

"Agricultural Resources in the Pan Handle of Texas." The sparsely settled Panhandle received a boost from the railroad lines that began to traverse the area. Unusual for railroad brochures of the time, this one had a named author, James Wilson, an Iowa farmer who traveled to Texas and recorded his impressions. Courtesy Center for American History, University of Texas at Austin.

specialized homes demonstrate a creative and unique marketing approach for that era.[20]

Yet another service provided by the railroads was the many individual company employees. They worked under a variety of labels—Land Agent, Passenger Agent, Colonization Agent, or Immigration Agent. Unfortunately in the lives of big corporations the story of the relatively insignificant employee often gets lost. A dearth of information exists concerning the agents themselves. But to the incoming settler, the railroad agent could be and probably was a very significant individual.

The various representatives working for the railroad did so for numerous motives, but the bottom line for most must have been salary. These transportation companies needed employees to do the nitty-gritty paperwork at the home offices. They needed people at each depot to coordinate the local business of the road. Railroads employed maintenance teams to keep the trains rolling, as well as train personnel such as conductor, engineer, and fireman. Some employees were specifically hired to lure immigrants to Texas. As the companies grew in size and administrative need, publicity departments with writers, editors, and secretaries developed. Hundreds of brochures created by such departments were issued. Often railroad enticement literature did not list a specific author. Individual credit for railroad publications was rare. A more typical credit for a leaflet or brochure merely read, "Passenger Department of the Santa Fe Railroad" or "Publicity Department of the MKT." But there were people behind the lines of those documents. Their decisions on what to include in copy influenced the shape of those brochures over the years, since they literally provided volumes of written material for potential immigrants to read.[21]

Serving as yet another source of information for immigrants were the individual agents each railroad listed in their many brochures. Over and over again railroads published the names of their agents and then added some phrase encouraging the reader to write a letter to obtain more specific, concrete information. Did potential immigrants ever take this suggestion to heart and write to a railroad agent? The persistence by the railroad companies in using brochure or pamphlet space to list such agents seems to suggest some success at putting people in contact with people. The technique may have been included in all these brochures as a ploy to suggest that a person-to-person relationship was possible with such a large corporation as a railroad. Maybe, in reality immigrants seldom took the opportunity to write. Speculation as to this letter-writing activity remains unresolved.

Who worked as an agent for the railroad? What would such a person be like? One recent family history chronicles the life of Thomas Wilson, an English immigrant, who came, lived, and eventually died as an adopted Texan. For a portion of his life Thomas Wilson worked for the GH&SA RR as an immigration agent. Whether or not his particular life fits the pattern of a typical railroad immigration agent, his history illustrates some of the activities of such agents. A small businessman in Rosedale, England, Thomas married and began raising a family. At one point he had an overseas subscription to the *San Antonio Express,* thus learning about Texas via the written word. Through acquaintance with Dr. William G. Kingsbury, Thomas was hired by the railroad and in 1879 gathered his family together for the voyage to Texas. The Wilson family began life in the state as occupants and operators of the "Immigrant House" established by the GH&SA RR. Thomas's job was to oversee the portion of the roadway from Columbus to Kingsbury, with other agents handling the line to its terminus in Galveston. Little else is known about Wilson's railroad job. He resigned in 1883, moved his family into a newly built permanent home in Luling, and went into business for himself. The fact that he owned thirteen farms when he resigned from the railroad position would indicate he was an energetic worker, both for the railroad and for himself. He developed several commercial enterprises with the help of his children, including at least two general stores, a furniture store, a real estate business, and a hotel. His experience as a public relations person for the railroad and operator of the immigrant house surely served to prepare him for his later personal business life.[22]

While not much is known about his specific duties for the GH&SA RR, several experiences recorded by his biographer give us an insight into this immigrant-turned-Texan as representative of other immigrants to the state. Early on, Thomas kept in contact with family and friends back in England, both by personal letters and published letters in English newspapers. In 1879 he also wrote an article entitled "Hunting in West Texas," for the English journal *The Field.* His description of the potential for hunters has all the earmarks of the era's booster literature. The article also encouraged the reader to contact W. G. Kingsbury, a railroad agent in London, for further information and passage arrangements.[23]

Thomas wrote for his hometown newspaper. In one such effort in 1891 he referred to his work at "managing the immigration movement" for the GH&SA RR in years past and wrote, "A well directed immigration movement would bring into our midst a better class of renters, who would arouse to more activity those already here, and cause them to quit renting and purchase for themselves homes." Clearly a person who valued real estate ownership, Wilson saw the importance of cooperative efforts to sell land in the county and improve the local economy. As a real estate booster he also wrote, "All good people who desire to come here, and make their homes with us, will find a hearty welcome; but to worthless people seeking a community to support them in idleness, we will say your room is preferred to your presence. Stay away." Then adding specifics about the lands he had for sale, he ended with the encouragement to write him for details. "Never wait until tomorrow what you can do today," Thomas wrote. Such words reveal clearly his philosophy of life and his willingness to share that view with others.[24]

Thomas Wilson's life story demonstrates the energy of an immigrant who used personal skills to encourage other people to move to Texas. He originally pursued that goal as a paid employee of an aggressive railroad company. Seeing real estate as a potential moneymaking endeavor, he then supported his large family through a multitude of business enterprises. Surely not all railroad agents match Wilson's accomplishments. But most agents were in a position to make similar contributions to the peopling of Texas. As more of their stories come to be told, their contribution to the population growth of Texas will become clearer.

Yet another dynamic railroad employee provides a different vision of an agent's field of endeavors. Dr. William G. Kingsbury may have begun his career as an immigration agent in the official capacity as Commissioner of Immigration in the Texas Bureau of Immigration. In 1874 the bureau's superintendent, Jerome B. Robertson, identified Kingsbury as Robertson's choice for a bureau position. Saying that his "ability, long residence in, and familiarity with the climate, soil and products of the Western portion of the State, qualified him for the duty," Robertson announced Kingsbury's appointment to the bureau's office in St. Louis, Missouri. Others spoke highly of Kingsbury's enthusiasm and hard work. The *Texas New Yorker* in 1875 called him "the active and efficient agent of the Texas Bureau of Immigration" who "has been the means of distributing information, printed, written and oral, which has been the cause of swelling our population several thousands."[25]

When the Texas Bureau of Immigration died due to lack of funding, Kingsbury used his connections with the railroads and his enthusiasm for immigration to develop another career in private enterprise. He became an agent for the GH&SA RR, spending much of his time working in London, England. Kingsbury believed in the power of the written word and was prolific at writing letters for publication and at communicating with Europeans and Texans alike. Information he provided to the *Anglo-American Times* in London became an article in the *St. Louis Texan* when the editors of the later newspaper lifted the earlier article. Thus by his industry, one moment's work was turned into information for many, varied readers. The *Galveston Daily News* was a frequent recipient of letters or announcements from Kingsbury. They used his copy to help fill their columns, since his boosterism complemented the newspaper's agenda. One interesting Kingsbury letter was published under the heading "Immigration Work in Europe." Boldly, Kingsbury said in this published letter, "Inasmuch as the railroads of Texas have been often charged with doing little or nothing in support of immigration, I wish to let your readers know what one at least has done." Sounding a bit defensive, Kingsbury then pointed to his own instrumental work at helping over six hundred immigrants to travel direct from Bremen to Galveston. He also bragged about distributing over forty-five thousand copies of a pamphlet and map "descriptive of Texas" in Germany, Sweden, Finland, Norway, and Holland. Calling upon Texans to support this effort, he optimistically wrote, "if the citizens of Texas will lend a helping hand by attentions and encouraging the new arrivals, strangers at your gates, and getting them to write good letters home, we shall make it a grand success."[26]

Using another publicity approach, Kingsbury took the written words of others and collated them for publication by his railroad. About 1878 his company published a fifty-three-page pamphlet entitled *The State of Texas,* ostensibly authored by Kingsbury. In reality it was a combination of gathered letters, articles, testimonials, and statistics proclaiming the glories of life in Texas for the industrious immigrant.[27]

Kingsbury's enthusiastic portrayal of Texas's potential also caught the eye of another Texas-based author, Alexander Edwin Sweet. Sweet was a journalist from San Antonio who in the late 1870s under the name "the sifter" started publishing columns heavily laced with sarcasm. Immigration agent Kingsbury came under criticism several times in Sweet's invectives. Hinting that Kingsbury could stretch the truth, Sweet acknowledged the influence Kingsbury had on immigration. At one point, Sweet wrote, "When you see an Englishman in Texas, who looks as if he needed medicine, you may be sure he is one of [immigration agent] Dr. Kingsbury's patients. At least, that is what all sick Englishmen in Texas claim." Sweet went on to write that one Englishman reported Kingsbury giving "a florid description of Texas, how pine apples [*sic*] grew on the prickly pear bushes, and boxes of oranges dropping ripe from the trees encumbered the sidewalks." Kingsbury's reputation was so solid that a satirist could use his name and know it would be recognized almost statewide.[28]

Kingsbury and Wilson are but two of the many railroad agents who worked to encourage immigration into Texas. One other name deserves notice here. Jerome B. Robertson has already been identified as the second superintendent of the Texas Bureau of Immigration (1874–76). But evidence supports the fact that he also served as a "Passenger and Emigration Agent" for the H&TC RR for several years in the late 1870s and that he worked as a land or real estate agent and railroad promoter in Waco from 1880 until his death in 1890. All three men indicate an intimate connection between railroad work and immigration promotion.[29]

In the period between 1876 and 1915 most Texas railroads shared similar strategies in luring immigrants to Texas. They advertised special rates. They targeted foreign and native born. They encouraged settling by colonies. And some offered the service of special lodgings. Through energetic, hard-working employees they multiplied the impact of the written word.

While the railroads presented a clearly focused plan to attract immigration, their geographical emphasis and the content of their message changed over time. A bare overview of Texas railroad growth in the early years points to the primarily eastern development of the state and the eastern growth of the road-ways. The early Anglo settlement of Texas moved across the land from east to west, also pushing slightly northwestward. Both the antebellum and post-

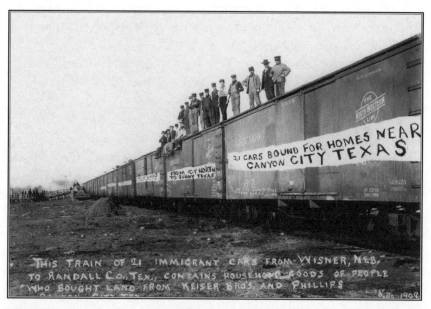

Immigrant trains were not a usual sight at the turn of the twentieth century. This one orig-inated in Nebraska. Note the banner declaring the importance of weather and climate on the decision to move. Courtesy Panhandle-Plains Historical Museum.

war migrations of people fit this standard trend. Transportation to the state was easiest by water through the Galveston port, although overland trails from Louisiana complemented the Galveston route. Thus, the lower southeastern portion of the state received most of the immigration, while the eastern counties along the Louisiana border also grew in population. Before railroads, travel by cart and wagon was the standard. But as the chaos and confusion of the Civil War and Reconstruction era faded, the railroad companies pushed to expand their track throughout the state. In these early postwar years, this expansion meant movement from Galveston inland to Houston and on to San Antonio. In time railroad growth also meant north/south lines like the I&GN RR through east Texas. Gradually, connections were made with St. Louis and there began a profitable two-way trade between Texas and Missouri and the lands in between.[30]

As the nineteenth century drew to a close, the western portions of Texas opened up to a major influx of ranchers and farmers. The stage for this movement had been set in 1876, when the Texas legislature took the last remaining territorial portions of the state land and carved it up into fifty-four counties. Images of buffalo and Indians yielding to the power of civilized government must have motivated the legislation. The act did serve to stimulate, to some extent, movement into the area. In the beginning mostly ranchers pushed into this land with their herds, but as the years passed more farmers sought the fertile land of the panhandle and west plains regions.[31]

Railroad publications of the 1870s and 1880s typically tried to lure newcomers to those areas of the state where the track already existed. Then a slight shift took place. Railroad publications dated 1888 or 1903 or 1911, more often than not, proclaimed the benefits of farming and settling in the relatively unsettled portions of the state: the panhandle, lands west of San Antonio toward El Paso, the plains west of Fort Worth but south of the panhandle, as well as lands on the far south border of Texas near Brownsville. These places in Texas had fewer people per square mile than the eastern half of the state. Yet these wide-open spaces also had fertile soil and real potential for ranching and farming. It was also in the self-interest of the roads to encourage movement westward since typically the state, when it granted land to the railroads, did not always grant land along the proposed routes of the roadbeds. Much of the land grants meant railroads had to market distant parts of west Texas. At the turn of the twentieth century an outpouring of rail publications proclaimed many advantages for farmers moving to the coastal lands of Texas or back to the eastern counties of the state.

One transitional leaflet was entitled *Texas: Her Resources and Attractive Features* (1883). It described various cities along the line of the Missouri Pacific (MP RR). Galveston, San Antonio, and Austin had often been described in earlier railroad literature. But this brochure covered those large cities plus added other vignettes of less commonly advertised towns. Weatherford in Parker County received attention for its healthfulness, its wool trade, and its flour mills. In addition, the accompanying illustration showed a farmer on the land with the caption, "January Plowing near Weatherford." Such visuals enhanced the readability of the pamphlet, plus in this case suggested the mild climate to be found. Abilene, first platted in early 1881, was touted by this same pamphlet as secure in its existence. Population and trade statistics were offered as proof. Two far western towns received notice also. The brochure advertised Big Springs noting its location near "two great natural wells." A young town only two years old, the writer praised Big Spring for its 1,800 inhabitants and "the best hotel on the line." Colorado City, located 232 miles west of Fort Worth, was described as a tent city in 1881, but a prosperous cattle-shipping center three years later. According to the brochure, in this far west town, "agriculture was not thought of at first, but the experiments of two years have been eminently successful, and have proven beyond all question that the soil of Northern Texas is as good as that of Kansas for wheat or any other crop." The copy in this railroad brochure clearly suggests the early stages of West Texas development in which agriculture came to be seen as a possibility for land that had been assumed a ranching domain exclusively.[32]

The Fort Worth and Denver City Railroad (FW&DC RR) encouraged West Texas development through its primary goal of connecting Denver, Colorado, to Fort Worth and on to Galveston. Once that line was in place the company turned to advertising the intervening land as ideal for farm settlement, even as they acknowledged not owning any land in the area. In publishing a specific West Texas pamphlet entitled *Agricultural Resources in the Pan Handle of Texas,* they claimed that the "Texas Pan Handle Route is to be a people's railroad, and the plow and the locomotive are to unite in a common purpose for a common end." The road placed General Robert A. Cameron in charge of an information bureau and he worked under the official title of "Commissioner of Emigration." The focus of this specific pamphlet was clearly agriculture. The railway company used a unique approach. They asked the Honorable James Wilson of Tama County, Iowa, who they billed as "an expert and practical farmer of large experience and known integrity" to tour the panhandle of Texas for two months and report on his findings. The idea

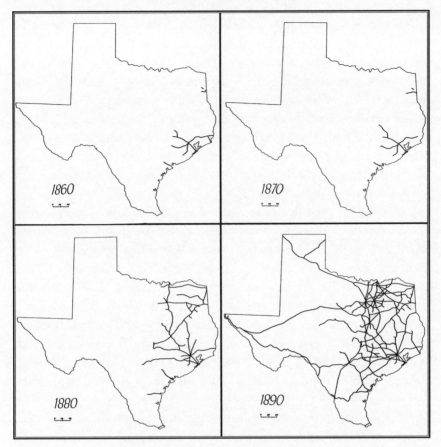

Growth of Railroad Mileage in Texas, 1860–1920. Railroad growth paralleled and spurred population in-migration. The railroad mileage reflected in these maps suggests extensive movement of people and products. From Charles P. Zlatkovich, *Texas Railroad: A Record of Construction and Abandonment.* Reprinted with permission by the Bureau of Business Research, McCombs School of Business, University of Texas at Austin.

of having a farmer from a major grain-producing area of the country make judgments about the Texas panhandle was a new tactic, and it aimed at verifying for the "doubting Thomases" of the world, the agricultural possibilities of the state. This fascinating pamphlet ends with the concluding sentence, "The farm is the natural place for the family, and Iowa people who will go south for a warmer climate can get homes in the Pan Handle [*sic*], where conditions for growing what it pays the farmer to raise are favorable."[33]

West Texas, as exemplified in panhandle Texas, was the object of extensive railroad enticement literature complemented by booster literature from the inhabitants of the land. Other railroad companies emphasized their own particular areas of the state. By the turn of the century the Texas southwest became a target for special publication efforts. The Southern Pacific (SP RR), utilizing their image-making label—the Sunset Route—published the work *Southwest Texas, from San Antonio to El Paso.* In this short leaflet, circa 1908, they noted development in this area saying that as "the older sections of the State become settled up[,] homeseekers and investors are rapidly pushing south and west in Texas." Then they added acknowledgment that there exists "a great demand for reliable information." The railways, as always, saw themselves as dispensers of that knowledge.[34]

The SP RR followed this smaller pamphlet with a longer thirty-two-page booklet demonstrating excessive booster optimism on its title page. Slogans added to the simple title, *Southwest Texas, An Agricultural Empire,* proclaimed "It offers a man a man's share of prosperity" and "Your opportunity is here, the time is now." Beekeeping, goat, sheep, and stock raising, as well as dry land farming and irrigation projects were only some of the topics discussed. A trek from El Paso to San Antonio was then described helping the traveler view the opportunities in Marfa, Alpine, Uvalde, and Lacoste. "Sunshine does it all. Sunshine all the year!" and "In Southwest Texas winter is almost winterless" claimed the bold railroad rhetoric. The writer declared that Texans in the southwest don't have to "farm against climate" anymore. "Southwest Texas is a land of surprises," stated the publicist, suggesting that if the reader only kept an open mind, he or she would discover the perfect place to build a home.[35]

This same pamphlet tackled the issue of irrigation head on. The topic had divided earlier publicists of the more arid or semiarid portions of Texas. To acknowledge the use of irrigation was to admit the land was less than a paradise for farmers. To discuss the potential use of windmills and irrigation could drive away the person unfamiliar with those newer technologies. Yet to not discuss the value of irrigation could doom to failure many farming ventures and potentially turn away many good farmers. In this particular publication, the railroad defined "irrigation" in two ways. First, they noted very scientifically that irrigation was the "conveyance of moisture to the soil by artificial means." But then they put it in human emotional terms by saying, "Irrigation means simply this: The farmer controls his own rainfall." The ability to plug into the feelings of the farmer, as well as his rational, statistical mindset may well have helped the railroad to lure people to southwest Texas. As they wrote in this 1911 brochure, "Southwest Texas Beckons to the Lover of Growing Things."[36]

Other railroads encouraged settlement in the "coast country" of Texas. Pamphlets used this label in attempts to encourage immigration to the more southern region of Texas, and they unanimously meant the land extending along the Gulf of Mexico from the Sabine River to the Rio Grande inland to a depth of about one hundred miles.[37] The dates on representative brochures indicate the time period of this specific drive by the railroads: 1896, 1902, 1903, 1906. Two key themes run through much of this particular enticement literature. The writers speak in glowing terms of the climate and they extol the potential for irrigated farming.

Warm skies, gentle breezes, moderate temperatures, and pleasant sun— these are the far superior qualities of nature's gift to the gulf coast of Texas. At least that is what the railroads were saying to potential immigrants. They addressed the "restless farmer of the north" who could come at any season and begin immediately to plant a crop. Imagine, says a pamphlet of the Southern Pacific Railroad, the "days of December, January, and February drift by, with perhaps an occasional frost to put a sauce upon the salad of such living, but no truant month slips past without seeing some crop confided to the ground or some harvest gathered to add to the abundant store that fills the land with plenty." To top off this description the writer admits to being a Yankee turned southerner, maybe in full testimony to the importance of fair weather on relocation. As a northerner turned Texan he could also make the argument for Texas sound plausible as he wrote, "The winters being winters in name only, the stock grower does not labor six months in the year to raise feed with which to 'carry his stock through' the other six." Pamphlets also stressed a variety of issues touching on the weather. "Here we have a country that requires no expensive buildings, where cold weather is almost unknown" and "No overcoats; very little fuel needed." Comparisons with the North were common. "When *you* are frozen up and *forced* to be idle, the Texas farmer is *plowing*. When you are *still* frozen up, *his* crops are *half grown*—when you are *starting* to plow, he is *harvesting* his *first* crop and getting the *high prices* that early products bring." Obviously in such comparisons, Texas won the contest handily.[38]

Good weather thus offered the first prerequisite for farming such fertile land in the southern and coastal regions. Abundant water was the next requirement. Artesian wells, ditching, and levees were terms included in these brochures of the later era. The availability of rivers, bayous, and lakes where water was also obtainable featured in some promotional literature. Railroad-sponsored booklets built around one crop also reinforced this acceptance of irrigation as a valid means to make the land bloom. The Southern Pacific published *Sugar Lands in Texas* and *Texas Rice Book*. Both handouts encouraged farmers to think in terms of crops that could be grown profitably in Texas soil, even though the techniques of growing them might be foreign to many northern or overseas immigrants.[39]

Both passenger trains and freight trains helped open up yet another part of the coast country to extensive farming—the far southern lands along the Rio Grande River. The tip of Texas received a great impetus for development when the St. Louis, Brownsville and Mexico Railroad (SLB&M RR) laid track southward from Corpus Christi through to Brownsville. Commonly called the Gulf Coast Line, this road provided inexpensive transportation not available earlier. This activity by the railroad between 1903 and 1904 pulled workers into the area and then helped encourage the irrigation of land and production of a widely diverse number of crops as fresh vegetables and fruit became more integral to the American diet.[40]

Another area of Texas that received special publicity efforts in the first decade of the twentieth century was, surprisingly, east Texas. This portion of Texas had grown tremendously during the early phases of the state's development. Railroads had laid track across the territory, moving typically north and south through the region. The booster publications of the early twentieth century assumed the existence of these various roadways as established means to markets elsewhere. Now they concentrated on suggesting new crops and new ways of thinking about the region's potential. The Cotton Belt Route issued a small leaflet (circa 1910) entitled *Profitable Products of East Texas*. The material explained, "That E in East Stands for Elbertas; That T in Texas for Tomatoes." Since many may never have thought of peaches and tomatoes as Texas crops, this railroad wanted to help farmers see the potential in growing fruits and vegetables. Their pamphlet reiterated the typical information about homeseeker excursions available on the first and third Tuesdays of each month saying, "After your season's work is over take a run down to East Texas." Sure that once immigrants saw the land, they would be won over to the move, the flier projected the future saying, "if he once gets a start in East Texas he is on a swift road to independence." Plugging into the old farmer's dreams of self-sufficiency, the railroads surely lured some farmers who heeded the message and moved to East Texas.[41]

East Texas was also prime locale in the brochure *Industrial Development, Central East Texas, The Fruit Belt of the State*. While the title suggests mechanical factories, the inside copy addresses mostly the agricultural production of the region. Twenty pages sketch the counties along the Houston East and West Texas Railroad and there is a definite "back to east Texas" flavor in the brochure. Referring to the recent Spindletop discoveries of 1901, the writer felt on solid ground when he wrote about tomatoes, fruit, and vegetables as "An East Texas Gold Mine" that was "Better than Gushers."[42]

In *East-South-East Texas,* the Texas and New Orleans Railroad (T&NO RR) touted the pine forests as a true asset. These forests had typically been viewed as detours to progress or obstacles to be overcome in tilling soil or planting crops. But this publication showed the money to be made in the lumber industry. Logging enterprises and existent sawmills were listed and described, in order to give the potential newcomer a clear idea of the possibilities. Truck farming and chicken raising also came in for their share of the suggestions offered.[43]

A major part of this "back to East Texas" movement was emphasis on the potential for success in truck farming. As with rice or sugar production in the coastal areas of Texas, truck farming was a type of agricultural work not familiar to most farmers. To those midwesterners, typically accustomed to growing grain crops, these must have seemed like new-fangled ways to make an agricultural living. Railroad publications attempted to ease some of this concern by publishing works directly aimed at explaining the truck farming industry. One such effort by the Southern Pacific was entitled *Ten Texas Topics by Texas Tillers and Toilers.* Its pages covered the ten subjects illustrated on the front cover: grapes, pecans, tobacco, alfalfa, beekeeping, fruits and vegetables, fish and oysters, hogs, rice, and angora goats. A later publication by the same railroad carried the title *Timely Tips to Texas Truckers.* Inside, twenty-one different articles by experts in their field extolled the possibilities of growing such things as English peas, celery, okra, spinach, watermelon, onions, garlic, asparagus, and peppers.[44]

While the geographic emphasis of railroad brochures may have shifted some over the course of the fifty years between the Civil War and World War I, the goal of peopling the state of Texas remained a constant. Within that constant, the messages inside these various brochures deserve attention as also showing a slight shift over the years. For example, irrigation and climate became prominent topics in the later nineteenth and early twentieth century. As the railroads pushed onto the semiarid lands of the panhandle, far west, or southwest Texas, dry farming techniques and irrigation procedures were included in the railroad's enticement literature for those areas. Picturing the climate as ideal in either location—far north Texas or extreme south Texas—typical railroad brochures noted the healthfulness of the climate and how different it was from the land of snow and ice in the northern states. When it spoke about the weather, enticement literature of the period from 1865 to 1876 reassured potential settlers concerning the notorious "Texas northers." The later material from 1890 forward rarely mentioned those cold winds of the Texas "northers." Rather they pointed to the vast contrast between winters in northern states and the more balmy seasons in Texas.

Experts were important to the pages of railroad enticement literature in this later era. As in earlier days, it was still assumed that some authoritative statement from a government official carried the most weight in the eyes of the potential immigrant. However, the background of such experts changed. The shift moved from messages by politicians and successful farmers to discussions of new agricultural technology from college professors and scientists. The state department of agriculture and the corresponding federal agencies issued material liberally quoted by the railroads, giving their presentations that aura of authority the companies desired.[45]

Often railroads created internal agricultural departments to supplement their land or immigration departments. Varying from railroad to railroad, the activities of such departments included establishing demonstration farms at various locations along the roadway and hiring agronomists to talk with and educate the farmers. Traveling cars on the tracks exhibiting various crops and techniques for planting provided education on wheels as yet an additional approach to reach farmers.[46]

Another shift in message was represented by railroad publicity directed at the healthseeker. One such brochure was entitled *West Texas beyond the Pecos, Her Health Giving Qualities.* This flier, issued by the Southern Pacific-Sunset Route, consisted mainly of reprinted articles by two medical doctors testifying to the benefits of camping, horseback riding, and the fresh air and water to be found in west Texas. Railroad brochures thus supplemented the message broadcast by city booster organizations and private resorts growing up around mineral springs or watering spots.[47]

Yet another potential target for the railroads was the tourist. While tourism could not provide major support for a railroad, it could contribute to the profitability of the road. Emphasis on the healthfulness of Texas and stories about the state's beautiful scenery probably served to entice some northerners to travel to Texas as a vacation spot. Frequently, pamphlets on San Antonio made reference to this possibility, by emphasizing the Alamo, past Texas history, the cosmopolitan population of the city, and the Hispanic element of architecture and culture. Other more specific brochures were aimed entirely at the tourist, such as the 1911 Sunset Route publications entitled *Louisiana and Texas for the Winter Tourist* and *Texas Tourist Points and Resorts, along the Sunset-Central Lines.*[48]

Galveston, early in the twentieth century, renewed its own interest in the potential for tourism. The erection of the Hotel Galvez overlooking the beach stimulated the Galveston economy and encouraged similar efforts at attracting visitors to this city as a resort destination. The *Galveston Daily News* gave the railroads credit for some of this development. Galveston saw this tourism as both good for the state and good for their city. The newspaper reported a visit to the island city from A. A. Allen, president of the MK&T RR. He promised support in advertising Galveston, saying the roadway could thus help encourage further growth of the gulf beach. This message must have been music to the ears of Galveston's boosters, and of course the railroad saw this also as a way to make money for themselves. The editor of the *News* was also sharp enough to see the potential of tourism. The "persons who come to rest and recreate will stay to invest and develop what they might never have appreciated if they had not been induced in the first instance to visit the state for pleasure." The interaction between railroad enticement literature, tourism, city boosters, and population growth reflected good business for all and ultimately resulted in an additional boon to the state's population increase.[49]

Railroad enticement literature during the last decade of the nineteenth century and the first two decades of the twentieth was significantly different from railroad publications in the 1870s. In the later era, the tendency to specialize on a particular geographic area became more common. The material inside the covers also changed. Photographs were introduced. Advertising brochures or pamphlets of whatever kind in the late nineteenth century almost always used visuals of some sort to help amplify their message. In the early years, closer to 1875, these visuals might be simple line sketches or more intricate woodcuts. The subject matter of these engravings and etchings most typically were pastoral scenes identifying luxurious tree growth, wide varieties of blossoms, and figures of people engaged at work or play in that energizing atmosphere. The fields demonstrated the productive Texas soil while the range scenes had contented livestock munching fresh grasses. Peace and serenity were the messages sent to the potential newcomer. Sometimes portraits of famous Texans were included with the perennial short history of the state included in many of those early pamphlets. Scenes showing ships or trains also sprinkled in a message of access to markets and ease of transportation. The railroads knew the value of illustrating their brochures. They enticed the potential migrant to Texas by joining the right words with a vivid visual image.[50]

As photographic equipment improved and the use of cameras became more commonplace, the railroads industriously appropriated this new technology to help spread their messages. The photographer most frequently went out to the field to document tall corn, hefty livestock, and busy farmers. The photos showed hogs, cattle, poultry, and horses—all in the prime of health. Crops such as alfalfa, corn, cotton, and wheat were shown row-upon-row as far as the eye could see. Close-ups of figs, oranges, tomatoes, and squash were meant to make the mouth water for fresh fruits and vegetables.[51]

Buildings were pictured in railroad literature as well. Some common portrayals included the state capitol building, the Alamo or other missions, the businesses on main street, and representative churches, schools, or residences. Of course when homes or businesses were photographed, the best each city had to offer were the only ones represented on the brochures' pages. The tendency to show a palatial home of the town's leading citizen and label it "representative residence" was not uncommon.

Some of these later railroad brochures included photographs depicting blacks as workers in the field or as sharing the spotlight with produce of the field. A few pictures of Japanese rice farmers and Mexican field workers can be found. Field pictures also show women as laborers. These groups—women, Mexicans, blacks—are not represented in the written descriptions or included in any significant way within the material of enticement. What is their purpose in the brochures? How were they viewed by prospective users of the railroad? Why were the marginalized people included visually, but not in words? These kinds of questions deserve greater research.[52]

One constant visual in almost every railroad brochure was some kind of map. These maps did not develop any special sophistication over the years, but typically located the rail route in question and identified stations and towns along the way. Sometimes connecting lines were included, especially as mergers prevailed and larger railroad "systems" evolved. Linkages with port transportation in Galveston or New Orleans might be demonstrated, but this was more unusual than common.

Railroads in Texas experienced almost a constant year-by-year increase in track mileage. While construction slowed at times when the nation's economy also slowed, it picked up quickly as the economy recovered from its downturn.

A correlation between increased railroad mileage and population growth in Texas appears clear. The statistics of track mileage and state population both show a steady and constant increase between 1865 and 1915. Representative years suggest this parallel growth:

Year	Track Mileage	People
1870	591	818,579
1880	3,244	1,591,749
1890	8,710	2,235,527
1900	9,867	3,048,710
1910	13,819	3,896,543[53]

To what degree the increase in one directly influenced the other is difficult to say. But it is clear that the railroads poured money and personnel into enticing people to Texas. The railroads perceived their task whether collectively or individually as requiring an aggressive publicity crusade. Central to the campaign was the publication of written materials that were meant to be produced and distributed widely. The rail lines were not diverted from that primary approach, for even when they tried such unique endeavors as immigrant homes or demonstration farms, these places in turn became also a distribution spot for that railroad's brochures, pamphlets, maps, leaflets, and fliers. Getting information to the potential immigrant kept railroad companies busy producing the kind of written material they felt would lure new people to Texas.

CHAPTER 9

❖

GALVESTON AND THE IMMIGRANTS

Enticed by words of encouragement from either official or unofficial sources, immigrants continued to flock to Texas in the mid- to late-nineteenth century. How did they arrive? Some came overland by train or wagon. Some came by ship.

Galveston had long been an immigrant port. People used the natural harbor on the west side of the island throughout the Anglo settlement of Texas. Sometimes the immigrant came by ship directly from Europe, but more typically the foreign-born arrived second hand, after first stopping at such places as New York, Boston, Baltimore, or New Orleans. Travel by water, the most economical means available, also enticed people living in the other states of the Union. Coastwise steamships proliferated and entered the market, carrying passengers as well as freight. These ships landed in several places along the Texas coast, but by far the majority used the Galveston harbor as their port of entry.[1]

As Galveston developed into the state's premier port, she publicized her value to shipping businesses far and wide. Lying heavily on the back of the cotton bale, traffic grew steadily through the port. As shipping lines vied to service the exporting of cotton, roadways in the water evolved into regular transportation lines to northern ports and European destinations. Galveston's focus on commerce and transportation linkages propelled her to seek bigger and better harbor facilities. The marketing associated with the wharves and ships supported movement of "things" in the form of products of the field, raw materials, and manufactured goods. The city's energies catered to the shipping and receiving of products. Human travel took a back seat to this freightage in terms of volume and in terms of the city's interest. Yet in the larger picture of Galveston's commercial aspirations for its port was the hope that it could develop its potential as an immigration destination—a hope that was fulfilled in the decade and a half before World War I.

The movement of people through Galveston contributed to the growth and advancement of Texas as a young state. The use of the preposition "through" is deliberate here, because Galveston did not view herself as a final destination for most homeseekers. It was not an industrial city with factories that needed large numbers of laborers. Galveston viewed herself as the funnel for goods and people. Since channeling people and products into and out of the state was her main objective, Galveston worked diligently to be a top-notch distribution point.

"Come to Texas!" the enticement literature from 1865 to 1915 repeated again and again. Pamphlets proclaimed, we have land that needs to be "tickled by the hoe." The sun shines on the hard work of the farmer, said many a booster brochure. How does Galveston fit into this larger picture of efforts to encourage immigration to the state? What specifically did Galveston contribute to this very concerted effort? Most significantly, she continued throughout this period to serve as a major access point for newcomers. She did not expend energy in the early years on developing specific facilities for disembarking passengers or promoting extensive procedures for moving people across the docks. There was an assumption that the flow of people was a natural, sporadic, and incidental aspect of the port's tremendous activity. Unlike the inland railroad system, which labored long and hard to entice newcomers to fill up the vast spaces of Texas's farm and ranch lands, Galveston and its port businesses did not produce hundreds of pamphlets, maps, and brochures extolling their services for immigrants.

Rather than focus primarily on producing written materials as was the case with railroads and land agents, Galveston businesses and citizens exploited her natural resource—the harbor—as their effort to bring in immigration. Continually they poured their individual and collective energies into that objective. To their way of thinking anything helpful to improving the harbor and port would be helpful to everything else they desired for the city.[2]

Thus, the story of encouraging immigration into and through Galveston parallels the development of efforts to obtain a deeper harbor for ocean-going vessels. As a deep channel became a reality in the mid-1890s and as migration from Europe to the United States reached peak years, Galveston turned to more focused efforts at improving the city's image as a point of entry for foreign-born immigrants. Those efforts included the building of a federal immigration station and the evolution of citizen-driven organizations to help the newly arrived immigrants during their stay in the city. Throughout the harbor changes, a steady stream of individual people arrived at the Galveston wharves and typically moved on to the hinterlands of the state. The movement of people continued throughout all the negotiations, arrangements, and political maneuverings that resulted in improvements aimed at making Galveston a first-class port.

Life in Galveston has always been dominated by its relationship to the ocean. The struggle for deep water in Galveston's harbor began early and continued throughout the later half of the nineteenth century. Reaching a channel depth over the bar of twenty-five feet in 1896 finally put Galveston well within the mainstream of ocean-going commerce. Improvements in Galveston's harbor and port depended primarily on the infusion of money from the federal government. There had been a few times when the city tried to raise funds on its own and implement dredging operations, but these had been stop-gap measures and unsuccessful in the long range. Understanding their limitations, the fledgling Galveston Chamber of Commerce submitted a memorial in 1870 to the United States Congress begging for help on the improvement of "the Channels, Bars and Harbors of Galveston Bay." Within the wording of the memorial lay a hint of the future direction of appeals to Washington. The memorial argued that Galveston harbor improvements would benefit all of Texas and indeed all of the trans-Mississippi West. Tucked in one small paragraph was the statement, "In addition to this vast servitude of Galveston Bay, we must add all that portion of the trade of the Rocky Mountain States, soon to teem with population, which is bound across our American desert toward the sea." The River and Harbors Act of July 11, 1870 provided $25,000 for Galveston's harbor. Subsequent appropriations followed over the years.[3]

This particular memorial to Congress and most succeeding efforts were city driven. It was not primarily the state of Texas that pursued deep water, but the local municipal contingent. Galveston and her business leaders provided the driving force for this endeavor. One student of the port's history stated, "In custom, in practice, and in law, the city became caretaker of the port. The port had given rise to the city, and together their fate hung." Publications of the time reflected this sense of Galveston shouldering the responsibility for the port's growth, in both commercial and immigrant trade.[4]

Galveston's fate as a viable commercial port also depended on the growth of railroads in the state and rail connections with the island. A detailed story of railroad/port interaction has been told in *Tracks to the Sea, Galveston and Western Railroad Development, 1866–1900*. It documents the vast energy citizens of Galveston invested in railroad development. Railways were a major business investment of the nineteenth century. Galveston investors heard from many would-be railroad men. One civil engineer, Caleb G. Forshey, presented his visions for a Galveston, Houston and Great Northern Railroad to Galveston's mayor and business leaders in an 1866 pamphlet. He dreamed of a great system of roads "that shall in time tie together with iron bands the in-

dustrial interests of our great trans-Mississippi territory" and, of course, benefit the port city. By 1870 this same Forshey was a member of the Galveston
Chamber of Commerce continually pushing the city's agenda to include railroad needs. In the early 1870s municipal leaders appointed a Citizens' Committee on Internal Improvements. Their chairperson, Colonel J. S. Thrasher,
headed a list of prominent Galvestonians that included W. L. Moody, N. B.
Yard, W. Jockush, and A. C. McKeen among others. They selected a civil engineer to conduct the needed harbor study. S. H. Gilman's research strongly
encouraged the Galvestonians to act on the issue of railroad development and
thus enhance the city's growth. He noted the interrelationship of port to railroad. Gilman's enthusiasm was reflected in one of his report's concluding
statements: "Galveston harbor can, must, and will be opened within three
years to admit steamers up to the wharves drawing twenty-five feet of water."
What he foresaw as happening in three years did not take place for more than
twenty years, but his written treatise did appear to inspire Galvestonians as
they continued efforts to improve their port.[5]

In the spring of 1882 the potential for linking rail and water routes took
concrete form when C. P. Huntington visited the city. He was in town checking on possibilities for his huge Southern Pacific railroad system and its Texas
and Mexico connections. Competition between New Orleans and Galveston

Port of Galveston. Before extensive dredging and the creation of deep water wharfs in
Galveston, "lighters" were used to move people and cargo between ship and shore. From
Edward King, *The Great South: A Record of Journeys* (Hartford, Conn.: American Pub-
lishing Co., 1879), courtesy Louisiana State University Press.

was part of the debate, and Huntington in sharp businesslike manner told the Galvestonians that they needed to get twenty-five feet of water over their bar and do it soon to insure excellent rail projections to the island.[6]

While railroads and railroad building remained a concern throughout the development of Galveston, the city primarily focused on its harbor. After the 1869–70 local efforts that eventually resulted in some federal appropriations, Galveston learned to turn to the national government for continuing support. The river and harbor bills down through the years have been the focus of growing lobbying efforts in the federal congress with the expectation of grand, log-rolling rewards. The 1870 bill included separate appropriations for eighty-nine different locations. The next year 112 locations received aid, and in 1872 the number was up to 146. As federal assistance for internal improvements expanded, Galveston's efforts to obtain a portion of that congressional pie intensified.[7]

Galveston received federal money throughout the 1870s and into the 1880s, but the 1883 river and harbors bill did not make it through Congress. At this critical point in time, the *Galveston Daily News* believing in the power of the written word published an exclusive edition supporting harbor interests. The special edition came out on December 1, 1884, and was packed with information from over eleven states and the various U.S. territories. Each western state and territory had amassed statistics and descriptions of its land that were meant to show its specific needs for a deep-water port. Despite newspaper boosterism and congressional debate, there followed a long financial dry spell from 1882 until August 5, 1886, when $300,000 was finally appropriated by the federal government for "continuing operations at outer bar" in Galveston harbor.[8]

This financial hiatus may have provided the major stimulus for the city to redouble its promotional efforts, but other factors also came into play. Commercial activity in the port was multiplying. Cotton and other crops increasingly found their way to the Texas coast for transport to European markets. A new board of army engineers arrived in Galveston in January 1886 and began to see harbor improvements with a fresh eye. Construction of jetties to help minimize shifting sand had always been part of the overall plan. But now stone in large quantities and at a reasonable cost became available from inland Texas for use on jetty construction. The developing lands west of the Mississippi, via railroad transportation east and west across the expanses to California, also entered into the picture at this time. As these new areas opened for settlement, farmers and growing towns found themselves very concerned about the lack of cheap and fair transportation alternatives. Frustrated with eastern and midwestern outlets, they began to look to the Gulf of Mexico and the Texas coastline.[9]

Visions of western settlement and harbor improvements led to a conference in Dallas that served as catalyst for ultimately obtaining deep water in Galveston Bay. The stated purpose for this December, 1887, assembly was "to consider means of effecting an influx of immigration and capital to Texas." An earlier discussion of this convention in chapter seven pointed to the written material produced by communities throughout the state to entice migration. Galveston, as a community, used the 1887 convention to fuel its work for the port.

In planning the event a committee of seven met on December 3, 1887, developed a set of resolutions, and then issued a call through the state's newspapers for an Immigration Convention of Texas to be held later in the month on the twentieth and twenty-first. Galveston citizens met at their cotton exchange on Friday, December 9, and held an animated discussion about the relevance of Galveston's participation in the convention. Seeing the "importance of immigration to Texas" as a "self-evident proposition," they appointed eight men as a committee to represent the city. The list included R. G. Lowe, W. L. Moody, John D. Rogers, M. Lasker, H. M. Trueheart, John Focke, E. T. Flint, and J. M. Skinner—all prominent businessmen on the island.[10]

As the date for the convention moved closer, the *Galveston Daily News* reported rumors from Dallas of potential conflict between the people of Texas and the railroad men. One interviewee discounted this supposed tension by saying that "cities can not grow nor the population and wealth increase very fast without immigrants and the railroad." The impetus for the immigration convention involved a strong element of railroad men, business interests, and land developers. They appeared to hold the belief that when their individual interests were met, all would benefit.[11]

This same *News* article in the December 13 issue addressed the problem of false stories that circulated abroad. Noting that some people held negative views of Texas due to inaccurate information, the paper pointed to the value of good information from appropriate official individuals. Reference was made to Governor Hubbard's address at the Philadelphia Centennial in 1876, wherein he dispelled negative criticism and conveyed a "correct impression" of the state. "Some of the biggest railroad officials of the state used it as immigration ammunition, and in a pamphlet form distributed the same all over the eastern and middle portion of the United States and in Europe," according to the *News*. Written documents were seen as an integral part of railroad endeavors to improve the profitability of their lines. The *Galveston Daily*

News had used its columns repeatedly over the years to spur Galveston and communities statewide to greater activity and involvement in luring immigration. The tradition continued as the newspaper reported glowingly on this special Dallas convention.[12]

The enthusiasm generated by the convention literally jumped off the pages of the *News* in its December 23 article. With a headline of "Immigration is Imminent. The Dallas Convention a Success," the paper had only praise for the convention's activities. Provision was made for a committee of thirty-one members to be known as the State Immigration Committee of Texas. Each senatorial district would have one member who would serve for a year. While the committee representative would receive no salary, his expenses were to be covered by his district. One major goal was to meet with "railroad authorities of the different systems . . . having connections into the State of Texas" and to arrange for the "best possible rates . . . for prospectors, excursionists and immigrants into and through Texas in every direction." Members created a mission statement saying, "It is the purpose of this organization to induce, by a truthful representation of the advantages and resources of Texas, the investment of capital in the State and the immigration to the State of all law-abiding people who may be seeking new homes."[13]

During convention proceedings a Mr. Browning submitted a series of resolutions relating to a seaport. This man was not part of the Galveston delegation. There is no indication anywhere in the official proceedings or in the newspaper account of the convention as to who this man was or what part of the state he represented. The record only comments that, "Mr. Browning said he had come from a country that needed immigrants." Part of his resolution stated that Texas was "without a seapoart [*sic*] of sufficient magnitude" and that "the agricultural and pastoral interests of the State have been retarded in a very large degree." It went on to state that "the cotton growers" and "grain growers" had been burdened by the lack of a first-class port. He criticized the federal government and the U.S. Army Corps of Engineers for wasteful and inefficient port efforts in the past. Then restating the purpose of the convention as one of bringing people of "honest labor and honest energy" to Texas, his resolution encouraged efforts to secure deep water for the state. The convention adopted the resolutions unanimously. In this fashion, interests for immigration and for a deep-water port on the Texas coast joined hands in a larger movement.[14]

The *Galveston Daily News* observed that many benefits came from the assembly. They listed "enthusiasm imparted to each delegate" as one benefit and the "acquaintance made between the sections of the state" as another.

The Galveston delegation returned home and made plans to form their local Galveston Immigration Committee.[15]

Dallas convention members empowered an executive committee to negotiate with the railroad people for improved transportation accommodations for immigrants. Believing that people would come to look for land and to settle if they had inexpensive rail rates into and through the state, the immigration committee fought for a cheap immigrant rate. The railroads as a group saw the request as too demanding, but agreed to set up immigration excursion cars beginning in January. These cars would allow prospective settlers to see the land and then go back home and make arrangements to come to Texas "in the fall, which is the season for immigration." This compromise seemed to meet the Texas need for "living witnesses" of the greatness of Texas for settlement. The railroad representatives also offered to distribute free of charge any written material or pamphlets that the immigration committees might produce, thus facilitating the distribution of information on the state's qualities.[16]

Galvestonians supported the efforts at negotiating with the railroads, but their main interest was rewarded more clearly in the work of the following year. On July 11, 1888, a deep-water convention met in Fort Worth. Convention delegates selected General R. A. Cameron of Denver, Colorado, as president, and in his speech Cameron declared that "we are here to create enthusiasm, to spread information, to develop inquiry and awaken the attention of the people . . . to inaugurate a trade between the north and south that will develop the country." The convention encouraged Denver to hold an interstate deep-water convention in August or September, with the aim of involving more people, more land, and more of the western territories in the effort to procure a deep-water port on the Gulf of Mexico. At the conclusion of the one-day conference in Ft. Worth, the Colorado delegates were invited to visit Galveston as guests of the city. The businessmen of the island community wanted to improve their image with western investors. Their efforts at good public relations paid off that August in Denver. The *Galveston Daily News* reported that Colorado "proposes to escape from eastern bondage via the Gulf of Mexico." Such anti–Atlantic Coast sentiment figured strongly in the August conference. Negative feelings were shared by many communities in the plains and trans-Mississippi west. The Galveston business community was to be represented by a twenty-five-member delegation at this first ever interstate deep-water convention.[17]

Hundreds of representatives from all over the West and Southwest met in Denver beginning on August 27, 1888. The official count said there were 644 regular delegates at the convention, of which 341 were from Texas. Lively conference debates covered a variety of topics relating to the deep-water issue itself. The Associated Press acknowledged the event and broadcast the story country-wide, noting Colorado Governor Alva Adams's words: "Against us will be arrayed the influence of the ports of the Atlantic and the many interests of the north and east." The newspaper accounts record a sense of empowerment on the part of the assembled group by virtue of their merely getting together en masse.[18]

Articles in the *Galveston Daily News* of September 5 and 9 were positively glowing over the implications of the deep-water convention for Galveston. The newspaper's analysis of the convention was so extensive and optimistic it is hard not to see this August, 1888, conference as crucial in Galveston's efforts to be the first-class port on the Gulf of Mexico and a strong contender as the entry port for immigration destined for much of the West. Frank Bowden Chilton received much of the coverage in the *News.* Serving as secretary of the Texas Immigration Association, Chilton was there "with four large chests of printed information about Texas." Noting the centrality of railway/port connections to would-be immigrants, he pointed to copies of a railroad folder that he said would be "placed in the waiting room of every railway station west of the Mississippi River, whereby home-seekers and capitalists may read and learn to love Texas." The reports of this Denver deep-water convention highlighted the potential for the integration of immigration efforts and deep-water concerns. For Galveston the convention meant that "a first-class deep water harbor on the Texas coast is no longer a visionary idea, but an assured event."[19]

The momentum generated in Denver and in the subsequent deep-water convention a year later in Topeka, Kansas, influenced congressional leaders and members to include Galveston in the 1890 River and Harbors Appropriation in a major way. Along with a specific appropriation, a provisional clause required that the work proceed continuously until completed. Thus they discarded the old driblet system of appropriations. A total sum of $6,200,000 was spent on the north and south jetties and in the dredging. As one historian noted, Galveston thus became "Denver's Deep-Water Port" and in the process western lands in Texas, Kansas, Colorado, and the other states of the trans-Mississippi west benefited from deep water. Galvestonians, with interrelated interests in human cargoes and commercial tonnage, had succeeded in a major accomplishment essential to the survival and growth of their city and their port. Their interest in immigration had helped fuel their efforts to get deep water, which in turn helped to stimulate immigration into and through the port.[20]

One interesting effort on the part of Galvestonians to influence immigration was the Northern Settler's Convention of 1905. As a full-blown public relations event it brought approximately six thousand visitors to the city over the course of four days in April, 1905. The Land and Immigration Department of the SP RR worked with city officials to coordinate what was intended to be a yearly meeting. Carloads of people arrived by train while the Business League and Chamber of Commerce set up an extensive welcoming effort and a public comfort bureau to facilitate lodgings and activities around the island. Most speeches praised the value of land in Texas and Louisiana and emphasized the fertility of the soil and the healthy climate. The forward-looking participants included one person who enthusiastically stated that "the tide of immigration is flowing surely and steadily to the South."[21]

Comprehensive coverage by Galveston's newspapers reflects editorial interest in this Northern Settler's Convention and fit perfectly with their booster efforts of years past. When one convention speaker said to the members of the vast audience, "You had just as well now arrange to come back, for Texas has got a cinch on you," the *News* was quick to record it. When he said that it doesn't matter what flag you fought under, "We quit fighting about forty years ago," the columns of the paper recorded that, too. The importance of the railroads, which had obviously brought almost every one of the visitors to Galveston in the first place, was touted long and hard in a very pro-railroad approach. Another delegate shared how he was quite unhappy with the railroads when he first arrived in Texas twenty-six years earlier, but that he now knew the importance of farmer and railroads working together. He also praised the media and was quoted as saying "The newspaper is the great window to let in the light. They tell of the resources of the country. The farmer takes the light shed by the newspaper, and the railroads make it possible to develop." All in all the Galveston newspaper had a field day, knowing that what they reported would be read throughout the state and beyond.[22]

In September, 1900, the island sustained the full fury of a gulf hurricane. It picked itself up, dried itself out, and rebuilt an economy and city still based heavily on commerce strongly dependent on the harbor as a natural resource. When the members of the Rivers and Harbors Committee of the U.S. House of Representatives visited the island city in June, 1901, they were favorably impressed with "the pluck of the Galveston people." They viewed damage to the jetties, but also saw the necessity for keeping the port open and fully accessible to ocean-going vessels. Appropriations developed through this committee continued into the twentieth century to help the Galveston channel and harbor keep deep water.[23]

Galveston did not see itself as primarily an immigrant port. Yet Galveston did endeavor to develop its immigrant trade as a part of the overall commercial picture. Once deep water was achieved, some of the city's attention shifted to specific efforts related to improving immigration facilities and immigration through the port. By the turn of the century Galveston had become a significant immigrant destination.

"Galveston has shipped her bar. That was Galveston's greatest accomplishment in 1896," stated the *Galveston Daily News* in its January 1, 1897, edition. Proud of their accomplishment in making their harbor a deep-water port, Galvestonians now expected increased commercial activity at their port, both in freight and human passengers. The North German Lloyd (NGL) Steamship line based in Bremen had always maintained connections with Galveston. She was the mainstay of direct immigration from Europe to Texas. So it was no surprise that the first immigrants to arrive in deep-water Galveston were aboard the *Halle,* an NGL ship that berthed on October 9, 1896. The newspaper recorded that a big crowd "largely composed of curiosity seekers" was on hand to meet her. A crew of government officers from Washington and New Orleans inspected the 116 passengers on board ship. The *News* labeled the passengers as "a superior looking set" that "looked like the ordinary German farm people, who know how to make a penny do the work of a nickel." Interpreters helped as passengers were asked questions about their destinations, future occupations, and family. Health inspectors checked each arrival, and then most immigrants headed off to the railroad cars that carried them farther inland. This pattern continued in the years to follow until the official immigration station opened in 1913.[24]

In 1896 the fee on the NGL line stood at $38.50 for steerage passage. Many of the future Texas farmers came over on prepaid tickets, attesting to the chain migration that was already in evidence in the United States. Other steamship companies soon noticed the increased availability of deep water at Galveston and responded. Negotiations with the Hamburg-American Packet Company were quite involved in the fall of 1898 when a representative of the line said, "The Company is anxious to do business at this port and will give their line a fair trial before they make any decision about the future. Of course the steerage passenger business will not maintain the line. It only helps to do so. Freights are what count."[25]

In the spring of 1907 the *Galveston Tribune* ran several articles announcing two Italian lines that "were coming to Galveston." Their ships would initially land at New York but in short time begin coming directly to Galveston. The evolution of Italian shipping and passenger lines was a direct result of the Italian Ambassador's visit to Galveston in April, 1905. Baron Mayor des Planches's visit was extensively covered by the *News* with headlines stating "Homes for Italy's Surplus" and "Visit Significant to Texas." The ambassador was on an extended "tour of inspection of the South" and had already stopped at Mobile and New Orleans as well as other South Atlantic states. Meeting transplanted Italians all along his journey, he repeatedly seemed impressed with the opportunities that southern agriculture already offered the Italian farmer. Comparisons with congested urban areas in the North were numerous, and the officials everywhere the ambassador traveled extolled the virtues of farm living.[26]

The stopover in Galveston afforded the city's leaders an opportunity to boast about Texas and their unique harbor. Mayor William T. Austin as well as C. R. Kitchell, president of the Chamber of Commerce, were among those pointing to "lands in abundance for industrious immigrants" and to Galveston as "of necessity one of the most important immigration ports for the South." One interesting anecdote points to the importance of the written word at communicating information about Texas. Garrett A. Dobbin, an agent of the Santa Fe Railroad, tried to give the ambassador a copy of *The News Almanac* and began explaining the county index, when the ambassador informed him that he had already obtained his own copy by sending in twenty-five cents "some time ago." Texas publishers were obviously successful at getting their information into the hands of people who would use it, even the diplomatic corps of foreign countries.[27]

German steamship lines were the first to offer passenger service into Galveston. But slowly other lines from other countries saw the Galveston potential. In addition to the Italian lines, Scandinavian countries with extensive shipping interests began to show an interest in Galveston and the Gulf of Mexico trade. In July, 1907, the Norway-Mexico Gulf Steamship Company announced its interest in passenger service between Christiania, Norway, and the Gulf Coast and its beginning freight service in October. The *News* predicted that in two years immigrants would arrive in Galveston "from practically every quarter of Europe, from Sunny Italy to Norway."[28]

European migrants to Texas sometimes arrived by a less than direct route. There was a substantial movement of immigrants via the coastwise trade aboard such carriers as the Mallory and the Morgan Lines among others. A hint of this coastwise business can be seen in a sixty-nine-page booklet entitled *The Port of Galveston, Texas, U.S.A., 1906–1907*. The booklet affirmed that it was "Issued as an advertisement of the magnificent Harbor facilities and Phenomenal growth of the Port's Export and Import trade." According to this source, coastwise steamships of the two major lines "have prospered" so that nearly every vessel entering the port or clearing the port has been loaded to the Plimsoll mark, while every available accommodation for passengers has been filled." This same document included an advertisement for the Mexican-American Steam Ship Company announcing regular service both freight and passenger, from Galveston to Mexico. Trade with neighbors in Central and South America was not typically viewed as trans-Atlantic trade. It was seen then as part of the coastwise shipping trade. This developing southward trade added to the optimism Galvestonians embraced when thinking about their port.[29]

Although the immigrant trade ranked a far second in importance to freight and consumer goods, the Galveston businessmen worked to develop the city's potential as an immigration port. Just as deep water over the bar was a major prerequisite for sustained port growth, a solid, separate immigration station was a must in developing Galveston as a landing spot for immigrants. Dialogue between Washington and Galveston continued over many years as arrangements were made for such a building, as well as a new federal quarantine station.

Primitive, if often nonexistent facilities, greeted earlier arrivals to this Texas port. Those coming in 1880 had to endure transshipment from ocean-going vessel to barges or lighters to reach the wharf proper. When forty or so immigrants arrived in 1880, they stayed overnight in "different boarding-houses" and then went by rail inland the following day to Schulenberg, San Antonio, Huntsville, and other Texas locations. The shift from ship to train was typical for most of these immigrants. When 532 steerage passengers arrived via the NGL *Hohenstaufen* on September 23, 1882, most left on a Santa Fe train, but many had to wait and so "bunked as best they could in the depot building" until morning departures. An 1885 landing of several hundred immigrants found many of them spending a night in a warehouse on the wharves before leaving Galveston.[30]

Once deep water was achieved in 1896 the number of immigrants increased, but the facilities did not improve. In May, 1906, over one thousand immigrants landed and were processed in a warehouse meant for storage of cargo. Edward Holman, U.S. immigration inspector in charge of the Galveston port, encouraged the Galvestonians to put together plans for building a station, then address those specific ideas to F. P. Sargent, Commissioner General of the National Bureau of Immigration. In February, 1906, Mayor H. A. Landes sent a telegram to Sargent. Signed also by the chair of the Deep Water Committee and presidents of the Chamber of Commerce, the Business League, the Cotton Exchange and Board of Trade, and the Maritime Association, this communication played the supplicant, asking for help. Sargent visited Galveston in June of that same year and was enthusiastically courted by Walter Gresham, chair of the reception committee, and Secretary Kitchell of the Chamber of Commerce among others. Commissioner Sargent used the newly built Honolulu immigration station as a major reference point with the Galvestonians and discussed hopes for cooperation between Galveston and Washington on the building.[31]

Sargent used his visit to observe the port and also to give some advice to the island's inhabitants and other Texans. He steadfastly encouraged Texas to provide a state commissioner of immigration with the intent of publicizing Texas in Europe and facilitating the easy flow of information.

> If the State of Texas, in my judgment, will take this matter up as a State, and establish a State immigration bureau, and spend a little money in advertising under the auspices of the State Bureau, the advantages that Texas offers to settlers, both at home and abroad, it would not be but a little time until we would have a substantial increase of immigration this way, and if the steamers are running direct from the ocean ports to Galveston the people in Europe will know that they can come to Galveston and arrive within a few hours' ride of where they are destined.

Sargent also pointed to the importance of letters written home by those who arrived in the United States.

> Another thing, and in connection with having an adequate immigration station here. If you have good facilities for receiving and treating these people, more will naturally follow. In writing home to their friends they will say: "We came to Galveston via the North German Lloyd. We recommend that you come that way." But if you have no facilities here you will get a black eye.

Sargent praised Galveston and Texas for its interest in commerce and shipping of merchandise, but then he admonished, "I want to see you take a little more interest in humanity."[32]

City leaders took Sargent's message to heart. However, knowing that the 1876 constitution proscribed state government involvement in developing immigration initiatives, Galvestonians launched their own sustained drive to get adequate facilities. Negotiations went back and forth between Galveston and Washington for several years. The issues were many. A major hitch developed when the powerful Galveston Wharf Company expressed reservations about giving up valuable shipping footage on the wharf to set up what seemed like a less remunerative immigration operation. This obstacle must have been overcome at least momentarily, for three months later detailed architectural plans were shipped to Washington stating that Galveston Wharf Company property between Thirty-third and Thirty-fourth Street would be the site of the station. A processing room large enough for 950 people, plus sleeping quarters for about three hundred immigrants, were included in the plans.[33]

Discussions continued for some time over the location of the immigration building—either on the wharves themselves or over on Pelican Spit, a small island in the harbor. The ultimate location on Pelican Spit was facilitated through federal government expenditure, deeding of the island from the state of Texas to the national government, and building of water mains by the Galveston municipal government to supply the island and thus the immigration station. Galvestonians followed the seesaw nature of these continuing negotiations through the pages of their newspapers.[34]

Sargent visited Galveston again on June 21, 1907, for a first-hand look at the potential use of Pelican Spit. Decisions needed to be made concerning the best use of federal appropriations, i.e., money already designated for the work. Representatives of numerous transportation interests were in town and the Galveston businessmen agreed verbally to the providing of light and water for the station on the Spit. In addition to business discussions, recreational activities were also on the agenda. Swimming in the afternoon and a fish fry in the evening provided the typical Galveston social ending for a day of business. Rabbi Henry Cohen was reported as attending the evening's entertainment. His interest in immigration through the Jewish Galveston Movement was growing and his work would be influential in the years ahead. The commissioner from Washington told a *News* reporter that the immigration figures listed two thousand foreigners as having arrived at the port in May, and he expressed a positive outlook for growth. Then Sargent left the island community with the statement, "Galveston now ranks fifth among the ports in the number of aliens landed annually, and stands at the head of all Gulf ports."[35]

The June visit by Sargent was followed up with a July visit by Walter Gresham to Washington, D.C. Gresham telegraphed back to the Galveston Chamber of Commerce a jubilant message that he was able to smooth over the differences and that Galveston would come out the winner. The national bureaucracy would provide for jetty repair and extension, a new dredge, continued construction of the seawall, and a new light for the lighthouse. The big news, of course, was that Commissioner Sargent accepted the location of the

Opened in 1913, the new Immigration and Lifesaving Station provided facilities to process the larger numbers of immigrants through the Galveston Port. Courtesy Rosenberg Library, Galveston.

immigration station on Pelican Spit. Galveston thought first-class immigrant port status was just around the corner.[36]

Unfortunately, things did not proceed that smoothly. Various details needed compromise. Building construction slowed and then halted, though later resumed. Appropriations did not come through on time. Even as late as March 28, 1912, Alfred Holt, an agent for the NGL, stated, "The present conditions of handling immigrants in Galveston are not all that could be desired. The aliens are landed on a bare freight wharf." Finally, the May 16, 1912 *Galveston Tribune* announced that the building was erected and ready for business except it had no furniture or fixtures—the appropriation having not been made by Washington.[37]

The immigration station finally opened in 1913. Little is known about the station from local sources. The buildings no longer exist. One 1929 newspaper source stated that the immigration station opened in 1913 and was abandoned in 1916. Why such a short life? Two reasons were suggested: first, the extensive damage to the station by the Gulf storm of 1915, and, second, the war raging in Europe had greatly restricted immigration to the United States. The location, building, and opening of a federal quarantine station parallels the development of work on the immigration station. They both ended up on Pelican Spit and opened about the same time.[38]

Throughout this era of station negotiations and construction, immigrants continued to arrive in Galveston. With or without any special facilities, each individual still had to undergo entry procedures into the country and the state. As this experience repeated itself again and again, the city re-envisioned itself as a major immigrant port. The pronouncements and judgments in the columns of the *Galveston Daily News* demonstrate the island's response to the immigration experience.

"Banner Immigrant Day" shouted a special box on the front page of the April 22, 1905, *News.* With pride and a sense of curiosity the paper went on to note that the 9,675 steerage passengers were the "largest number ever passed in quarantine in one day." Exhibiting a full-blown curiosity about these new arrivals, the article went on to record the reporter's impressions. "It was a study to stand near the gangway and watch these prospective American citizens. . . . While undoubtedly of the peasant class, they did not look like the scum of the earth, as immigrants have often been described . . . a healthy, strong-looking lot of men, women and children . . . the children jumped and capered around like lambs in a field of clover." The reporter's observations filled the columns of the paper. He pointed out that each person carried bundles of possessions and frequently heavy coats from a much colder climate. All newcomers had to be moved off the ship and onto waiting railroad cars, which "would whirl them further into the new and strange country to which they had come." This journalist continued his observations: "There were 330 people known as homeseekers, or, in other words, men looking for work. As the demand for labor was greater than the supply, the 330 were placed in an enclosure and the railroad agents and others looking for labor were passed in among them and began a lively bidding for the employment of the men." He went on to note that, "As fast as an agent secured a set of men they were ushered out and placed in charge of another man who secured railroad tickets for them and watched over them to see that some other agent did not get them away from his." Some were detained for a more thorough inspection. One couple began life in their new country together after a marriage aboard the ship.[39]

Subsequent arrivals and landings mirrored many of these experiences. Down the gangplank always came the cabin passengers first, then the steerage people with prearranged transportation, and lastly the "homeseekers" defined as "not ticketed through to any destination." Class differences existed in treatment both in disembarkation and in expectations. Potential brides landing from cabin passage were allowed to travel on inland and marry later. Those

coming out of steerage had to be met by a responsible party and married before leaving the ship.[40]

In a labeling that would startle us in the twenty-first century, headlines read
"Aliens were Landed" and "Thousands of Aliens Come Via Galveston to
American Homes." More with a sense of curiosity than fear, these newspaper
articles highlighted the growing self-image of the port city. By 1910 Galveston
viewed itself more and more as an immigrant disembarking station. The
Greater Galveston Publicity Committee issued a thirty-eight-page pamphlet
proclaiming the pluses of their city, bragging that 4,539 immigrants arrived
during 1909, and that construction of both an immigration and a quarantine
station were slated for 1910. Yet another Galveston booster organization
known as the Commercial Association urgently wrote to their Washington
representative, Congressman A. W. Gregg, suggesting that he use his "best influences" to help Galveston obtain the needed appropriations to finish the station construction "for the arrivals of immigrant aliens here are constantly increasing and the importance of Galveston as a port of immigrant entry is
constantly growing." A survey of the *Galveston City Directory* in the first fourteen years of the twentieth century reflects this growing, albeit small, sense of
self as an immigrant port. The list of steamship lines increased greatly, reflecting passenger service improvements. The *Directory* noted that the federal
immigration inspectors maintained offices and residences on the island. It also
provided statistics on numbers of immigrants arriving at the port.[41]

Proof positive of Galveston's existence as an immigrant port and its potential for expansion was its selection as the port of entry for an organized effort
to direct Jewish immigrants to the southwest and western lands of the United
States. The Galveston Movement evolved as a highly structured and organized program initiated by philanthropic Jews in New York. Using contacts on
the European mainland and in England as well as Rabbi Henry Cohen's expertise and interest in Galveston, about ten thousand Jews came through
Texas between 1907 and 1914. The intent of the program was to help Jews
move into the interior of the country rather than coming in such large numbers to remain in the ghettos of New York City. Instead these Jewish immigrants were to arrive at Galveston and then travel by train to a destination
where supportive Jewish people or communities would help with jobs and
settlement. Iowa, Missouri, Nebraska, Minnesota, and Texas received the majority of these immigrants.[42]

The Galveston Movement blossomed at a propitious time in this country's
history. As more immigrants entered the United States, the vast majority of
them chose to settle in urban areas of the northeast. This concentration of

A North German Lloyd vessel delivers immigrants from Europe to the Galveston wharfs, ca. 1900. Note the tags on the individuals, presumably for help at disembarkation. Courtesy Rosenberg Library, Galveston.

Rare photograph of immigrants arriving in Galveston in 1907. Enticed by the Jewish Immigrants Information Bureau as part of the Galveston Movement, most immigrants traveled inland, dispersing throughout Texas and the midwest. Courtesy Temple B'nai Israel, Rabbi Jimmy Ressler, Galveston.

people often resulted in congestion in the cities. Often these cities seemed unable to absorb such large numbers and were unable to provide all the services needed by these urban dwellers. One suggestion praised by many reformers was the diversion of some of these people to other parts of the United States. National leaders such as Terrence Powderly and Theodore Roosevelt had supported such discussions earlier. Talk of labor needs in the developing New South fueled these suggestions. Expansion into previously unclaimed territory in the western states also stimulated action on these proposals. Galveston's earlier successful drive for a deep-water port allowed her to meet these needs very conveniently.[43]

Into this atmosphere of northeastern frustration with huge numbers of immigrants and various philanthropic or religious groups willing to help change the flow of these people, the Galveston Movement fit snugly. The island city of Galveston seemed to relish its task as port of entry for these people. Just as the New York Jewish leaders viewed the movement as a funneling of their religious compatriots into the country's hinterlands, so also the Galvestonians saw themselves conveniently as that funnel. The papers' notice of the first arrival of these Jewish immigrants reflects this sense of serving as a conduit inland. Praising the work of the Jewish Immigration Information Bureau (J.I.I.B.), the reporter stated that through their efforts, "all the Jewish Immigrants arriving on the . . . steamship . . . yesterday morning are well on their way to the various destinations assigned them by the bureau, all having left the city on the afternoon and evening trains with the exception of about eight, who will be ticketed to their several destinations this morning."[44]

Utilizing the NGL lines already in place, the first eighty-six of these immigrants arrived July 1, 1907, on the *Cassel*. They were met by Rabbi Cohen and helpers of the J.I.I.B. Even Mayor Landes turned out to greet this first contingent of Jewish newcomers. Later immigrants arriving through the auspices of the J.I.I.B. received similar treatment. Special provisions were made for those arriving on high holy days, as local Jews worked to minimize the burdens of the new arrivals. The *Galveston Daily News* continued to chronicle the arrival of these ships over the years as the J.I.I.B. remained an active presence on the island. Rabbi Cohen had only high praise for the way the media vied "with one another in their enthusiasm" to cover the various arrivals and departures.[45]

The Galveston Movement officially ended in the fall of 1914. The local office closed and its paid workers moved off to other locations and employment. However, Jewish supporters on Galveston island continued in an informal way to help their co-religionists arriving on later ships. One sustaining effect of the Galveston Movement was the chain migration it helped set in motion. For once immigrants begin movement toward a location, there is a tendency for that stream to continue even if in small numbers.[46]

Yet another agency assisting immigrants was the Methodist Immigration Information Bureau, which maintained an office and corps of workers similar to the J.I.I.B. This bureau, also called the "Methodist Mission" or the "Galveston Immigrant's Home" opened its doors in July, 1908, with the Reverend F. Bruckmann originally in charge and living on the premises with his family. Serving as a mission arm of the Methodist Episcopal Church South, the building provided lodgings, food, and interpreters as needed. Its location at Twenty-first Street and the Strand provided twenty-four cots for women on the second floor. Since male immigrants outnumbered women about three to one, they were housed in a larger area on the third floor. Meals cost twenty-five cents and a night's lodging the same amount. Two years later these services were offered more cheaply, with twenty cents for food and fifteen cents for a night's stay. Most immigrants remained in the facilities and on the island for a very short time, often proceeding via train into the interior within twenty-four hours of landing.[47]

Goals for both Methodist and Jewish bureaus were similar. As an outgrowth of their respective religious beliefs, these bureaus labored to help people adjust to a new country. Overcoming language barriers and solving employment problems were typical tasks. Sometimes they provided basic food and shelter needs. In helping newcomers these organizations served a crucial need in an ever-growing immigrant port. The initial religious mission became a secular influence on Galveston as well. Galvestonians individually supported the work of the established bureaus. They also supported a mission to the sailors in town establishing a Seaman's Home on the Strand as well. Galvestonians had a right to be proud of these agencies and their work. Their newspapers also lauded the endeavors of Albion L. Barkman, a federal agent of the U.S. Department of Immigration with offices in Galveston who set up an "Information Bureau." Barkman's aim was to furnish information about employment for the arriving immigrants.[48]

In 1914 the outbreak of warfare in Europe constricted immigrant flows to all of the United States. Galveston, too, experienced that same reduction.[49] Although their immigration station was in place and able to function efficiently by this time, the immigrant stream became a mere trickle. Businessmen of Galveston spearheaded efforts to improve their port all through the last half of the nineteenth century. Their interest in developing an immi-grant port meshed with their efforts for deep water over the sandbar and easy access to the harbor and wharves by ocean-going vessels. While the interest in immigration was secondary, it nonetheless served in the mid-1880s as the catalyst to push for the final accomplishment of deep water, which meant in-creased commercial activity for Galveston in both freight and human cargo.

CHAPTER 10

TEXAS, THE IMMIGRANT STATE

In 1920 Texas boasted a total population of 4,663,228 people, a 19 percent increase over the 1910 figure. Such an increase simply continued the post–Civil War growth of Texas. Between 1860 and 1920 the population increased more than 671 percent.[1] But statistics tell only one part of the development of the state. They do not convey the energy expended by Texans in seeking to encourage people to come to Texas.

Why did people migrate to Texas between 1865 and 1915? What did they hear or see that caused them to consider relocating to Texas rather than somewhere else or anywhere? What enticements held out the strongest appeal? What kind of people came during those years? How were they received by those who had arrived earlier? Did they move in one long-distance jump, or did they move by increments, gradually deciding where to put down roots and settle? The migratory process contains so many factors that an analysis of the total picture can be overwhelming. But the tremendous increase in population in Texas from 1865 to 1915 justifies an attempt to come to some conclusions about these multiple questions.

This continuity in population growth presents Texas as an "immigrant state" in a way not usually perceived by the public. It is important to keep in mind that the term "immigrant" is being defined in the nineteenth-century way as anyone who moved to Texas, whatever his or her place of origin. Images of cotton, cowboys, and oil wells have overwhelmed the image of Texas as an "immigrant state." Yet the reality remains that from its antebellum beginnings until today, Texas has grown and developed by the infusion of many, differing peoples and through the lure of its natural resources.

An extensive history of Texas focusing on migration and immigration would incorporate events like the discoveries at Spindletop, the introduction of the automobile as a new and important means of transportation, the financial Panics of 1873 and the 1890s, and the Mexican Revolution of 1910. These events had tremendous influence on the state. Looking at only one variable—written words of enticement—presents only one thread in the fuller cloth, one influence in this tremendous movement of people, one of many aspects to the total tapestry. Yet it is a crucial piece of the whole story.

Words of enticement originated with people. Luring people to Texas with images created through words on paper was an active endeavor to create a change. It was people-driven. It was aimed at the individual. It was meant to move folks. To the Texans who continued to feverishly produce the written word, it worked. Or at least, it appeared to work. The constant influx of new-comers to the state, repeatedly and in ongoing fashion, suggested a building momentum. The perception that their words were moving people sustained the efforts. The strong belief that concrete, specific information in the hands of potential migrants would sway their minds and result in their moving to Texas underlay this multiplicity of voices.

This belief, reinforced by swelling population, carried the energy. There is no way to quantify cause and effect. There is no way to prove that so many words translated into so many people. But the perception that words would move people kept the enticement efforts coming. Texans, both native and adopted, worked to encourage other people to join them living in the Lone Star State. Committed Texans did this with a vigor, a persistence, and a cre-ativity not always found in other states or United States territories. Many Texans participated in this activity in response to the state's constitutional prohibition, others out of a desire to have relatives and friendly people as neighbors, still others hoped through immigration to bring increased pros-perity to the state. Whatever their motivation, people wrote letters, pam-phlets, books, newspapers, and made personal connections in an effort to broadcast their message of enticement. Texans, as a whole, put out the wel-come mat once they built their own homes and settled in.

When the Civil War ended in 1865, Texas began a new era. Using the land as a lure, Texans publicized their state as the place of renewal—the place of new beginnings. In the first five years after Appomattox, Texas reasserted its antebellum message of "Come to Texas."

Whether directly because of the written efforts of enticement or not, the population of Texas grew. Texans were encouraged by the arrival of newcom-ers and as a result continued their cordial-welcome-image. Their Bureau of Immigration was but one part of that image projection and that bureau be-lieved in using enticement rhetoric to produce their brochure *Texas: The Home for the Emigrant, From Everywhere.* While records demonstrate this ac-tivity, there is no measurable way of knowing exactly how much influence the bureau actually had on migration to Texas. Its existence and its work, though, indicate an interest on the part of many Texans at encouraging an influx of newcomers.

Government activity was but one part of the overall endeavor to bring new people to the state. Many private companies, agencies, and organizations constituted an informal network of efforts to write and publish literature intended to attract immigrants. Again, the key point is that people felt they could channel the movement of other people to their state. They had faith in the power of their words to move people. Personal letters also had an immeasurable impact on potential settlers to the state. The links they provided among those far apart from one another often made the move more palatable and also commonly served to encourage the chain migration that contributed significantly to the state's growth. Crucial to understanding the influence of a letter is the realization that most letters typically received more than a "once-over" glance by the reader. As one newly arrived Texan in 1866 wrote to Mississippi relatives, "I have read Tommie's letter over twenty times."[2] Often a letter on the receiving end was shared, in whole or in part, with other family members or friends and was no doubt discussed for days on end. As each person heard or read the words, the influence of the written message multiplied. Both negative and positive responses or impressions could thus develop and in turn cause these readers to rethink their own decision to remain where they were or to relocate.

People of the time were aware of the influence their words had on others. The *Houston Telegraph* told its readers in 1869, "Let us be alive to our own interest and soon will there be a flood of immigration pouring down upon us to obtain the advantages, which our State and her railroads will offer." Emphasizing the importance of individual action, the article continued, "The Legislature has much to do to foster this matter, but we should not expect it to do the half that may be done. Every citizen can give substantial help with little trouble or expense. Two cents to send a paper or three cents for a letter may bring a dozen good citizens." In booster fashion the writer moved into bolder rhetoric saying, "Let every man and woman in Texas feel that it is a part of his or her duty to induce others to come here. . . . Let us work and do it actively, and within a year we will see very astonishing returns."[3]

Throughout Texas's history, she has competed with other states and territories for newcomers. In the late-nineteenth and early-twentieth century some Texans spread beguiling paragraphs—words intended for any potential reader with the slightest spark of interest in relocating. The descriptions and explanations of Texas were meant to entice people into making a change in their lives, into leaving whatever place they called home to set up a new home in Texas. During the debates at the 1875 constitutional convention, one delegate felt that to "advertise Texas,"[4] as he put it, was a waste of time and money. To his way of thinking Texas could do that just by its existence and as word spread of its fame and territory. But in fact Texans in the field and in the cities did not agree with him. Their outpouring of written "advertisements" continued and at times even increased throughout the late nineteenth and early twentieth century.

When the 1876 state constitution became the law of the land, the constitutional prohibition officially pulled the state government out of the "immigration business." But this was not a dead-end event. The impulse to prepare written material continued. In fact the prohibition in Section 56 served as a springboard to inspire public citizens to do their own work at enticing newcomers to the state. Stepping into the perceived vacuum created by the constitutional provision, various groups and individuals began to produce their own written words of enticement. Indeed the strength of their belief in the power of the words is represented concretely by surreptitiously circumventing restraining provisions of the basic law. How did they do this? People within state agencies such as the Department of Insurance, Statistics, and History and the later Department of Agriculture, Insurance, Statistics, and History produced volumes of information gleaned from statewide surveys. Under the cover of preparing this information for intrastate use, these agencies published works that then were used to "get out the message" of what Texas had to offer the potential emigrant or homeseeker.

Concern for good transportation also helped to propel energies directed ultimately at facilitating the movement of people. The continued construction of railroad mileage stimulated greater ease of travel statewide. In 1865 the state had 395 miles of track. Ten years later that total reached 1,685, and by 1895 it had climbed to 9,291.[5] This transportation web across the state attracted the attention of newcomers, in essence grabbing them and channeling them into and throughout the state. Key to this expansion of transportation access was the assumed need to print, publish, and distribute the written word to augment the construction of the rails. Throughout this entire time, railroad publicity departments issued forth a steady stream of written materials. Similar efforts by those interested in improving transportation into Galveston, the state's premier port, became evident in the city's own outpouring of written information. As a commercial trade center of long standing, Galvestonians had always known the value of "advertising" and they applied this to their port improvements and to their efforts to create a strong immigrant destination.

Throughout the period between the Civil War and World War I, Texans believed in the production of mass amounts of written material to entice new-comers to the state. The increase in population and the perception, justified or not, that the words influenced the movement kept the stream of words coming. However, as the twentieth century advanced, Texans were frustrated with the limits imposed on their collective efforts.

SIGNIFICANT POSTSCRIPT

On December 20, 1956, the public relations firm of Syers, Pickle, and Winn, Incorporated, presented the findings from its nine-month study to the orga-nizational committee of the newly established Texas Tourist Foundation (T.T.F.). The complete report, which reads like a short history of the or-ganization of the T.T.F., conveyed its belief that Texas needed some kind of private agency with the aim of drawing tourists and "new Texans by adoption" to the state. It also included survey results obtained by canvassing private state organizations, as well as research into the work of other states in pro-moting themselves for potential tourism.[6] What were some of the findings and conclusions?

Most conspicuous in the report were the characterizations of Section 56

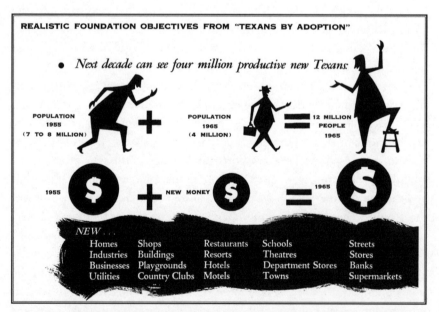

The Austin-based public relations firm of Syers, Pickle, and Winn created an eighty-two-page report (precise year unknown) for the Texas Tourist Foundation that proposed a plan for attracting tourists and newcomers. This image was part of the report. Courtesy Texas State Library and Archives Commission.

of the state's constitution: "antiquated clause," "eighty-year-old stumbling block," "silly, horse-and-buggy law," "ridiculous, hampering and long outmoded clause," "archaic, 80-year-old Constitutional prohibition." From the very beginnings of the T.T.F. and the subsequent survey it commissioned, the 1876 prohibition against "selling Texas" served as a strong focal point of reference.[7]

Fascinating statistics concerning promotional budgets for other states and United States territories were also presented. According to Syers, Pickle, and Winn, the state of Florida overwhelmingly took the lead with a recent yearly expenditure of $1,000,000 in state funds. Hawaii came in second with an advertising budget of $649,000. North Carolina spent $293,484, Tennessee $162,000, and Alabama $110,000. Texas with its state constitutional prohibition could not even be included on the list. These representative figures helped lead the study organizers to draw the conclusion that, "All of the 47 other States now have statewide development programs . . . Texas alone has NONE."[8]

According to the Syers, Pickle, and Winn written report, a group of interested people met in Austin on March 22, 1956. This gathering was an outgrowth of an earlier February meeting held by the Petroleum Marketers Association. The petroleum industry had a vested interest in procuring a wider market for their products by encouraging tourism. The oilmen originally intended to form a Tourist Information Service, but after much discussion and subsequent gatherings they arranged a July 12, 1956, meeting in which the Texas Tourist Foundation became a more broadly based organization. The list of participants at that July meeting reveals much about the support for such an endeavor. Over one hundred persons were present. The assembly included representatives from Humble Oil & Refining Company, Texas Motor Bus Association, Magnolia Petroleum Company, the *Houston Post,* the Texas Historical Foundation, the Associated Texas Service Stations, the Lower Rio Grande Valley Chamber of Commerce, and the Texas Good Roads Association. Not surprisingly, the Southern Pacific Railroad and the Burlington Railway had delegates at the meeting, thus reflecting a continued interest on the part of the railroads in helping develop the state's economic growth. But somewhat surprising was the presence of the Director of Information of the Texas Highway Department and the Director of the Texas State Parks Board. One wonders if they attended as interested observers or as formal representatives of their state agencies? The person holding the reins of this not-for-profit organization was F. W. Burton, who was also serving as the current president of the Petroleum Marketers Association. The listing of meeting participants and later nominations for the advisory board reinforces the statement by Syers, Pickle, and Winn that the T.T.F.'s "support and leadership is drawn equally from all groups concerned with bringing more people to Texas, temporarily or permanently."[9]

The final report by this Austin-based public relations firm illuminates the evolution of a program from an original effort to provide information about Texas through private businesses to a public foundation tackling a major constitutional prohibition. By December, 1956, the T.T.F. viewed 1957 as the beginning of a three-year campaign in which its "Number One Project" was to change Texas laws. As it projected the near future, the organization would expend its energies at pushing for an amendment to the state constitution in 1958. Then it would lobby in 1959 for enabling legislation to authorize the expenditure of state money to attract people to Texas. In 1960, T.T.F. expected the government to establish a "State Development Commission" to carry out the goal of continually advertising Texas.[10]

The fight to allow the state government to invest in tourism and immigration ultimately succeeded. On November 4, 1958, Texas voters accepted the argument of the T.T.F. and changed the 1876 constitution. The new provision read:

> Sec. 56. The Legislature of the State of Texas shall have the power to appropriate money and establish the procedure necessary to expend such money for the purpose of developing information about the historical, natural, agricultural, industrial, educational, marketing, recreational and living resources of Texas, and for the purpose of informing persons and corporations of other states through advertising in periodicals having national circulation, and the dissemination of factual information about the advantages and economic resources offered by the State of Texas.[11]

While the adoption of a new amendment represents a break with the past it also demonstrates a continuity of interest. Two examples illustrate this point. A change in the wording of the amendment took place between the 1955 version and the one finally adopted in 1958. The addition of the word "historical" indicates an awareness on the part of lawmakers of the chances for exploiting the state's historical past as a way to lure more people to visit Texas. Enticement literature of the late-nineteenth and early-twentieth century overwhelmingly included references to Texas history as part of their message. This later twentieth-century effort thus clearly follows in the footsteps of earlier enticement literature.

Another parallel to those earlier efforts is reflected in the two-fold goal of tourism's literature in the late twentieth century. First, the rhetoric was meant to bring visitors to the state. This means money spent on travel, lodgings, food, and entertainment. Money spent in this way enriched the state's economic growth. Second, the hope existed in a vision of "once a visitor, later a resident." The earlier attempts by railroad brochures to suggest a visit to the state by a farmer to see for himself or herself the potential in Texas are thus matched by the later efforts to get people to see Texas for themselves and thus plant the seed in their minds that this might be the place to which they want to move permanently.

With this constitutional amendment, Texas moved into a new era. She dramatically increased her promotional power to draw more people to Texas. Private companies, businesses, city and county chambers of commerce, and booster organizations continued to convey their individualized information. But now once again the state government could move aggressively into a campaign of words saying to people far and wide, "Come to Texas."

NOTES

CHAPTER 1

1. James M. Smallwood, *Time of Hope, Time of Despair: Black Texans during Reconstruction,* 32–33.

2. Slave narratives compiled in Texas suggest the freed persons desire to express their independence by moving. See Ronnie C. Tyler and Lawrence R. Murphy, eds., *The Slave Narratives of Texas,* 113, 115, 118. Pages 113–27 of these slave narratives offer a fuller picture of those immediate months following emancipation.

Scholars of the southern black migration reinforce the message of the freed slaves. See Carter G. Woodson, *A Century of Negro Migration;* Daniel M. Johnson and Rex R. Campbell, *Black Migration in America;* William Cohen, *At Freedom's Edge: Black Mobility and the Southern White Quest for Racial Control, 1861–1915.*

3. White people's fears of losing their property increased the anxiety among Texans. One Texas resident landowner wrote to a friend who was also a northern congressman saying, "let me know about confiscation. The idea is being spread among the negroes that the lands of the whites will be taken and given to them." See "The Bryan-Hayes Correspondence," *Southwestern Historical Quarterly* 25 (April 1922): 292.

4. Vera Lee Dugas, "Social and Economic History of Texas," 102; Merline Pitre, *Through Many Dangers, Toils and Snares,* 199.

5. William H. Harris, *The Harder We Run: Black Workers since the Civil War,* 7; E. Merton Coulter, *The South during Reconstruction, 1865–1877,* 92–101.

6. F. W. Loring and C. F. Atkinson, *Cotton Culture and the South, Considered with Reference to Emigration,* 4–5.

7. Loring and Atkinson, *Cotton Culture,* 68, 69, 70.

8. First quotation is from the *Texas Almanac* for 1868, 109–10; second quotation is from the 1867 almanac as quoted in William R. Johnson, "A Short History of the Sugar Industry in Texas," *Texas Gulf Coast Historical Association Publications* 5 (April 1961): 40.

9. Affleck to his Uncle Hannay in Scotland, November 14, 1865, 223; Affleck to a businessman in Liverpool, November 22, 1865, 239; Affleck to C. S. Longcope, a merchant in Houston, August 30, 1865, 215. All Affleck letters are from Fred C. Cole, "The Texas Career of Thomas Affleck." Starr's letter to W. S. Fisk, dated September 7, 1866, is quoted by Larry Earl Adams, "Economic Development in Texas during Reconstruction, 1865–1875," 138–39.

10. General William H. Hamman to sister Caroline in Virginia, November 18, 1865, in Hamman Collection, Fondren Library, Rice University. Martha Ann Otey at Washington-on-the-Brazos to her mother, M. F. Nolley in Mississippi, July 15, 1866, Sam Houston State University, Huntsville, Tex.

11. First quotation is from the *Tyler Reporter* as quoted in *Dallas Herald,* January 18,

1870, by Winston Lee Kinsey in "The Immigrant in Texas Agriculture during Reconstruction," *Agricultural History* 53 (January 1979): 136. Subsequent quotation from *Daily Austin Republican* of June 14, 1866, as quoted by Larry E. Scott in *The Swedish Texans*, 113.

12. *Galveston Daily News,* August 13, 1865, 1, hereinafter cited as *GDN; Texas Almanac* for 1867, 272–73. A detailed account of Affleck's involvement with this company can be found in Cole, "Texas Career of Thomas Affleck," 311–13, 322–46. Another prominent Texan, Ashbel Smith, physician, was on the board as well.

13. *GDN,* August 18, 1865, Supplement.

14. *GDN,* May 19, 1866, 2; August 30, 1867, 2; August 5, 1868, 3; August 6, 1868, 2; August 7, 1868, 2; December 2, 1868, 1, 2; October 29, 1869, 3; March 4, 1874, 2.

15. *GDN,* May 19, 1866, 2; *Flake's Bulletin,* March 30, 1866, 4. Flake's support of immigration efforts continued in later issues. See February 13, 1867, *Flake's Bulletin,* for his praise of Bishop Dubois's efforts to direct Polish immigration to Texas.

16. Dugas, "Social and Economic History of Texas," 351–52. One historian calls the *Texas Almanac* for 1867, "a revealing documentation of planter prejudices." See James A. Baggett, "The Rise and Fall of the Texas Radicals, 1867–1883," 61. For Washington County information and quote, see pp. 171–72.

17. *GDN,* July 31, 1867, 2; Kinsey, "Immigrant in Texas Agriculture," 134–35; *GDN,* November 18, 1865, 1.

18. Undated obituary by E. J. Hooper of Cincinnati, Ohio, in Thomas Affleck Papers at Rosenberg Library, Galveston, Texas; Robert W. Williams, "Thomas Affleck: Missionary to the Planter, the Farmer, and the Gardener," *Agricultural History* 31 (1957): 40–48.

19. *GDN,* August 9, 1865, 1; May 19, 1866, 1; August 10, 1865, 1; see also *GDN,* March 25, 1866, 4.

20. *GDN,* August 10, 1865, 1; "Texas and Her Resources," Thomas Affleck, pamphlet in the Affleck Papers, Rosenberg Library, Galveston, Texas, see pp. 2 and 9 for respective quotes.

21. *GDN,* March 25, 1866, 4.

22. *GDN,* May 19, 1866, 1; "Immigration and Labor," Thomas Affleck, pamphlet in the Affleck Papers, Rosenberg Library, Galveston, Texas; printed letter and contracts dated August 1, 1866, from Glenblythe, near Brenham in the Affleck Papers.

23. Ultimately Affleck was unable to consummate a sustained plan that actually brought large numbers of immigrants to Texas. However, it is difficult to discount the potential impact his written material and personal visits to Europe had on influencing individuals to eventually immigrate to Texas. See Kinsey, "Immigrant in Texas Agriculture," 128.

24. An excellent historiographical overview of reconstruction in Texas is available in Walter L. Buenger and Robert A. Calvert, eds., *Texas through Time: Evolving Interpretations,* chap. 8, "Statehood, Civil War, and Reconstruction, 1846–76," by Randolph B. Campbell.

25. H. P. N. Gammel, comp. *The Laws of Texas, 1822–1897,* 5: 900. Thomas Affleck lobbied in August of 1866 before the eleventh legislature for the passage of a bill naming him to the position of Commissioner of Statistics, for the Promotion of Immigration. He hoped to mesh his personal interest in immigration with a governmental title and thus receive authority to prosecute such an endeavor. While the bill passed the Texas House, it

failed passage in the Senate, thus ending Affleck's dreams of formally representing the state in Europe. See Cole, "Texas Career of Thomas Affleck," 347–59.

26. Gammel, *Laws,* 5: 1375–77, 1459.

27. Gammel, *Laws,* 7: 420.

28. *Journal of the Reconstruction Convention,* which met at Austin, Texas, June 1, A.D., 1868, 1: 15; Betty Jeffries Sandlin, "The Texas Reconstruction Constitutional Convention of 1868–1869," 186; Seth Shepard McKay, *Seven Decades of the Texas Constitution of 1876,* 18.

29. *Journal . . . Reconstruction Convention,* 1: 17.

30. *Journal . . . Reconstruction Convention,* 1: 25, 106, 419, 533–35; Sandlin, "Reconstruction Convention," 249–61. Biographical information for all convention delegates is available in an appendix to Sandlin's work. Most Immigration Committee member information is drawn from that material. For additional information on black legislators see J. Mason Brewer, *Negro Legislators of Texas.* Pitre, in *Through Many Dangers, Toils and Snares* identifies Curtis as a carpenter, aged sixty years. See p. 10 of her work.

31. *Journal . . . Reconstruction Convention,* 1: 164 for quotation. See pp. 162–69 for the complete recommendation and report.

32. *Journal . . . Reconstruction Convention,* 1: 163, 166; Gammel, *Laws,* 7: 420.

33. *Journal . . . Reconstruction Convention,* 1: 163, 167–68.

34. *Journal . . . Reconstruction Convention,* 1: 168.

35. The newspaper quotation is recorded by James Marten in *Texas Divided: Loyalty and Dissent in the Lone Star State,* 138.

36. *GDN,* August 2, 1868, 2; August 4, 1868, 2.

37. Marten, *Texas Divided,* 137; U.S. Congress, House of Representatives. Misc. Doc. #127. 40th Cong., 2nd Sess., "Communication from Governor Pease of Texas, Relative to the Troubles in that State," May 11, 1868; See Sandlin, "Reconstruction Convention," chap. 4, "The Convention's Action on Lawlessness" for a good overview of the subject and pp. 74–77 for reference to the special committee's report.

38. Ernest William Winkler, ed., *Platforms of Political Parties in Texas,* III, 112–15.

39. Baggett, "The Rise and Fall of the Texas Radicals," 197, 217; Winkler, *Platforms,* 122–23; *Proceedings of the Democratic State Convention,* held in the Representative Hall in Austin, on January 23, 24, 25, 26, 1871, 8.

40. The best account of the division issue for Texas on this time period can be found in Ernest Wallace, *The Howling of the Coyotes: Reconstruction Efforts to Divide Texas.*

41. Sandlin, "Reconstruction Convention," 215–37.

42. Donald B. Dodd and Wynelle S. Dodd, *Historical Statistics of the South, 1790–1970,* 54. It is interesting to note that the relative ratio of blacks to whites remained fairly constant during the decade's growth. In 1860 whites constituted 69.66 percent of the total population, and in 1870 that figure stood at 68.99 percent.

CHAPTER 2

1. *General Laws of the Twelfth Legislature of the State of Texas,* 1st Sess., 1871, 127–28; *Constitution of the State of Texas,* adopted by the Constitutional Convention, 33. Copies of these documents also available in Gammel, *Laws,* 6: 1029 and 7: 420. Rowland T. Berthoff in his study of immigration in the South mistakenly states that Texas organized in 1871 a bureau with agents, "though the state constitution forbade appropriations of

funds for the purpose." In actuality state money supported the bureau until the 1876 constitution prohibited such expenditures. See Berthoff, "Southern Attitudes toward Immigration," 338.

2. Texas *Laws.* 12th Legislature, 1st Sess., 1871, 127–28.

3. Ibid.

4. *Vernon's Annotated Constitution of the State of Texas,* vol. 3, p. 460 has an account of Davis's message. The 1876 Constitution is found in its entirety in Gammel, *Laws,* vol. 8. See pp. 779–834 for the entire 1876 constitution and p. 834 for this specific provision.

5. *Constitution of the State of Texas,* (1869), 33; Loeffler's activity is documented by Baggett, "The Rise and Fall of the Texas Radicals," 167; *House Journal of the Twelfth Legislature, State of Texas, First Session,* p. 23 contains record of Governor Davis's address.

6. See Loeffler entry in Ellis A. Davis and Edwin H. Grobe, eds., *The New Encyclopedia of Texas,* 1666; *Houston City Directory,* 1866, 33, 84; *Houston City Directory,* 1873, 20; Loeffler's first name is listed differently in various places: Gustav, Gustave, or Gustaf.

7. Texas Bureau of Immigration, *Report,* (1870), 3, 5. Reports were printed by various publishing houses in Austin. All further references to these reports will be by year report covers and under TBI.

8. According to Dugas in "A Social and Economic History of Texas," written information about immigration frequently identified December and January as the best months for migration to Texas. See pp. 50–54. Statistics can be found in TBI, *Report,* (1870), 4.

9. TBI, *Report,* (1872), see especially pp. 3–4.

10. Ibid., 5, 7–8.

11. Ibid., 7.

12. Ibid., 10–27.

13. Ibid., 23, 24.

14. Hertzberg's communication can be found in TBI, *Report,* (1872), 16–19, while Parson's information is on pp. 25–27.

15. TBI, *Report,* (1873), 9; *C. J. H. Frensz's Tariff Investigator of the United States, Enumerating Steamboat, Sail Vessels, Express, Steamships, Immigration, Canal, Railroad, Telegraph,* 1, 33.

16. *Frensz's Tariff Investigator,* 33. The only copy of such a certificate that this author has been able to locate exists in the 1872 Bureau of Immigration Report where Loeffler includes what he labels a facsimile of such a certificate.

17. *Frensz's Tariff Investigator,* 33.

18. Ibid.

19. *Frensz's Tariff Investigator,* 33; Texas *Laws.* 12th Legislature, 1st Sess., 1871, 127–28.

20. *GDN,* August 25, 1871.

21. *Notes on Texas and the Texas and Pacific Railway.* Schedule of rates is on pp. 39–40.

22. *Notes on Texas,* 44–48.

23. Texas Bureau of Immigration, *Texas: The Home for the Emigrant, From Everywhere.*

24. Gammel, *Laws,* 6: 1463–64; Texas *Laws.* 12th Legislature, 1st Sess., 1871, 325–26; Gammel, *Laws,* 6: 1574–75; Gammel, *Laws,* 7: 152–53; Texas *Laws.* 12th Legislature, 1st Sess., 1871, 42; Gammel, *Laws,* 7: 211–12, 1047–49, 1124–26, 1508; Texas *Laws.* 12th Legislature, Called Session, 1870, 127.

25. Walter Keene Ferguson, *Geology and Politics in Frontier Texas, 1845–1909.* The

economic point and analysis is aptly made by Lee Van Zant in *Early Economic Policies of the Government of Texas,* Monograph No. 14 in Southwestern Studies Series, vol. 4, 1966. See entire article, pp. 1 through 48. The inclusion of the Homestead legislation in multiple documents published to attract immigrants to Texas, testifies to the perceived significance of this legislative provision on influencing people to make Texas their home. Repeatedly these laws, copied verbatim from the legal codes, were inserted somewhere in the text of pamphlets or booklets extolling the advantages of settling in Texas.

To what extent these laws were utilized by women is the subject of an intriguing study by Florence C. Gould and Patricia N. Pando. In *Claiming Their Land, Women Homesteaders in Texas,* the authors compiled from Texas Land Office documents lists providing the number of women and their claims between 1845 and 1898. If nothing else, the study shows that women did arrive as immigrants to Texas and participated in the process of claiming and settling the land. This helps rectify the "invisibility" of women as immigrants to the state.

26. William S. Speer, ed., *The Encyclopedia of the New West,* 548–50.

27. Speer, *Encyclopedia,* 549; Harold B. Simpson, *Touched with Valor, Civil War Papers and Casualty Reports of Hood's Texas Brigade,* 7–9, 19; Robertson also actively worked for the Texian Veterans, in addition to his interest in the smaller Hood's Brigade. The *1873 Proceedings* of this organization indicate extensive commitment to the veterans of Texas by Robertson and thus also a readymade network system of people with which Robertson interacted. Such connections probably enhanced Robertson's effectiveness as Bureau Superintendent. See *Proceedings of the Convention of Texian Veterans,* held at Houston, May 13, 14, 15, 1873.

28. "Governor Coke, January 12, 1875," *Governor's Messages, Coke to Ross,* edited by and for the Archive and History Department of the Texas State Library, 1916, 110. Future references to this volume will be by title, speaker, date of address, and page number in volume; *Revised Map of the State of Texas,* published by the Houston & Texas Central R.R. This is a one-sheet map with copy on the reverse side. The written material identifies Robertson as a former superintendent of the Texas "Bureau of Emigration" and encourages potential settlers to write him for information sent free of charge; see advertisement for H&TC RR in *Waco Daily Examiner,* June 27, 1877; Speer, *Encyclopedia,* 549.

29. TBI, *Report,* (1874), 5–6; TBI, *Report,* (1872), 3; TBI, *Report,* (1873), 9; TBI, *Report,* (1875), 3.

30. TBI, *Texas: Home,* (1875).

31. TBI, *Texas: Home,* (1875), 26.

32. Ibid., 5–8, 24, 33–34, 41–43.

33. Ibid., 37–38, 34, 20, 13, 36, 10.

34. Ibid., 24, 8–9, 19.

35. Ibid., 4, 15–16, 35.

36. Ibid., 26, 28.

37. *Report,* Bureau of Immigration, 1875, 5.

38. Ibid., 6.

39. *Governor's Messages,* Governor Coke, January 15, 1874, 6; January 26, 1874, 17–18; March 16, 1874, 49; January 12, 1875, 105–106.

40. *Governor's Messages,* Governor Coke, January 12, 1875, 108–109.

41. Ibid., 105–10.

CHAPTER 3

Chapter epigraph from Gammel, *Laws,* vol. 8. See pp. 779–834 for the entire 1876 constitution and p. 834 for this specific provision. For a more detailed account of the 1876 Texas constitution and the Bureau of Immigration see Barbara J. Rozek, "Words of Enticement: Efforts to Encourage Immigrants to Texas, 1865–1914" (Ph.D. diss., Rice University, 1995).

1. A more complete view of the political battles swirling around the Republican Party can best be obtained in reading Carl H. Moneyhon, *Republicanism in Reconstruction Texas* and John Pressley Carrier, "A Political History of Texas during the Reconstruction, 1865–1874" (Master's thesis, Vanderbilt University, 1971); McKay, *Seven Decades of the Texas Constitution of 1876,* 48.

2. John Walker Mauer, "Southern State Constitutions in the 1870's: A Case Study of Texas," 108–109, 134; Ernest Wallace, *Charles DeMorse, Pioneer Editor and Statesman,* 176; "Governor Coke's Message to Texas Senate and House of Representatives, March 16, 1874," *Governor's Messages, Coke to Ross,* edited by and for the Archive and History Department of the Texas State Library, 1916, 43, and "Governor Coke's Message to the Texas Legislature, January 12, 1875," 73–74. Future references to this volume will be by title, speaker, date of address, and page number in volume.

It would seem that the Republicans were also unsure about the value of holding a separate constitutional convention. On the whole they opposed such an endeavor. One scholar suggests that Ex-Governor Davis wavered in his support of calling a convention, but finally concluded that the potential in the 1869 Constitution concerning "the colored people, condemning Secession, establishing Schools, encouraging immigration &c &c [*sic*] will continue a dead letter" unless the Democrats are forced to make a clear statement of their commitments and philosophy of government. See Lawrence D. Rice, *The Negro in Texas, 1874–1900,* 17–18, for this argument and quote.

3. *Journal of the Constitutional Convention of the State of Texas,* 1875, 15–16, 21; *Walsh & Pilgrim's Directory of the Officers and Members of the Constitutional Convention of the State of Texas, A.D.* 1875, 1–6. Walsh's contemporary list identifies only four blacks at the convention. Recent research suggests there were five blacks. See John Mitchell in the *New Handbook of Texas.* An excellent source for biographical information on numerous legislators involved in the state convention is the *NHT.*

4. McKay's comment in *Seven Decades* (p. 181) that "it was generally conceded that the new constitution was a Granger product. . . ." has been the basis for many conclusions including the supposition about anti-immigrant feelings. See Van Zant, *Early Economic Policies of the Government of Texas,* 40, and Simpson, *Touched with Valor,* 20.

5. Alwyn Barr, *Reconstruction to Reform,* 9, 22; McKay, *Seven Decades,* 69–70.

6. McKay, *Seven Decades,* 70; Mauer, "Southern State Constitutions in the 1870's," 210–12.

7. Numbers seem to vary slightly depending on the source. A combination of information from *Walsh & Pilgrim* along with the Nat Henderson Directory recorded by Ericson in his article are sources for this information. It is interesting to note here that the two main historical sources for the floor debate record no Republican voice heard. The identifiable speeches came from Democrats, both those holding Grange membership and those not members of the Grange.

8. *Journal,* Convention 1875, 44; *Walsh & Pilgrim,* 3.

9. *Journal,* Convention 1875, 240–41.

10. *Journal,* Convention 1875, 275; *Walsh & Pilgrim,* 1–3.

11. *Journal,* Convention 1875, 288–90.

12. Ibid.

13. *Journal,* Convention 1875, 300.

14. Ibid.

15. *Journal,* Convention 1875, 299–302; George D. Braden et al., *The Constitution of the State of Texas: An Annotated and Comparative Analysis,* 2: 797. This analysis of Section 56 is authored by David A. Anderson.

16. *Journal,* Convention 1875, 353–54; Seth Shepard McKay, ed., *Debates in the Texas Constitutional Convention of 1875,* 239–40.

17. *Journal,* Convention 1875, 401–402.

18. *Walsh & Pilgrim,* 2; *Journal,* Convention 1875, 402.

19. Ben H. Proctor, *Not without Honor: The Life of John H. Reagan,* passim and especially pp. 208–10 concerning the 1876 constitution.

20. *Walsh & Pilgrim,* 3, McKay, *Debates,* 275.

21. *Walsh & Pilgrim,* 1; McKay, *Debates,* 276.

22. McKay, *Debates,* 276, 277, 278. McKay notes his source for King's speech as the version published in the Austin paper, the *State Gazette,* for October 31, 1875.

23. McKay, *Debates,* 27–79.

24. Ibid., 279–80.

25. *Walsh & Pilgrim,* 3; McKay, *Debates,* 283.

26. McKay, *Debates,* 285–86; *Journal,* Convention 1875, 402–403.

27. Stockdale was originally from Kentucky. He was not a Grange member and was forty-eight years old at the time of the convention. *Walsh & Pilgrim,* 3; *Journal,* Convention 1875, October 20, 1875, 424; October 27, 1875, 501–502; October 28, 1875, 510. The second and third readings of the provision came on November 1, 1875 (*Journal,* 531), and November 5, 1875 (*Journal,* 571). The final vote on the Constitution en toto came on November 24, 1875. Only sixty-four of the potential total of ninety delegates registered their votes. The result was fifty-three yeas and eleven nays (*Journal,* 818).

28. *Proceedings of the Second Annual Session of the Texas State Grange, Patrons of Husbandry,* held at the City of Dallas, Tex., Aug., 1875, 18.

29. The 1874 Superintendent's Report for the Bureau of Immigration does not specifically cite A. B. Kerr as one of its agents. However, it does identify Robertson's appointment of twelve unpaid agents for the bureau. Kerr's report to the Grange suggests therefore that he was one of those appointees of the Texas Bureau of Immigration who did not receive a salary for their work. See TBI, *Reports,* (1875), 9; *Proceedings . . . Texas State Grange,* 1875, 31–33.

30. *Proceedings . . . Texas State Grange,* 1875, 31–33.

31. Ibid.

32. See *Proceedings . . . Texas State Grange* for the years 1876–81 as documentation on official Grange interest in immigration. Also see Roscoe C. Martin, "The Grange as a Political Factor in Texas," *Southwestern Political and Social Science Quarterly* 6 (March 1926): 382, and Ralph A. Smith, "The Grange Movement in Texas, 1873–1900," *Southwestern Historical Quarterly* 42 (April 1939): 301, 313; final quote is from Solon Justus Buck, *The Granger Movement,* 297.

33. Claude Hunter Nolen, "Aftermath of Slavery: Southern Attitudes toward Negroes,

1865–1900," 189; "Colored Men's Convention, July 3–4, 1873," in Frederick Eby, comp., *Education in Texas*, 584.

34. This analysis depends on integration of two sources: The final vote as listed in the *Journal* of the Constitutional Convention, 1875, 403, and the biographical information furnished in the *Walsh & Pilgrim*, 1–3.

35. McKay, *Seven Decades*, 135, 147–48.

36. McKay, *Seven Decades*, 134; Winkler, ed., *Platforms*, 163–72 for complete address. Quotations are from p. 172.

37. McKay, *Seven Decades*, 108.

38. *Dallas Weekly Herald*, October 23, 1875, 1, 2.

39. Newspaper information in McKay, *Seven Decades*, 108–109.

40. Winkler, ed. *Platforms*, 177; Barr, *Reconstruction to Reform*, 19–20.

41. *GDN*, December 19, 1875, 1; January 4, 1876, 4; Mauer, "Southern State Constitutions," 252.

42. *General Laws of the State of Texas, Passed at the Session of the Fifteenth Legislature*, 317.

43. *Revised Statutes of Texas: Adopted by the Regular Session of the Sixteenth Legislature*, A.D. 1879, 95–97.

44. Randolph B. Campbell, *Grass-Roots Reconstruction in Texas, 1865–1880*, 17, 25, 1.

CHAPTER 4

1. *Proceedings of the Immigration Convention of Texas*, convened in Dallas, Tex., December 20–21, 1887, and *of the State Immigration Committee of Texas*, convened in Dallas, Tex., December 29, 1887, 33; *The Immigrant's Guide to Texas, Giving Descriptions of Counties, Towns and Villages, with Valuable Historical and Statistical Information*, 26; *Grimes County Directory, 1904*, ad on back cover of publication; *Houston Telegraph*, December 7, 1869, 4.

2. Thomas J. Schlereth, *Victorian America*, 7, 9.

3. Kenneth Cmiel, *Democratic Eloquence*, 17, 57–63, 122.

4. Robert J. Robertson, *Her Majesty's Texans*, 29.

5. J. T. Ashton in Galveston, Texas, to his sister in Wigan, England, March 19, 1878, J. T. Ashton Manuscript Collection, Rosenberg Library, Galveston, Texas; Bergman's letter as quoted by Larry E. Scott, *The Swedish Texans*, 51. Other representative letters from the Bergman brothers to their sister in Sweden can be found in H. Arnold Barton, *Letters from the Promised Land, Swedes in America, 1840–1914*, 179–86, 238–48; letter from George and Catherine Davies in New Philadelphia, Texas, to their parents and friends, December 8, 1879, in Alan Conway, ed., *The Welsh in America, Letters from the Immigrants*, 153; letter from Martha Ann Otey in Washington County, Texas, to her sister Eliza Thomas Nolley near Durant, Mississippi, June 22, 1866, in bound volume under the title "A Journey from Mississippi to Texas 1866," Manuscript Collection, Sam Houston State University Library, Huntsville, Tex.

6. *Bryant's Texas Almanac and Railway Guide, 1882*, 52; R. B. Hubbard, *Centennial Oration of Governor R. B. Hubbard, of Texas, Delivered at the National Exposition, September 11, 1876*, 13. A copy of this speech is at the Texas State Library, bound in a volume with multiple printed works. No publication information or title page to the sixteen-page

pamphlet was included, although a one-page preface of explanation for publication was listed as written by W. G. Kingsbury, London, England.

7. *Bryant's Texas Almanac, 1882,* 20.

8. *Houston Telegraph,* December 7, 1869, 4; November 8, 1871, 6; reproduction of brochure originally written by Charles Herndon, *Smith County, Texas, The Land of Diversified Farms and the Heart of the Great Fruit and Truck Belt* (n.p., 1908), 35, under title, "Come and Share Our Plenty," *Chronicles of Smith County, Texas* 9 (fall 1970): 29–46.

9. Statistics compiled from data in *The Statistical History of the United States from Colonial Times to the Present,* 1965, which is a comprehensive overview of federal census material.

10. Liz Carpenter, *Getting Better All the Time,* 148.

11. Some exceptions to this inactivity by historians include: Alwyn Barr, "Occupational and Geographic Mobility in San Antonio, 1870–1900," *Social Science Quarterly* 51 (September 1970): 396–403; Susan Jackson, "Movin' On: Mobility through Houston in the 1850s," *Southwestern Historical Quarterly* 81 (January 1978): 252–82; Terry G. Jordan, "A Century and a Half of Ethnic Change in Texas, 1836–1986," *Southwestern Historical Quarterly* 89 (April 1986): 385–422; Homer L. Kerr, "Migration into Texas, 1860–1880," *Southwestern Historical Quarterly* 70 (October 1966): 184–216; Barnes F. Lathrop, *Migration into East Texas, 1835–1860: A Study from the United States Census.*

12. Extensive material from Austin and his efforts at publicizing Texas's opportunities can be found in manuscript collections at the Center for American History, the University of Texas at Austin, and the San Jacinto Museum of History, San Jacinto Museum near Houston.

Multiple published works of antebellum letters exist. They illustrate the fact that written material was sent, received, and discussed by those "back home." Mary Austin Holley's letters (Mattie Austin Hatcher, *Letters of an Early American Traveller*) and those of Elise Waerenskjold, *The Lady with the Pen,* are representative of the genre. Examples of antebellum immigrant guidebooks are also numerous. David Woodman, *Guide to Texas Emigrants,* and Arthur Ikin, *Texas: Its History, Topography, Agriculture, Commerce, and General Statistics* are two good examples. An excellent secondary source on this antebellum era is Robin W. Doughty's *At Home in Texas: Early Views of the Land.*

13. Ellis Turner, "In the Trail of the Buffalo: A Descriptive Bibliography of the Oregon, California, and Texas Guidebook, 1814–1860," 32, 63; J[acob] de Cordova, *Texas: Her Resources and Her Public Men,* 20–21. Two years earlier de Cordova had written *The Texas Immigrant and Traveller's Guide Book,* from which these quotations were lifted word for word.

14. Turner, "Trail of Buffalo," 10; De Cordova, *Texas: Her Resources,* 20; and De Cordova, *The Texas Immigrant,* 8.

15. *Western Texas, the Australia of America,* 208.

16. Roderick P. Hart, *Modern Rhetorical Criticism,* 18.

17. *Texas New Yorker,* July, 1872, 260. Hereinafter cited as *TNY.*

18. *FREE!,* Missouri, Kansas and Texas Railway, 7, 8, 4, 6.

19. TBI, *Texas: Home,* 1875, 22; Hart, *Modern Rhetorical Criticism,* 18.

20. William Warren Rogers, ed., "From Planter to Farmer: A Georgia Man in Reconstruction Texas," *Southwestern Historical Quarterly* 72 (April 1969): 528; Theodore C. Blegen, ed., *Land of Their Choice,* 369.

21. *Texas: Its Climate, Soil, Productions,* 31.

22. An interesting epilogue to the story of this Texas city exists. The 1870s was the high point of development for Jefferson. The city would not work with Jay Gould and the potential railroad construction he offered. The city was left with water transportation heading toward New Orleans, but no rail connection with the rest of the state or country. This contributed heavily to the city's failure to evolve into the growing metropolis fore-seen by city boosters.

23. A secondary theme in immigration studies that has received little attention is the extent to which multiple moves were common and an assumed part of the migration pro-cess. John Bodnar's work emphasized that European immigrants often made repeated moves before crossing the Atlantic to the United States. The place moves of Europeans were replicated once they arrived in the United States by their willingness to move again, once here, as they continued that search for happiness and success. Urban studies of this phenomenon are common. Clearly a parallel exists between the city worker moving from apartment to apartment and the southern rural farm worker who frequently moved from farm to farm on a yearly basis pursuing similar goals as the city worker. While seldom did geographic mobility translate into social mobility or economically more remunerative jobs, the constant movement of people from place to place ought not to be ignored by his-torians. Unfulfilled hopes are hopes nonetheless and contribute to changes in individual lives as much, if not more, than hopes fulfilled.

Terry Jordan in his work on Texas notes that the "southerners who populated Texas were traditionally footloose, with a long heritage of moving from place to place, and the roots they put down in any given piece of land were shallow. Theirs was essentially a mo-bile society." See Terry G. Jordan, "The German Settlement of Texas after 1865," *South-western Historical Quarterly* 73 (October 1969): 198.

24. John Bodnar, *The Transplanted;* Oscar Handlin, *The Uprooted.*

25. *Texas State Register,* 1879, 50; W. N. Bryant, *Bryant's Railroad Guide,* 84; *Austin, The Capital of Texas and Travis County,* 4–5.

26. *Houston Telegraph,* December 7, 1869, 4; H. C. Mack, *Texas. Information for Em-igrants,* 15; W. C. McCarty, *A Few Practical Remarks about Texas,* 20.

27. *Texas State Register,* 1879, 43.

28. TBI, *Texas: Home,* 28–29.

29. M. Whilldin, comp., *A Description of Western Texas,* 92.

30. *Free Guide to Texas,* Missouri, Kansas & Texas Railway. Document consists of one folded sheet.

31. Hart, *Modern Rhetorical Criticism,* 16; *FREE!,* 2.

32. *Houston Telegraph,* November 8, 1871, 6; *TNY,* July 1872, 260; *Texas State Regis-ter,* 1876, 73.

33. *FREE!,* 2; Mack, *Texas,* 141.

34. McCarty, *A Few Practical Remarks,* 3; *Texas: Its Climate, Soil, Productions,* 28, 5–6.

35. Hubbard became governor of Texas in December 1876. Governor Coke resigned his state position to take on the challenge of new tasks as United States Senator; Hubbard, *Centennial Oration,* 11, 7.

36. Hubbard, *Centennial Oration,* 14.

37. Hubbard, *Centennial Oration,* "Preface," no pagination listed. It is not known how many copies were printed by the Galveston, Houston and San Antonio Railroad or distributed overseas.

38. *Circular of the Texas Colonization, Land & Trust Company,* 6; *Texas State Register,* 1876, 61; *Texas State Register,* 1872, 78.

For a short, general explanation of the norther's impact on the history of Texas, see Edward Hake Phillips, "The Texas Norther," *Southwestern Historical Quarterly* 59 (July 1955): 1–13.

39. Mack, *Texas,* 131–33.

40. TBI, *Texas: Home,* 35.

41. Jane Lenz Elder, *The Literature of Beguilement,* exh. cat., De Golyer Library.

CHAPTER 5

1. *GDN,* September 14, 1865, 2, 3; August 30, 1867, 1, and *Flake's Bulletin* on January 2, 1866; *Gonzales Inquirer* as quoted in *Houston Telegraph,* November 1, 1871, 4.

2. *Houston Telegraph,* October 26, 1871, 2, 5; October 27, 1871, 5.

3. *Houston Telegraph,* December 7, 1869, 4; October 20, 1869, 5; October 26, 1871, 6.

4. Masthead description comes from an October, 1871, copy of the *Texas New Yorker,* the earliest extant issue available to this author.

5. *TNY,* October 1871.

6. *TNY,* November 1871, 50; January 1872, 102.

7. *TNY,* May 1872, 198, 210; July 1872, 248.

8. *TNY,* November 1871, 51; December 1871, 75.

9. *TNY,* May 1872, 193; June 1872, 234; April 1872, 183.

10. *TNY,* January 1872, 101.

11. This information is from an advertisement in the back pages of a book entitled *Southern and Western Texas Guide.* The work was authored by James L. Rock and W. I. Smith, proprietors of the *St. Louis Texan.* This author has knowledge of only three extant issues of this paper published during the spring of 1878. They are currently located in the Center for American History's Newspaper Collection, Austin, Texas.

12. *St. Louis Texan,* February 9, 1878, 2, 1; Homestead Laws repeated in February 9, 1878, 4; March 9, 1878, 4; and March 16, 1878, 4; response to New Yorker's inquiry in March 16, 1878, 4. Hereinafter this publication will be referred to as *SLT.*

13. *SLT,* February 9, 1878, 2, 3; March 9, 1878, 3; March 16, 1878, 3. Some of the railroad advertisements listed emigrant rates, others only their first-class ticket rates.

14. *SLT,* March 9, 1878, 2; March 16, 1878, 1.

15. *SLT,* March 16, 1878, 1.

16. Lawrence H. Larsen, *The Urban West at the End of the Frontier,* 33.

17. Stuart McGregor, "The Texas Almanac, 1857–1873," *Southwestern Historical Quarterly* 50 (April 1947): 419–21, 427. The next issue of this almanac after 1873 was in 1904 when interestingly a change in title reflects a change in emphasis for the publication. The 1904 volume became the *Texas Almanac and State Industrial Guide,* a name that remains through to the present yearly editions. See non-paginated Introduction by Walter Moore to the volume *The Texas Almanac, 1857–1873, A Compendium of Texas History,* compiled by James M. Day.

18. *GDN,* August 4, 1868, 1; McGregor, "Texas Almanac," 426; *GDN,* August 30, 1867, 4.

19. *Texas Almanac,* 1872, Preface, n.p.

20. Ibid., Preface, n.p., and 149–51.

21. *Texas Almanac*, 1872, 150; *Texas State Register*, 1872, 66; *Texas State Register*, 1876, 3.

22. *Texas Rural Register and Immigrants' Hand-Book, for 1875*, title page; *Burke's Texas Almanac and Immigrant's Hand Book, for 1879*. A Facsimile Reproduction (1969). See non-paginated Introduction by Dorman H. Winfrey for explanation of the full run of *Burke's Almanac*.

23. *Texas Rural Almanac and Immigrants' Hand Book, for 1876*. See front cover also. Map is folded and tucked inside back cover.

24. *Texas Rural Almanac*, 1876, 31.

25. Ibid., 91.

26. Hart, *Modern Rhetorical Criticism*, 3.

27. John W. Forney, *What I Saw in Texas*.

28. *Texas: Its Climate, Soil, Productions, Trade, Commerce, and Inducements for Emigration.*

29. McCarty, *A Few Practical Remarks*, 27, 26.

30. Mack, *Texas*, 16.

31. *The Mortgage Bonds, (7 per cent, Gold or 8 per cent. Currency.) of the New Orleans, Mobile and Texas Railroad Company.*

32. *Mr. Greeley's Letters from Texas and the Lower Mississippi*, 25.

33. Blegen, ed., *Land of Their Choice*, 368–71.

34. Norwood Stansbury, "Letters from the Texas Coast, 1875," James P. Baughman, ed., *Southwestern Historical Quarterly* 69 (April 1966): 499–501.

35. Stansbury, "Letters," 507.

36. Stansbury, "Letters," September 15, 1875, 511, and February 6, 1875, 503.

37. *Houston Telegraph*, November 25, 1871, 4.

38. *Mobile Alabama Daily Register*, September 28, 1870, 3.

39. *Alabama Register*, September 28, 1870, 3; Statistics for Petty County come from a work by B. F. Riley, *Alabama as It Is: Or, The Immigrants' and Capitalist's Guide Book to Alabama*. Bradley's comment that blacks in his new home (Columbus in Colorado County, Texas) were "comparatively few" is interesting for the census records identify heavy black population in that county, i.e. in 1870 out of a total county population of 8,326 people, 3,701 were "colored" and 4,625 were white; in 1880 the same county had a total population of 16,673 people, 7,686 were "colored" and 8,987 were white. The relative balance between the races in Colorado County, Texas, must have seemed to Bradley as a significant improvement over the three-to-one ratio of black to white in Perry County, Alabama, which was the home from which he emigrated. For census figures, see *Statistics of the Population of the United States, Ninth Census* and *Tenth Census*.

40. *TNY*, June 1872, 235.

41. Lois E. Myers, *Letters by Lamplight: A Woman's View of Everyday Life in South Texas, 1873–1883*, 6.

42. Mitchell Daniel, Paris, Texas, to Raleigh Travers Daniel, Richmond, January 29, 1877, in Robert A. Brock Collection, Box 82, Folder 66, Huntington Library, San Marino, Calif.

43. Camilla Davis Trammell, *Seven Pines: Its Occupants and Their Letters, 1825–1872*, 232–33.

44. M. A. Otey to Mary Frances Nolley, March 16, 1866; M. A. Otey to E. T. Nolley, March 22, 1866; M. A. Otey to E. D. Nolley, March 22, 1866. Otey Collection, SHSU.

45. Genie E. S. Williamson to Martha A. Otey, March 26, 1866; M. A. Otey to M. F. Nolley, April 25, 1866; M. A. Otey to M. F. Nolley, June 29, 1866; M. A. Otey to M. F. Nolley, July 15, 1866. Otey Collection, SHSU.

46. Photocopy of original letter held by the Baker family of Fort Worth, Texas, is in the possession of the Texas Seaport Museum, Galveston, Texas. Mary Taylor of Hewitt, Texas, donated the photocopy and is a granddaughter of one of the children mentioned as coming to Texas in that 1871 group.

47. Baker Family letter, Texas Seaport Museum, Galveston.

CHAPTER 6

1. Dodd and Dodd, *Historical Statistics of the South,* 54–55.

2. Alex E. Sweet and J. Armory Knox, *On a Mexican Mustang, Through Texas, From the Gulf to the Rio Grande,* 666–69.

3. Hubert Howe Bancroft, *History of the Pacific States of North America,* vol. 11: *Texas* vol. 2, 1801–1889, 516.

4. *TNY,* March 1876, 200.

5. B. J. Gautier to L. L. Foster, May 17, 1889, in Department of Agriculture, Insurance, Statistics, and History Files, Texas State Library, Austin, Texas. File Number 001-1, Statistics, Files 8–14; File Number 001-2, Statistics, Files 1–3. Letters are arranged alphabetically by first initial of surname or name of institution and the bulk of this correspondence is dated from January 1889 to December 1891. Further references to letters in these files will be listed by letter writer followed by D.A.I.S.H. Statistics File, TSL.

6. TBI, *Texas: Home.*

7. *The Home for the Emigrant. Texas: Her Vast Extent of Territory, Fertility of Soil, Diversity of Productions, Geniality of Climate, and the Facilities She Affords Emigrants for Acquiring Homes.* See pp. 16–17 for school information.

8. Examples of these incorporated letters can be found on pp. 22–23 and 24–25 of *Texas: The Home for the Emigrant, From Everywhere.* The quotation about bureau activities comes from p. 37 of the same document. This type of material (i.e. letters and references to the Bureau of Immigration) does not appear in the 1877 publication retitled *The Home for the Emigrant.* This author estimates that the later publication is a 75 percent direct copy of the earlier document.

9. *The Home for the Emigrant,* 1877, 35–36, and title page.

10. *The Revised Statutes of Texas: Adopted by the Regular Session of the Sixteenth Legislature,* A.D., 1879, 653–54.

11. A. W. Spaight, *The Resources, Soil, and Climate of Texas.*

12. Spaight, *The Resources,* iii–iv.

13. Ibid., v.

14. Ibid.

15. This fold-out map was found loose between the pages of the Spaight Report, located in the Masterson Collection, Fondren Library, Rice University.

16. Bourbon conservatism versus New South reformism is a major theme in southern political postbellum history. See Eric Foner, *Reconstruction: America's Unfinished Revolution, 1863–1877,* especially pp. 548–50; C. Vann Woodward, *Origins of the New South, 1877–1913,* 58–66; Edward L. Ayers, *The Promise of the New South: Life after Reconstruction,*

44–46. For Texas specifically, see Robert A. Calvert and Arnoldo De León, *The History of Texas,* 146–51; Randolph B. Campbell, "Statehood, Civil War, and Reconstruction, 1846–76," in *Texas through Time: Evolving Interpretations,* especially pp. 191–96.

17. Marvin E. De Boer, ed., *Destiny by Choice: The Inaugural Addresses of the Governors of Texas.* First Inaugural Address, January 21, 1879, 125–37, especially p. 131 for long quote; Second Inaugural Address, January 18, 1881, 138–45, especially p. 139.

18. Barr, *Reconstruction to Reform,* 58–59.

19. *Governor's Messages.* Lieutenant Governor Sayers. Address to State Senate at the convening of the Seventeenth Legislature, January 11, 1881, 335–40, especially p. 338.

20. Winkler, *Platforms,* 204, 203.

21. *Governor's Messages.* Lieutenant Governor L. J. Storey, Inaugural Address, January 18, 1881, 348–57, especially pp. 351, 352.

22. Winkler, *Platforms,* 196, 214, 188, 199.

23. Southern state agencies participated in this movement. For a detailed account of this work see Rozek, "Words of Enticement."

24. *Proceedings of the Third Annual Session of the Texas State Grange, Patrons of Husbandry,* held at the city of Tyler, Tex., January, 1877, 26; Gammel, *Laws,* 9: 98–99.

25. *Governor's Messages.* Governor John Ireland. January 11, 1887, 528–53, see especially p. 552.

26. *Governor's Messages.* Governor Ross. January 20, 1887, 574–95, especially, pp. 586–87.

27. Ibid.

28. Gammel, *Laws,* 9: 98–99.

29. Department of Agriculture, Insurance, Statistics, and History, *First Annual Report of the Agricultural Bureau of the Department of Agriculture, Insurance, Statistics, and History, 1887–88.* The transmittal letter is on pp. v–xi; the long quote is from pp. vii–viii.

30. *Governor's Messages.* Governor Ross, January 13, 1891, 657–98, especially p. 683.

31. D.A.I.S.H., *First Annual Report of the Agricultural Bureau,* 1–250.

32. See files of the Department of Agriculture, Insurance, Statistics, and History at the Texas State Library, Austin, Tex. Letters are arranged in chronological order as received by the department.

33. Terry G. Jordan, "The Forgotten Texas State Census of 1887," *Southwestern Historical Quarterly* 85 (April 1982): 401–408.

34. Gammel, *Laws,* 9: 67; 10: 111.

35. Hiram Clawson to Governor, January 22, 1889, D.A.I.S.H. Statistics File, TSL.

36. Conrad Doering of Davison County, Dakota, to "Dear Sir" June 23, 1889, D.A.I.S.H. Statistics File, TSL.

37. W. S. Chapin of Montgomery City, Missouri, to "Dear Sir" October 19, 1889, D.A.I.S.H. Statistics File, TSL.

38. G. W. Alexander to L. L. Foster, March 23, 1889; Nicholas Baggs to L. L. Foster, April 26, 1889; A. P. Cogswell & Son to Secy of the State Board of Agriculture, January 15, 1890, D.A.I.S.H. Statistics File, TSL.

39. Postcard from Borsari of Napoli, Italy, to Secretary of the Texas Agricultural Bureau, November 8, 1889; Letter from En. D. Desi of Manchester, England, to "Gentlemen," December 24, 1890; Letter from Wm. W. Lang of Hamburg, Germany, to L. L. Foster, January 24, 1889; J. G. Myer of Round Rock, Texas, to L. L. Foster, September 28, 1889, D.A.I.S.H. Statistics File, TSL.

40. Subsequent reports of this agency show growth in the size of their publications and the implementation of new ideas. See D.A.I.S.H. Reports: *Fourth Report,* 1890–91; *Fifth Report,* 1891–92, John E. Hollingsworth Commissioner.

CHAPTER 7

1. Documents list this company in a variety of ways, using South and Western as separate words, or sometimes as one hyphenated word, or sometimes as a single compound word. No clear delineation seems to exist, but this author will uniformly refer to the organization as the South Western Immigration Company. South Western Immigration Company, *Texas: Her Resources and Capabilities,* 3–5.

2. SW Immigration Co., *Texas,* 6, 4.

3. Ibid., title page, 5–6, 10.

4. SW Immigration Co., *Texas.* See pp. 68, 247, 249, 66, 154, for representative headings included in the larger division that extends from page 159 to 246; Robertson noted on pp. 67–68.

5. *TNY,* September 1875, 8; November 1875, 72; February 1876, 167.

6. *TNY,* April 1876, 254.

7. *Echo* article quoted by Naomi Kincaid, "The Founding of Abilene, The 'Future Great' of the Texas and Pacific Railway," *West Texas Historical Association Year Book* 22 (October 1946): 20.

8. Anna J. Hardwicke Pennybacker, *A New History of Texas for Schools,* 165. A later edition of this text continued to include the "Immigration Movement" as a significant event during the administration of Governor Ross. The verb tense shifted from present to past stating, "Strong efforts were made during 1888 to bring more immigrants into Texas" and then concluding the paragraph with "The movement was a success." However one judges the movement itself, the author of this textbook very obviously felt as strongly about it in 1908 as she had when writing the 1888 edition. See Anna J. Hardwicke Pennybacker, *A History of Texas for Schools,* rev. ed., 261.

9. The drought was extensive, but affected certain portions of the state more severely than others. Two sources for an overview of the 1886–87 drought include, W. C. Holden, "West Texas Drouths," *Southwestern Historical Quarterly* 32 (October 1928): 103–23 and J. W. Williams, "A Statistical Study of the Drouth of 1886," *West Texas Historical Association Year Book* 21 (October 1945): 85–109.

For a primary source on the immigration convention see *Proceedings . . . Immigration Convention,* 1888, 4.

10. *Proceedings . . . Immigration Convention,* 1888, 3–7, 23; *GDN,* December 10, 1887, 8, and December 13, 1887, 2.

11. *Proceedings . . . Immigration Convention,* 1888, 7–15.

12. *Proceedings . . . Immigration Convention,* 1888, passim. A variety of names were used to identify this organization. The convention was held in December of 1887 and after that organizational meeting newspapers, media, and people variously used such labels as State Bureau of Immigration, State Immigration Committee, Committee for Immigration to Texas, and Executive Committee on Immigration. Since no official governmental body existed at the time, all these labels referred to the organization that evolved from the 1887 convention that included numerous smaller committees within the association.

13. *Proceedings . . . Immigration Convention,* 1888, 24, 25–26, 28.

14. Ibid., 24, 30, 39.

15. *GDN*, January 13, 1888, 8; January 12, 1888, 2; January 12, 1888, 4; March 1, 1888, 8.

16. [R. S. Neblett], *Texas. Description of Navarro County. Her Resources, and Inducements Offered to Immigrants,* 29, 21; R. W. Haltom, *History and Description of Angelina County, Texas,* 41, 44; *Facts for Immigrants: A Truthful Description of the Town of Palestine and Anderson County, Texas,* title page, preface page, 30, 24.

17. *Statistics and Information Concerning the State of Texas, with Its Millions of Acres of Unoccupied Lands.*

18. *New Birmingham, Texas.*

19. [Immigration Society of Cooke County, Texas], *Cooke County: Its People, Productions and Resources,* p. 2 of an unpaginated document.

20. [Immigration Society], *Cooke County,* 2–5 of an unpaginated document.

21. [Immigration Society], *Cooke County,* 13, 19 of an unpaginated document.

22. Waco Immigration Society, *The Immigrant's Guide to Waco and McLennan County Texas.* Reproduction of this seventeen-page document originally compiled by Charles Herndon in 1908 can be found under the title, "Come and Share our Plenty," *Chronicles of Smith County, Texas* 9 (fall 1970): 29–46.

23. *Grimes County Directory,* 1904, preface page of an unpaginated document.

24. *Kerrville, U.S.A.,* n.p. Quote from section subtitled, "Sociology."

25. *The Industries of Austin, Texas; The Industries of Dallas, Her Relations as a Center of Trade;* [Andrew Morrison], *The Port of Galveston and the State of Texas; A Souvenir of Galveston; Galveston, Texas,* B.P.O.E., No. 126, n.d., a pamphlet in archival collection at Center for American History, Austin, Tex.; *San Antonio, Texas: The City of Missions,* 66; *San Antonio as a Health and Pleasure Resort: Climatic Conditions which Have Made this City the Health Seekers Earthly Paradise;* Chatfield, W. H., comp., *The Twin Cities of the Border . . . and the Country of the Lower Rio Grande;* two examples of joint efforts include, *The Story of San Antonio* and *Facts about El Paso and Adjacent Country.*

26. *GDN,* November 2, 1888, 8.

27. *GDN,* December 12, 1888.

28. *GDN,* December 12, 1888; *Vernon's Annotated Constitution,* 3: 460.

29. *Proceedings of the Southern Interstate Immigration Convention,* 1888, 2, 3.

30. South Carolina was the location for one of these state conventions. See *Proceedings of the Immigration Convention,* held at the Academy of Music, Charleston, S.C., on May 3, 4, 5, 1870. An example of newspaper editorializing in support of efforts to attract immigration can be found in the *Greensboro Patriot* of North Carolina. See August 24, 1871, 2; November 30, 1871, 1, 2; December 7, 1871, 2. For a fairly definitive listing of state laws and agencies relating to immigration prior to 1911 see vol. 39 of the 42 volume set, *U.S. Congress, Senate Immigration Commission,* (1911). An early attempt at joint efforts to attract immigrants to the South took place in 1884. See Southern Immigration Association of America, *Address of A. J. McWhirter, Pres't, at Vicksburg, Miss. November 21st, 1883* and *Proceedings of the First Annual Session of the Southern Immigration Association of America,* held at Nashville, Tenn., on, March 11, 12 and 13, 1884.

31. *GDN,* December 13, 1888, 1; *Proceedings . . . Southern Interstate Immigration Convention,* 1888, 10.

32. *GDN,* December 13, 1888, 1; December 14, 1888, 2.

33. *Proceedings . . . Southern Interstate Immigration Convention,* 1888, 17.

34. *Proceedings . . . Southern Interstate Immigration Convention,* 1888, 3.

35. *Proceedings. . . Southern Interstate Immigration Convention,* 1888, 4, 11, for Chilton quotes. See all fifty pages of the *Proceedings* for an overview of the transportation issue.

36. *Proceedings . . . Southern Interstate Immigration Convention,* 1888, 34, 43–50.

37. Multiple examples of southern interstate efforts exist in Department of Agriculture, Insurance, Statistics and History Files, Texas State Library, Austin, Texas. See File Number 001–1, Statistics, Files 8–14; File Number 001–2, Statistics, Files 1–3.

38. Information about the Texas exhibit in Chicago can be gleaned from the *Chicago Tribune,* June 16, 1893, 12; September 16, 1893, 4; September 17, 1893, 8; Edward Hake Phillips, "Texas and the World Fairs, 1851–1935," *East Texas Historical Journal* 23 (1985): 5–6; Hubert Howe Bancroft, *The Book of the Fair,* 797, 796; Chris Meister, "The Texas State Building: J. Reilly Gordon's Contribution to the World's Columbian Exposition," *Southwestern Historical Quarterly* 48 (July 1994): 1–24.

39. Texas Commercial Secretaries' Association, *Industrial Texas,* 1, 5; Texas Commercial Secretaries' Association, *The Master Builder,* 8–9, 6–7.

40. Texas Commercial Secretaries' Association, *Industrial Texas,* 21–22, 31, 29; Texas Commercial Secretaries' Association, *The People, Population 3,896,542,* 1–6.

41. Carl Blasig, *Building Texas,* 17, 19, 24; *Texas Almanac and State Industrial Guide,* 1912, 390–93.

42. *El Paso Herald,* August 17, 1907, 2, hereinafter referred to as *EPH; GDN,* August 17, 1907, 8; *EPH,* August 17, 1907, 2. Copies of these membership-oriented leaflets were found glued inside the pages of the Five Million Club document entitled *Texas from A to Z,* located in the Texas State Library, Austin, Tex. Quotes from those small leaflets were obtained from that source.

43. Texas Five Million Club, *Texas from A to Z, A Compendium of Information.*

44. *GDN,* August 17, 1907, 8.

45. *EPH,* August 15, 1907, 3; August 15, 1907, 1; August 16, 1907, 2; August 17, 1907, 1; see August 16, 1907, 3 for an account of Miller's talk.

46. Blasig, *Building Texas,* 55. For newspaper coverage of Huntsville's efforts see *Huntsville Post-Item,* November 30, 1906, 1; December 7, 1906, 1; January 4, 1907, 1; February 1, 1907, 2.

CHAPTER 8

1. *Texas, Empire State of the Southwest; Texas; Greater Texas and the Coast Country: Houston-Galveston District, the Winter Garden,* 4th ed.; *West Texas, Its Soil, Climate and Possibilities, from San Antonio to El Paso.*

2. James B. Hedges, "The Colonization Work of the Northern Pacific Railroad," *Mississippi Valley Historical Review* 13 (December 1926): 311; *Mission Route—The San Antonio and Aransas Pass R'y.* This document is a one-sheet map. The backside of the map has multiple sections. This quote is from a section with heading "Statistics of the Lone Star State."

3. The complete story of railroading in Texas has yet to be told. The classic account is by S. G. Reed, *A History of the Texas Railroads,* and Reed claims to have built upon the research of Charles S. Potts in the University of Texas, Bulletin No. 119 (March 1, 1909) entitled *Railroad Transportation in Texas.* See also Charles P. Zlatkovich, *Texas Railroads: A Record of Construction and Abandonment* for a more recent account of railroad growth and stasis.

4. The smaller railroad story of each community along a rail line has not often been documented. One fine effort at describing this rhythm of development is John S. Garner, "The Saga of a Railroad Town: Calvert, Texas (1868–1918)," *Southwestern Historical Quarterly* 85 (October 1981): 139–60. He notes the pull by the construction efforts for the Houston and Texas Central Railway of approximately 250 Chinese workers into the community for at least a period of time. He also points to an 1870 statistic that 7 percent of Calvert's population was foreign-born immigrants who had arrived to work on the railroad or open businesses in town. Further research into other communities would surely demonstrate this pull factor between population growth and railroad development.

5. The Iron Mountain Route was a label applied to a combined effort by three different railroads: the International & Great Northern (I&GN RR), the Texas & Pacific (T&P RR), and the St. Louis, Iron Mountain & Southern. By 1911 these three railway companies made an affiliated effort they called the Joint Texas Immigration Bureau. One of their pamphlets identified T. C. Kimber as their general immigration agent located in St. Louis. See *Sunny Southwest Texas,* 4th ed. Long quote is on p. 18.

6. For an example of this technique of inserting letters or portions of them, see H. S. Kneedler, *The Coast Country of Texas,* 40–43. For testimonials from the common people settling the state see *Immigrants Guide to Western Texas,* especially pp. 35–42. A document that represents the ultimate in "cut and paste" or total appropriation of another persons' words, is Walter B. Stevens, *Through Texas, A Series of Interesting Letters,* by the passenger department of the Missouri Pacific Railway Company in 1892. For examples of excerpts from newspapers see *Texas,* Houston and Texas Central Ry, 12 (*Waco Examiner*) and (*Clarendon News*); 15 (*Morgan Sentinel*); 16 (*Calvert Democrat*); 19 (*Brazoria Independent*) and (*Cleburne Chronicle*); *Sunny Southwest Texas,* 18.

7. Whilldin, comp., *A Description of Western Texas,* 92; *FREE!,* 9–10; Rock and Smith, *Southern and Western Texas Guide,* 25; *Homes in Texas, on the Line of the International and Great Northern R.R., 1880–1,* 8; [James Wilson], *Agricultural Resources in the Pan Handle of Texas on the Line of the Texas Pan Handle Route; A Description of the State of Texas Traversed by MK and T;* Norman G. Kittrell, *Texas Illustrated or the Romance, the History and the Resources of a Great State,* 22–23, 29.

8. Reed, *Texas Railroads,* 196. Texas may have been treated differently than other western states in regard to lower fares for immigrants. It was not uncommon for western-directed railroads to put "immigrant cars" on their tracks. These cars were no-frills versions of other passenger cars and varied from company to company. One historian refers to them by saying they "bore the same relationship to Pullman cars that steerage aboard ship bore to first class stateroom accommodations." The trains pulling "immigrant cars" often sat at sidings while express trains pulled through, thus helping to justify in the mind of the railroad a lower rate. A comparison of westbound trains of the 1870s and 1880s with Texas-bound trains might illuminate whether such cars were ever used crossing into and through Texas territory. See Oscar Osburn Winther, *The Transportation Frontier: Trans-Mississippi West, 1865–1890,* 123–25; *The Lone Star Guide, Descriptive of Counties on the Line of the International and Great Northern Railroad of Texas,* see advertisement next to map; *Immigrants Guide to Western Texas,* 55; *The Through Car Line,* a one-page timetable and map with information on the reverse side; *Homeseekers' Fares to Texas,* 1911.

9. W. D. Mauldin, "The Coming of Agriculture to Dallam County," *West Texas Historical Association Year Book* 13 (October 1937): 108–109.

10. Standard Land Company information as quoted in *God, Grass & Grit: History of the Sherman County Trade Area,* comp. and ed. Marylou McDaniel, 78; Soash Land Company information is from Garry L. Nall, "Panhandle Farming in the 'Golden Era' of American Agriculture," *Panhandle-Plains Historical Review* 46 (1973): 71.

11. *Texas,* H&TC RR, 44.

12. *New Farming Opportunities in Northwest Texas along the Santa Fe,* 30; David B. Gracy II, "A Preliminary Survey of Land Colonization in the Panhandle-Plains of Texas," *Museum Journal* 11 (1969): 67; *Plains Farmer: The Diary of William G. DeLoach, 1914–1964,* ed. Janet M. Neugebauer, 42–43.

13. *Sud und Sudweft Texas.*

14. *Texas,* H&TC RR, 43; *New York, New Orleans, Southern Pacific, Atlantic Steamship Lines,* [Time Table], 59–60; *Texas Voran! Handbuch von Texas.*

15. See *Texas Via the H and TC,* May, 1890, a timetable and a map; *A Description of the State of Texas Traversed by the MK and T,* 1.

16. *Texas,* 36; *Lands Originally Granted to the Houston & Texas Central; Galveston, Harrisburg & San Antonio; Texas & New Orleans; and Gulf, Western Texas & Pacific Railway Co's in Texas,* 17–18.

17. For an example addressing issue of loneliness, see Kneedler, *Coast Country,* 71. Other examples of movement by colony can be found in W. C. Holden, "Immigration and Settlement in West Texas," *West Texas Historical Association Year Book* 5 (June 1929): 66–85. See "European Folk Islands in Northwest Texas," in vol. 56 of the *Panhandle-Plains Historical Review* (1983). This volume contains ten separate articles about representative "folk island" communities in the panhandle region. These multiple articles express the diversity of such streams of migration and highlight an intriguing aspect of the development of far west and far north Texas.

Another excellent example of ethnic colonization is in the work of Peter L. Peterson, "A New Oslo on the Plains: The Anders L. Mordt Land Company and Norwegian Migration to the Texas Panhandle," *Panhandle-Plains Historical Review* 49 (1976): 25–54. For an account of French colonization see Robert Robertson, "Texas: La Terre Promise," *West Texas Historical Association Year Book* 73 (1997): 11–30.

For a good overview of the colonization movement see David B. Gracy II, "Survey of Land Colonization," 52–79. For an idea of how one such religious colony evolved see John R. Hutto, "The German and Catholic Colony of Mariensfeld," *West Texas Historical Association Year Book* 9 (October 1933): 24–34.

18. Huff, "Work Done by Railroad Companies to Encourage Immigration," 39–41. She quotes information from a railroad pamphlet entitled *Notes on Northern Texas* with an 1889 publication date; Robert L. Martin, *The City Moves West: Economic and Industrial Growth in Central West Texas,* 21; L. L. Blackburn, "Early Settlers and Settlements of Callahan County," *West Texas Historical Association Year Book* 23 (October 1947): 18–19; John C. Rathbun, *The "Cephallanographissiment" or a Truthful Description of the Staked Plain,* 17.

19. Francis W. Wilson, *Advocate for Texas, Thomas Wilson,* 15, 17–18, 26. Huff in her study "Work Done by Texas Railroad Companies to Encourage Immigration" mistakenly states that "no mention of an Immigrant's House" exists for the GH&SA RR. See p. 73 of her thesis. Published documents suggest a different conclusion. Dr. Kingsbury as agent for the European Land and Emigration Department of the GH&SA RR issued a four-page

leaflet that included extracts from letters. In one of the letters the president of the line, Thomas Peirce, expressed his plans for the future, including the building of a "temporary Home for Immigrants" in Luling while he noted the existence of one already in New Philadelphia. See leaflet in a multi-volume bound book at the Texas State Library, Austin, Tex. No title page is included and thus no specific publication information is available.

20. *Homes in Texas, on the Line of the International and Great Northern R.R., 1880–1,* 6; *Texas, the Short Line to Texas is Via the I&GN RR.* This map folded down to a convenient size for carrying in a pocket and was covered with helpful information and visuals on the opposite side. Yet another publication by the I&GN RR trumpeted the Immigrant's Home. See *The Lone Star Guide,* 2–3. This pamphlet also took note of a group of "Grangers" in Waverly, Texas who "are proposing to erect a building for free use by immigrants" (p. 9). The railroad may have hoped that such endeavors would have grown and multiplied across the state.

There is some indication that a few communities did, for a time, establish immigrant homes to help encourage immigration to their area. Bryan in the Brazos River valley area built an immigrant's home using as part of their money funds raised at a concert in February of 1875. See Elder Grade Marshall, "The History of Brazos County, Texas," 107; Valentine J. Belfiglio, "Italians in Small Town and Rural Texas," in *Italian Immigrants in Rural and Small Town America,* ed. Rudolph J. Vecoli, 33.

21. A few examples of authors receiving credit for their promotional writing in a railroad publication do exist. See *The Coast Country of Texas (Annual), a Wonderland Illustrated,* by W. W. Dexter for the Southern Pacific in 1903; *Southwest Texas, an Agricultural Empire,* by Allen Maull for the Sunset-Central Lines [1911(?)]; *The Coast Country of Texas,* by H. S. Kneedler for a joint effort by the H&TC RR, T&NO RR, and the GH&SA RR in 1896; *Texas Illustrated,* by Norman G. Kittrell for the Sunset-Central Lines in 1911. Even though these railroad promotions had listed authors, frequently their content included extensive "cut and paste" material by other writers.

22. Wilson, *Advocate,* 7, 10–12. All the information about this immigration agent comes from this one source, which also includes extensive primary documents as appendices to the written account of Wilson's life.

23. Wilson, *Advocate,* 8–9, 88–89, 83–87.

24. Ibid., 112–13, 92–93.

25. TBI, *Report,* (1974), 5; *TNY,* December 1875, 105.

26. *SLT,* March 9, 1878, 2; *GDN,* November 11, 1880, 4.

27. W. G. Kingsbury, *The State of Texas.*

28. Excerpts from the *Texas Siftings,* December 24, 1881, are quoted in a compiled work by Eisenhour entitled *Alex Sweet's Texas,* 119.

29. The best source documenting Robertson's involvement with the railroad is the *Revised Map of the State of Texas,* a one-sheet map published by the H&TC RR in 1876, DeGolyer Collection at Southern Methodist University.

30. Reed, *Texas Railroads,* 208–209, 364, 376.

31. R. C. Crane, "The Claims of West Texas to Recognition by Historians," *West Texas Historical Association Year Book* 12 (July 1936): 25–27.

32. *Texas: Her Resources and Attractive Features.* The arrival of railroad tracks and the accompanying activity typically spurred land boosterism. A symbiotic relationship existed between the community and its railroad or railroads. See David L. Caffey, "We Have the

Land: Now for the People, Boosterism in Frontier West Texas," *Permian Historical Annual* 21 (December 1981): 49–57.

33. [Wilson], *Agricultural Resources of the Texas Pan Handle,* 4, 9, 15.

34. Examples of other railroad brochures dealing with the far west and panhandle Texas include: *Resources and Attractions of the Texas Panhandle for the Homeseeker,* 3rd ed., as quoted in Huff, "Work Done by Railroad Companies to Encourage Immigration," 91; *Shallow Water Country of Northwest Texas.* See also Jan Blodgett, *Land of Bright Promise: Advertising the Texas Panhandle and South Plains, 1870–1917; Southwest Texas, from San Antonio to El Paso,* Southern Pacific Railroad, 4.

35. *Southwest Texas, an Agricultural Empire,* quotations from title page, 2–3.

36. *Southwest Texas, an Agricultural Empire,* 16, 17, 2. El Paso also received some attention in this later time period from the railroad brochures. One example would be *Facts about El Paso and Adjacent Country.*

37. An interesting example of second-time migration relates to this later railroad effort to lure people southward. Terry Jordan in his research on Germans in Texas in the postbellum period documents the migration of Germans in large number from more northerly counties like Washington and Fayette to more southern areas such as Fort Bend County and Wharton County. These were Germans who had already been part of the Texas quilt of ethnic groups, but who probably responded to the promotional advertising by the Southern Pacific Railroad. See Jordan, "The German Settlement of Texas after 1865," 193–212 and especially p. 201. The documentation of these second moves by the Germans can't help but make us believe this was more common than typically assumed. The high geographic mobility that pulled many people to Texas in the first place also facilitated the not so uncommon practice of moving once, twice, or three times after first arriving within the state's borders.

38. Kneedler, *Coast Country of Texas,* 74–76, 44; *The Coast Country of Texas* (Annual), 149. Title page identifies W. W. Dexter as editor, but also notes distribution free of charge by the Southern Pacific Passenger Department; *Gulf Coastings,* Gulf, Colorado and Santa Fe Railroad, n.p.; *Texas, Empire State of the Southwest,* 34.

39. Kneedler, *Coast Country of Texas,* 44; *Texas Rice Book; Sugar Lands in Texas.*

40. One example of promotional literature can be found in vol. 3 (April 1908) of the *Gulf Coast Magazine* with William Doherty as editor.

Studies of this southern area of Texas and the influence of the railroad reinforce the close connection of the two. See for example, the earlier works by J. L. Allhands, *Gringo Builders; Railroads to the Rio;* and *Uriah Lott.* See also J. Lee Stambaugh and Lillian J. Stambaugh, *The Lower Rio Grande Valley of Texas.*

A well-researched study of lower Texas is Dale Lasater, *Falfurrias: Ed C. Lasater and the Development of South Texas.* The connection of the Falfurrias Immigration Company and its promotional literature meshes neatly with the railroad's development southward.

41. *Profitable Products of East Texas, Orchards and Gardens,* 3, inside back cover.

42. *Industrial Development, Central East Texas, the Fruit Belt of the State,* 38.

43. *East-South-East Texas, On Line of the Texas & New Orleans Railroad.*

44. *Ten Texas Topics by Texas Tillers and Toilers; Timely Tips to Texas Truckers.*

45. Patrick J. Brunet, "'Can't Hurt and May Do You Good': A Study of the Pamphlets the Southern Pacific Railroad Used to Induce Immigration to Texas, 1880–1930," *East Texas Historical Journal* 16 (fall 1978): 38–39.

46. *Scenes along the Houston North Shore Railway,* 25; Steven F. Mehls, "Garden in the Grasslands Revisited: Railroad Promotional Efforts and the Settlement of the Texas Plains," *West Texas Historical Association Year Book* 60 (1984): 61–62.

47. *West Texas beyond the Pecos, Her Health Giving Qualities.*

48. *Louisiana and Texas for the Winter Tourist; Texas Tourist Points and Resorts, along the Sunset-Central Lines.*

49. *GDN,* March 7, 1911, 6.

50. Representative pamphlets that best illustrate the use of pre-photographic visuals include: *Texas: Her Resources,* passim; *Texas,* passim; Whilldin, *A Description of Western Texas,* passim; *Homes in Texas, on the Line of the International and Great Northern R.R., 1880–1,* passim.

51. For representative pamphlets that illustrate photography of the field see: *Southwest Texas, An Agricultural Empire,* passim; *The Coast Country of Texas,* passim; *Texas, Along the Line of the Texas & Pacific Ry,* passim.

52. For representative railroad brochures see: *The Coast Country of Texas,* 3, 9, 37; *Southwest Texas, an Agricultural Empire,* 6, 9, 24; *East-South-East Texas, On Line of the Texas & New Orleans Railroad,* 4.

53. The statistics presented are a combination of track mileage from Reed, *Texas Railroads,* 517, and population numbers from *The Statistical History of the United States.*

CHAPTER 9

1. Direct foreign immigration into Galveston is more easily documented than the general movement of people into Galveston via water. Travel by water has always been the least expensive mode of travel. It was thus used for freight and passengers along the coast of the United States as a mainstay of transportation. While records were and are kept by the government for the initial arrival of any foreign-born person, their second, third, or subsequent moves are not recorded. Individuals and family units, whether foreign-born or native to the United States, frequently traveled by coast-wise shipping during the entire nineteenth century and into the twentieth century. Coastal steamers were not required to provide lists of passengers, thus depriving us of a numerical account of people arriving at any one port. Thus a real void exists in the story of population movement through Galveston.

2. See Earle B. Young, *Galveston and the Great West* for an extensive account of Galveston's efforts at developing its port.

3. *Memorial of the Galveston Chamber of Commerce to the Congress of the United States for the Improvement of the Channels, Bars and Harbors of Galveston Bay,* 8; *Laws of the United States Relating to the Improvement of Rivers and Harbors, from August 11, 1790 to March 4, 1913,* 3 vols., 184, 195.

4. Kathleen E. Lazarou, "A History of the Port of Galveston: A Constitutional-Legal Overview," *Houston Review* 2 (summer 1980): 84. Newspaper articles and state almanacs often referred to Galveston as the force behind its own destiny. See the *Texas State Register* of 1877, 94–96, for one such example.

5. Caleb G. Forshey, *Texas Rail Roads,* 1; [S. H. Gilman], *The Tributary and Economical Relations of the Railway Systems of the United States to the Commerce of Galveston: Considered Geographically, Topographically and Economically,* 1, 3, and Appendix, 5, 6.

6. *GDN,* March 21, 1882.

7. *Laws of the United States Relating to the Improvement of Rivers and Harbors,* 184, 195, 205.

8. Lynn M. Alpern, *Custodians of the Coast: History of the United States Army Engineers at Galveston,* 48; *GDN,* December 1, 1884, 12 pages; U.S. Congress, Senate, Misc. doc. #111. 48th Cong., 1st Sess., 16.

9. U.S. Army Corps of Engineers, *Galveston Harbor, Texas.* 61st Cong., 2nd Sess., H. of R., Doc. #328, 1909.

10. *Proceedings . . . Immigration Convention of Texas,* 3; *GDN,* December 10, 1887, 8. Refer to chapter seven for additional information and another perspective on this conference.

11. *GDN,* December 13, 1887, 2.

12. Ibid.

13. *GDN,* December 23, 1887, 4; *Proceedings . . . Immigration Convention of Texas,* 28–29.

14. *Proceedings . . . Immigration Convention of Texas,* 22, 31, 32.

15. *GDN,* December 23, 1887, 4; December 24, 1887, 8.

16. *GDN,* December 30, 1887, 1–2.

17. *GDN,* July 12, 1888, 1; July 20, 1888, 8.

18. *GDN,* August 29, 1888, 2; August 30, 1888, 1; August 31, 1888, 1.

19. *GDN,* September 5, 1888, 5; September 9, 1888, 6.

20. *Laws of the U.S. Relating to the Improvement of Rivers and Harbors,* 532; Alpern, *Custodians,* 53–55; Ruth Evelyn Kelly, "'Twixt Failure and Success': The Port of Galveston in the 19th Century," 98–99; Bernard Axelrod, "Galveston: Denver's Deep-Water Port," *Southwestern Historical Quarterly* 70 (October 1966): 217–28. One national publication of the time picked up on this story and labeled Galveston as "The Great Seaport of the Southwest," giving it credit for confidence in the inherent value of its harbor and noting its involvement with the western states in securing federal moneys. This article entitled "Galveston Harbor" in *Frank Leslie's Illustrated Newspaper* (May 31, 1890): 365–68, reported that the bill to secure full appropriations had passed the Senate "without a dissenting vote" and was currently before the House with the full approval of the River and Harbor Committee.

21. *GDN,* April 21, 1905, 4; April 22, 1905, 4; April 23, 1905, 6–7. A souvenir program from the *Northern Settler's Convention* provides titles and names of speakers for the event. A copy of this program is at the Rosenberg Library, Galveston, Texas.

22. *GDN,* April 23, 1905, 6–7; April 26, 1905, 12.

23. Clarence Ousley, ed., *Galveston in Nineteen Hundred.* See *GDN,* June 9, 1901, 2, for account of the visit by the Congressional Committee. *Laws of the U.S. Relating to the Improvement of Rivers and Harbors,* 963 (1902), 1038 (1903), 1058 (1904).

24. *GDN,* January 1, 1897, 6; October 10, 1896. Along with the immigrants, the *Halle* arrived with a lower deck cargo of cement.

25. This sum of $38.50 in the fall of 1896 was $2.00 more than the trip from Bremen to New York. Competition between the North Atlantic ports and the Gulf port of Galveston was an issue for the NGL. She had to negotiate with the transportation forces in New York and rescind an earlier offer of a $34.00 trip from Bremen to Galveston. Rates had increased some by 1912 when NGL advertisements hawked a Galveston to Bremen

charge of $35.00 steerage or $67.50 cabin and then suggested, "Bring Your Relatives from Europe by the Same Route, $67.50 Cabin, $40.50 Steerage." See *GDN*, July 9, 1896, 10; October 16, 1896, 4; December 25, 1896, 8; *Galveston Tribune*, May 16, 1912. The Hamburg-American quote is from *GDN*, September 22, 1898, 6.

26. *Galveston Tribune*, May 14, 1907, 2; June 3, 1907, 7; *GDN*, April 26, 1905, 12; April 27, 1905, 12.

27. *GDN*, April 27, 1905, 12.

28. *GDN*, July 24, 1907, 10.

29. *The Port of Galveston, Texas, U.S.A., 1906–1907*, 33, back cover. The booklet includes a short, two-page article entitled "Immigration," written by H. H. Haines, then Secretary of the Chamber of Commerce.

30. *GDN*, November 11, 1880, 4; October 7, 1881, 4; September 24, 1882, 4; October 1, 1884; September 30, 1885, 8; October 5, 1885. These ships delivering passengers also carried various other loads. The *Hohenstaufen* after landing in Galveston continued on to New Orleans where eighty other passengers disembarked. The steamer also sailed for New Orleans with 150 tons of oil cake on board.

31. *GDN*, February 1, 1906, 12; June 12, 1906, 5.

32. *GDN*, June 11, 1906, 4.

33. *GDN*, June 20, 1906, 5; October 9, 1906, 12.

34. *GDN*, March 8, 1907, 5; *Galveston Tribune*, May 23, 1907, 7; *GDN*, March 30, 1907, 14.

35. *GDN*, June 21, 1907, 7.

36. *GDN*, July 23, 1907, 1.

37. *GDN*, October 6, 1907, 26; October 13, 1907, 16; November 1, 1907, 12; October 6, 1909, 10; May 11, 1910, 1; March 28, 1912, 12; *Galveston Tribune*, May 16, 1912.

38. *GDN*, March 28, 1912, 12; *Galveston Tribune*, November 26, 1929; for a fuller story of the quarantine station see Larry J. Wygant, "The Galveston Quarantine Stations, 1853–1950," *Texas Medicine* 82 (June 1986): 49–52; and *GDN*, July 11, 1907, 14; July 17, 1907, 6.

39. *GDN*, April 22, 1906.

40. *Galveston Tribune*, June 10, 1907, 8; May 16, 1912; *GDN*, July 2, 1907, 10; December 8, 1907, 16; September 18, 1909, 10.

41. *GDN*, December 8, 1907, 16; *Galveston Tribune*, May 16, 1912; pamphlet entitled *Galveston* dated 1910, (no publication information and no author) in Rosenberg Library, Galveston; *GDN*, March 28, 1912, 12.

42. The Galveston Movement is well documented. The most comprehensive source is Bernard Marinbach's book *Galveston: Ellis Island of the West*.

43. A few selective articles in the newspapers of the time discussed this issue of diverting immigrants southward and identified President Taft's support of such endeavors. See *New York Times*, August 21, 1910, 2, and October 22, 1910, 10. For Galveston's look at this issue see *Galveston Tribune*, May 25, 1907, 10; *GDN*, May 6, 1906, 14; January 22, 1908, 6; April 25, 1908, 12; March 18, 1909, 12.

44. *GDN*, July 2, 1907, 9. The *Galveston Tribune* (May 16, 1912) painted a much bleaker picture of life on the island if the various immigrant agencies did not help out in this funneling process. "The result would be a congestion in Galveston; the port of entry would soon be crowded with immigrants who in due course of time would form Hebrew

quarters, German quarters, or whatever their nationality would demand, and they would be little if any better off than before they left their old home."

45. *GDN,* July 2, 1907, 9; July 2, 1907, 10; March 15, 1908, 28; *Galveston Tribune,* October 11, 1913, 9. Many articles in Galveston newspapers told the story of this continuing Galveston Movement, of which the following are only representative: *GDN,* July 2, 1907, 9; July 21, 1912, 14; October 2, 1914, 7; *Galveston Tribune,* October 11, 1913, 9. As this immigrant flow continued, numerous other agencies responded to the need of the immigrants coming through Galveston or settling in the city. One example would be the Council of Jewish Women, which organized in February of 1913 with fifty members, some of whom served as a "department of aid to immigrant girls." See *GDN,* February 17, 1913, 10.

46. *GDN,* September 27, 1914, 24; October 2, 1914, 7; Ronald A. Axelrod, "Rabbi Henry Cohen and the Galveston Immigration Movement, 1907–1914," *East Texas Historical Journal* 15 (1977): 33–34. The American Jewish Historical Society in Waltham, Massachusetts has papers dealing with the Galveston Immigration Plan and the Industrial Removal Office, which kept follow-up records on persons distributed throughout the United States through the efforts of the agency. These follow-up letters, Collection I-91, Industrial Removal Office, describe a wide variety of placements in Texas and hint at the work by adopted Texans in helping place immigrants.

47. *GDN,* July 19, 1908, 5; September 17, 1908, 10; March 15, 1909, 10; February 17, 1910, 2.

48. *GDN,* February 27, 1910, 2; *Galveston Tribune,* May 16, 1912.

49. *GDN,* January 3, 1915.

CHAPTER 10

1. These computer-generated statistics are based on the census data published in *The Statistical History of the United States from Colonial Times to the Present,* 12–13. If 1850 (the first federal census to include Texas) instead of 1860 were used as the base line for this analysis of population growth in Texas, the increase in population between 1850 and 1920 would represent a 2093 percent change. The counted population in 1850 was 212,592, while the 1920 figure was 4,663,228.

2. Letter from Martha Ann Otey in Washington County, Texas, to her mother, Mary Frances Nolley in Mississippi, June 29, 1866, Sam Houston State University.

3. *Houston Telegraph,* November 6, 1869, 4.

4. These words came from W. T. G. Weaver of Gainesville, Texas. McKay, ed., *Debates,* 285.

5. Reed, *A History of the Texas Railroads,* 517.

6. Texas Tourist Foundation, Final Report of the Texas Tourist Committee, unpublished mimeographed copy with cover letters dated December 20, 1956. Material is located at the Texas State Library in Austin, Texas, in Miscellany File, 2–23/1056. The document consists of three portions: Section A—Letter of Introduction; Section B—Part One, "Organization" and Part Two, "Research"; Section C—Conclusions and Recommendations. Since pagination is divided by Section, endnotes will reflect section and page number in that fashion and will hereinafter be listed under TTF; TTF, Section A, 3; TTF, Section B, Part One, 36. Section B, Part Two included the results of eight separate surveys.

7. TTF, Section B, Part One, 6, 24, 26; Section C, 5.

8. TTF, Section B, Part One, 36, and Section C, 1.

9. TTF, Section B, Part One, 9, 11–17; TTF, Section A, 1.

10. TTF, Section C, 5–8.

11. *Vernon's Annotated Constitution,* vol. 3, 399. According to one analyst of this amendment, Section 56 "now states in substance what the minority wanted to say in 1875." The efforts by a minority voted down in the 1875 constitutional convention thus were vindicated nearly eighty years later by the ratification of the new amendment in 1958. See George D. Braden, *The Constitution of the State of Texas: An Annotated and Comparative Analysis,* 798.

BIBLIOGRAPHY

MANUSCRIPTS, SPECIAL COLLECTIONS, GOVERNMENT DOCUMENTS

Affleck, Thomas. Papers. Rosenberg Library, Galveston, Tex.

Ashton, J. T. Letters. Rosenberg Library, Galveston, Tex.

Baker Family Letters. Texas Seaport Museum, Galveston, Tex.

Brock, Robert A. Collection. Huntington Library, San Marino, Calif.

Constitution of the State of Texas, adopted by the Constitutional Convention. Austin: Printed at the Daily Republican Office, 1869.

Department of Agriculture, Insurance, Statistics, and History Files. Texas State Library, Austin, Tex.

Department of Agriculture, Insurance, Statistics, and History. *Reports.* 1889 (First) and Years following.

Gammel, H. P. N., comp. *The Laws of Texas, 1822–1897.* Vols. 5–10. Austin: Gammel Book Company, 1898.

General Laws of the State of Texas, Passed at the Session of the Fifteenth Legislature. Galveston: Shaw & Blaylock, 1876.

General Laws of the Twelfth Legislature of the State of Texas, First Session—1871. Austin: J. G. Tracy, 1871.

Hamman, William H. Collection. Woodson Archives, Fondren Library, Rice University, Houston, Tex.

House Journal of the Twelfth Legislature, State of Texas, First Session. Austin: Tracy, Siemering & Co., 1870.

Industrial Removal Office (IRO) Collection. American Jewish Historical Society, Waltham, Mass.

Journal of the Constitutional Convention of the State of Texas, begun and held at the city of Austin, September 6, 1875. Galveston: Printed for the Convention at the "News" Office, 1875.

Journal of the Reconstruction Convention, which met at Austin, Texas, June 1, A.D., 1868. 2 Vols. Austin: Tracy, Siemering & Co., 1870.

Laws of the United States Relating to the Improvement of Rivers and Harbors, from August 11, 1790 to March 4, 1913. 3 Vols. Washington, D.C.: Government Printing Office, 1913.

Otey, Martha Ann. Letters and Diary. Sam Houston State University Library, Huntsville, Tex. Material bound in volume, entitled "A Journey from Mississippi to Texas 1866."

Railroad Ephemera. Collection. DeGolyer Library, Southern Methodist University, Dallas.

Revised Statutes of Texas: Adopted by the Regular Session of the Sixteenth Legislature, A.D., 1879. Published by the Authority of the State of Texas.

Spaight, A. W. *The Resources, Soil, and Climate of Texas.* Galveston: A. H. Belo & Co., Printers, 1882.

Statistics of the Population of the United States, Ninth Census. Vol. 1. Washington, D.C.: Government Printing Office, 1872.

Statistics of the Population of the United States, Tenth Census. Vol. 1. Washington, D.C.: Government Printing Office, 1883.

Texas Bureau of Immigration. *Report.* 1870, 1872, 1873, 1874, 1875.

———. *Texas: The Home for the Emigrant, From Everywhere.* Houston: A. C. Gray, State Printer, 1875.

Texas Tourist Foundation. Final Report of the Texas Tourist Committee. Texas State Library, Austin, Tex.

U.S. Army. Corps of Engineers. *Galveston Harbor, Texas.* 61st Cong., 2nd Sess. House of Representatives. Doc. #328. 1909.

U.S. Congress. House of Representatives. Misc. Doc. #127. 40th Cong., 2nd Sess. "Communication from Governor Pease of Texas, Relative to the Troubles in that State." May 11, 1868.

U.S. Congress. Senate. Misc. Doc. #111. 48th Cong., 1st Sess.

U.S. Congress. Senate Immigration Commission. 1911. Immigration Commission Report, 61st Cong., 3rd Sess., S. Doc. #747. 42 Vols.

BOOKS, ARTICLES, TEXAS ALMANACS, RAILROAD PUBLICATIONS

(Railroad publications are listed by title unless specific author is identified in publication.)
Allhands, J. L. *Gringo Builders.* Privately published, 1931.

———. *Railroads to the Rio.* Salado, Tex.: The Anson Jones Press, 1960.

———. *Uriah Lott.* San Antonio: The Naylor Company, 1949.

Alpern, Lynn M. *Custodians of the Coast: History of the United States Army Engineers at Galveston.* Galveston: Galveston District, U.S. Army Corps of Engineers, 1977.

Austin, The Capital of Texas and Travis County. N.p.: DuPre & Peacock, n.d.

Axelrod, Bernard. "Galveston: Denver's Deep-Water Port." *Southwestern Historical Quarterly* 70 (October 1966): 217–28.

Axelrod, Ronald A. "Rabbi Henry Cohen and the Galveston Immigration Movement, 1907–1914." *East Texas Historical Journal* 15 (1977): 24–37.

Ayers, Edward L. *The Promise of the New South: Life after Reconstruction.* New York: Oxford University Press, 1992.

Bancroft, Hubert Howe. *History of the Pacific States of North America.* Vol. 11: *Texas* Vol. 2, 1801–1889. San Francisco: The History Company, Publishers, 1889.

———. *The Book of the Fair: An Historical and Descriptive Presentation of the World's Science, Art, and Industry, as Viewed through the Columbian Exposition at Chicago in 1893.* Chicago: The Bancroft Company, Publishers, 1895.

Barr, Alwyn. "Occupational and Geographic Mobility in San Antonio, 1870–1900." *Social Science Quarterly* 51 (September 1970): 396–403.

———. *Reconstruction to Reform: Texas Politics, 1876–1906.* Austin: University of Texas Press, 1971.

Barton, H. Arnold. *Letters from the Promised Land: Swedes in America, 1840–1914.* Minneapolis: University of Minnesota Press, 1975.

Berthoff, Rowland T. "Southern Attitudes toward Immigration, 1865–1914." *Journal of Southern History* 17 (August 1951): 328–60.

Blackburn, L. L. "Early Settlers and Settlements of Callahan County." *West Texas Historical Association Year Book* 23 (October 1947): 13–20.

Blasig, Carl. *Building Texas.* Brownsville, Tex.: Springman-King Co., 1963.

Blegen, Theodore C., ed. *Land of Their Choice: The Immigrants Write Home.* Minneapolis: The University of Minnesota Press, 1955.

Blodgett, Jan. *Land of Bright Promise: Advertising the Texas Panhandle and South Plains, 1870–1917.* Austin: University of Texas Press, 1988.

Bodnar, John. *The Transplanted: A History of Immigrants in Urban America.* Bloomington: Indiana University Press, 1985.

Braden, George D., et al. *The Constitution of the State of Texas: An Annotated and Comparative Analysis.* Vol. 2. Austin: Texas Advisory Commission on Intergovernmental Relations, 1977.

Brewer, J. Mason. *Negro Legislators of Texas and Their Descendants: A History of the Negro in Texas Politics from Reconstruction to Disfranchisement.* Dallas: Mathis Publishing Co., 1935.

Brunet, Patrick J. "'Can't Hurt and May Do You Good': A Study of the Pamphlets the Southern Pacific Railroad Used to Induce Immigration to Texas, 1880–1930." *East Texas Historical Journal* 16 (fall 1978): 35–45.

"The Bryan-Hayes Correspondence." *Southwestern Historical Quarterly* 25 (April 1922): 274–99.

Bryant, W. N., ed. *Bryant's Railroad Guide: A Literary and Informational Work.* Published quarterly. N.p., n.d.

Bryant's Texas Almanac and Railway Guide. 1882.

Buck, Solon Justus. *The Granger Movement: A Study of Agricultural Organization and its Political, Economic, and Social Manifestations, 1870–1880.* Cambridge: Harvard University Press, 1933.

Buenger, Walter L. and Robert A. Calvert, eds. *Texas through Time: Evolving Interpretations.* College Station: Texas A&M University Press, 1991.

Burke's Texas Almanac. 1879.

Caffey, David L. "We Have the Land: Now for the People, Boosterism in Frontier West Texas." *Permian Historical Annual* 21 (December 1981): 49–57.

C. J. H. Frensz's Tariff Investigator of the United States, Enumerating Steamboat, Sail Vessels, Express, Steamships, Immigration, Canal, Railroad, Telegraph. Galveston: Galveston News Steam Print, 1873.

Calvert, Robert A. and Arnoldo De León. *The History of Texas.* Arlington Heights, Ill.: Harlan Davidson, 1990.

Campbell, Randolph B. *Grass-Roots Reconstruction in Texas, 1865–1880.* Baton Rouge: Louisiana State University Press, 1997.

Carpenter, Liz. *Getting Better All the Time.* College Station: Texas A&M University Press, 1993.

Chatfield, W. H., comp. *The Twin Cities of the Border: Brownsville, Texas, and Matamoros, Mexico, and the Country of the Lower Rio Grande.* New Orleans: E. P. Brandao, 1893, reprinted in Brownsville by the Herbert Davenport Memorial Fund, Brownsville Historical Association, Lower Rio Grande Valley Historical Society, 1959.

Circular of the Texas Colonization, Land & Trust Company, with a Brief Description of Texas, Northwestern Texas and Young County. N.p., 1873.

Cmiel, Kenneth. *Democratic Eloquence: The Fight over Popular Speech in Nineteenth-century America.* New York: William Morrow & Co., 1990.

The Coast Country of Texas. Southern Pacific. N.p., n.d.

Cohen, William. *At Freedom's Edge: Black Mobility and the Southern White Quest for Racial Control, 1861–1915.* Baton Rouge: Louisiana State University Press, 1991.

"Come and Share Our Plenty." *Chronicles of Smith County, Texas* 9 (fall 1970): 29–46. Reproduction of brochure written by Charles Herndon entitled *Smith County, Texas, The Land of Diversified Farms and the Heart of the Great Fruit and Truck Belt.* N.p., 1908.

Conway, Alan, ed. *The Welsh in America: Letters from the Immigrants.* Minneapolis: University of Minnesota Press, 1961.

Coulter, E. Merton. *The South during Reconstruction, 1865–1877.* Baton Rouge: Louisiana State University Press, 1947.

Crane, R. C. "The Claims of West Texas to Recognition by Historians." *West Texas Historical Association Year Book* 12 (July 1936): 11–33.

Davis, Ellis A. and Edwin H. Grobe, eds. *The New Encyclopedia of Texas.* Dallas: Texas Development Bureau, n.d.

Day, James M., comp. *The Texas Almanac, 1857–1873: A Compendium of Texas History.* Waco, Tex.: Texian Press, 1967.

De Boer, Marvin E., ed. *Destiny by Choice: The Inaugural Addresses of the Governors of Texas.* Fayetteville: University of Arkansas Press, 1992.

De Cordova, Jacob. *Texas: Her Resources and Her Public Men.* Philadelphia: E. Crozet, 1858.

———. *The Texas Immigrant and Traveller's Guide Book.* Austin: De Cordova and Frazier, 1856.

A Description of the State of Texas Traversed by the MK and T. N.p., 1892[?].

Dexter, W. W. *The Coast Country of Texas (Annual), A Wonderland Illustrated.* Distributed by the Southern Pacific Passenger Dept. Orange, Tex.: Rein Litho. Co., 1903.

Dodd, Donald B. and Wynelle S. Dodd. *Historical Statistics of the South, 1790–1970.* Tuscaloosa: University of Alabama Press, 1973.

Doughty, Robin W. *At Home in Texas: Early Views of the Land.* College Station: Texas A&M University Press, 1987.

East-South-East Texas, On Line of the Texas & New Orleans Railroad. Sunset Route logo on title page. N.p., 1906[?].

Eby, Frederick, comp. *Education in Texas: Source Materials.* University of Texas Bulletin, No. 1824. Austin: The University of Texas, 1918.

Elder, Jane Lenz. *The Literature of Beguilement: Promoting America from Columbus to Today.* Exh. Cat., DeGolyer Library. Dallas: Southern Methodist University, 1992.

Eisenhour, Virginia, ed. *Alex Sweet's Texas: The Lighter Side of Lone Star History.* Austin: University of Texas Press, 1986.

"European Folk Islands in Northwest Texas." *Panhandle-Plains Historical Review* 56 (1983).

Facts about El Paso and Adjacent Country. [Texas and Pacific Railway]. El Paso, Tex.: Hull's Printing House, 1899.

Facts for Immigrants. A Truthful Description of the Town of Palestine and Anderson County,

Texas. Published by the Citizens of the County. [Palestine]: Palestine Advocate Job Printing Office, 1888.

Ferguson, Walter Keene. *Geology and Politics in Frontier Texas, 1845–1909.* Austin: University of Texas Press, 1969.

Foner, Eric. *Reconstruction: America's Unfinished Revolution, 1863–1877.* New York: Harper & Row, 1988.

Forney, John W. *What I Saw in Texas.* Philadelphia: Ringwalt & Brown, Prs., [1872].

Forshey, C. G. *Texas Rail Roads.* Letter to Mayor of Galveston on the Galveston, Houston, and Great Northern Rail Road. July 13, 1866.

Free Guide to Texas. Missouri, Kansas & Texas Railway. Chicago: Rand McNally & Co., 1876.

FREE! Missouri, Kansas & Texas Railway. N.p., 1877.

Galveston. 1910. N.p.

"Galveston Harbor." *Frank Leslie's Illustrated Newspaper* (May 31, 1890): 365–68.

Galveston, Texas. B.P.O.E., No. 126, n.d.

Garner, John S. "The Saga of a Railroad Town: Calvert, Texas (1868–1918)." *Southwestern Historical Quarterly* 85 (October 1981): 139–60.

[Gilman, S. H.]. *The Tributary and Economical Relations of the Railway Systems of the United States to the Commerce of Galveston: Considered Geographically, Topographically and Economically.* Galveston: News Steam Book and Job Office, 1871.

Gould, Florence C. and Patricia N. Pando. *Claiming Their Land: Women Homesteaders in Texas.* El Paso: Texas Western Press, 1991.

Governor's Messages, Coke to Ross. Edited by and for the Archive & History Department of the Texas State Library, 1916.

Gracy II, David B. "A Preliminary Survey of Land Colonization in the Panhandle-Plains of Texas." *Museum Journal* 11 (1969): 52–79.

Greater Texas and the Coast Country: Houston-Galveston District, the Winter Garden. 4th ed. Iron Mountain Route. N.p., n.d.

Grimes County Directory, 1904. Anderson, Tex.: The Grimes County Record, 1904.

Gulf Coast Magazine. [St. Louis, Brownsville and Mexico Railway]. Houston: Cumming & Sons Printers. April 1908, Vol. 3.

Gulf Coastings. Gulf, Colorado & Santa Fe Railroad. N.p., 1907[?].

Haltom, R. W. *History and Description of Angelina County, Texas.* 1888, reprint, Austin: Pemberton Press, 1969.

Handlin, Oscar. *The Uprooted: The Epic Story of the Great Migrations that Made the American People.* New York: Grosset & Dunlap, 1951.

Harris, William H. *The Harder We Run: Black Workers since the Civil War.* New York: Oxford University Press, 1982.

Hart, Roderick P. *Modern Rhetorical Criticism.* 2nd ed. Boston: Allyn & Bacon, 1997.

Hatcher, Mattie Austin. *Letters of an Early American Traveller: Mary Austin Holley, Her Life and Her Works, 1784–1846.* Dallas: Southwest Press, 1933.

Hedges, James B. "The Colonization Work of the Northern Pacific Railroad." *Mississippi Valley Historical Review* 13 (December 1926): 311–42.

Holden, W. C. "West Texas Drouths." *Southwestern Historical Quarterly* 32 (October 1928): 103–23.

———. "Immigration and Settlement in West Texas." *West Texas Historical Association Year Book* 5 (June 1919): 66–86.

The Home for the Emigrant. Texas: Her Vast Extent of Territory, Fertility of Soil, Diversity of Productions, Geniality of Climate, and the Facilities She Affords Emigrants for Acquiring Homes. Austin: Institution The For [*sic*] Deaf and Dumb, 1877.

Homes in Texas, on the Line of the International and Great Northern R.R., 1880–1. Buffalo, N.Y.: Mathews, Northrup & Co., 1880.

Homeseekers' Fares to Texas, 1911. Issued by the Passenger Department, Sunset Route. Houston: Cumming & Sons, Printers, 1911.

Houston City Directory. 1866, 1873.

Hubbard, R. B. *Centennial Oration of Governor R. B. Hubbard, of Texas, Delivered at the National Exposition, September 11, 1876.* Copy in bound volume at Texas State Library, with no publication information.

Hutto, John R. "The German and Catholic Colony of Mariensfeld." *West Texas Historical Association Year Book* 9 (October 1933): 24–34.

Ikin, Arthur. *Texas: Its History, Topography, Agriculture, Commerce, and General Statistics.* Waco, Tex.: Texian Press, 1964.

The Immigrant's Guide to Texas, Giving Descriptions of Counties, Towns and Villages, with Valuable Historical and Statistical Information. Dallas: L. A. Wilson, 1888.

Immigrants Guide to Western Texas, Sunset Route. [Galveston, Harrisburg, and San Antonio Railway]. N.p., n.d.

[Immigration Society of Cooke County, Texas]. *Cooke County: Its People, Productions and Resources.* Gainesville, Tex.: N.p., 1898.

Industrial Development, Central East Texas, the Fruit Belt of the State. Published by the Passenger Department, Houston, East & West Texas Railway. Houston: N.p., 1902.

The Industries of Austin, Texas. Philadelphia: Levy Type Co., 1885.

The Industries of Dallas, Her Relations as a Center of Trade. Galveston: M. Strickland & Co., 1887.

Jackson, Susan. "Movin' On: Mobility through Houston in the 1850s." *Southwestern Historical Quarterly* 81 (January 1978): 252–82.

Johnson, Daniel M. and Rex R. Campbell. *Black Migration in America: A Social Demographic History.* Durham, N.C.: Duke University Press, 1981.

Johnson, William R. "A Short History of the Sugar Industry in Texas," *Texas Gulf Coast Historical Association Publications* 5 (April 1961): 40.

Jordan, Terry G. "The German Settlement of Texas after 1865." *Southwestern Historical Quarterly* 73 (October 1969): 193–212.

———. "A Century and a Half of Ethnic Change in Texas, 1836–1986." *Southwestern Historical Quarterly* 89 (April 1986): 385–422.

———. "The Forgotten Texas State Census of 1887." *Southwestern Historical Quarterly* 85 (April 1982): 401–408.

Kerr, Homer L. "Migration into Texas, 1860–1880." *Southwestern Historical Quarterly* 70 (October 1966): 184–216.

Kerrville, U.S.A. Kerrville, Tex.: J. E. Grinstead, n.d.

Kincaid, Naomi. "The Founding of Abilene, The 'Future Great' of the Texas and Pacific Railway." *West Texas Historical Association Year Book* 22 (October 1946): 15–26.

Kingsbury, W. G. *The State of Texas.* N.p., n.d.

Kinsey, Winston Lee. "The Immigrant in Texas Agriculture during Reconstruction." *Agricultural History* 53 (January 1979): 125–41.

Kittrell, Norman G. *Texas Illustrated or the Romance, the History and the Resources of a Great State*. Issued and Distributed: Sunset-Central Lines. N.p., 1911.

Kneedler, H. S. *The Coast Country of Texas*. Cincinnati: A. H. Pugh Printing Company, 1896.

Lands Originally Granted to the Houston & Texas Central; Galveston, Harrisburg & San Antonio; Texas & New Orleans; and Gulf, Western Texas & Pacific Railway Co's in Texas. Chicago: Rand McNally & Co., 1892.

Larsen, Lawrence H. *The Urban West at the End of the Frontier*. Lawrence: Regents Press of Kansas, 1978.

Lasater, Dale. *Falfurrias: Ed C. Lasater and the Development of South Texas*. College Station: Texas A&M University Press, 1985.

Lathrop, Barnes F. *Migration into East Texas, 1835–1860: A Study from the United States Census*. Austin: Texas State Historical Association, 1949.

Lazarou, Kathleen E. "A History of the Port of Galveston: A Constitutional-Legal Overview." *Houston Review* 2 (summer 1980): 84–95.

The Lone Star Guide, Descriptive of Counties on the Line of the International and Great Northern Railroad of Texas. St. Louis, Mo.: Woodward, Tiernan & Hales, Printers, 1878[?].

Loring, F. W. and C. F. Atkinson. *Cotton Culture and the South, Considered with Reference to Emigration*. Boston: A. Williams & Co., 1869.

Louisiana and Texas for the Winter Tourist. Sunset Route. N.p., 1911.

Mack, H. C. *Texas. Information for Emigrants*. Franklin, Tenn.: Haynes & Figuers, Publishers, 1869.

Marinbach, Bernard. *Galveston: Ellis Island of the West*. Albany: State University of New York Press, 1983.

Marten, James. *Texas Divided: Loyalty and Dissent in the Lone Star State, 1856–1874*. Lexington: University Press of Kentucky, 1984.

Martin, Robert L. *The City Moves West: Economic and Industrial Growth in Central West Texas*. Austin: University of Texas Press, 1969.

Martin, Roscoe C. "The Grange as a Political Factor in Texas." *Southwestern Political and Social Science Quarterly* 6 (March 1926): 363–83.

Mauldin, W. D. "The Coming of Agriculture to Dallam County." *West Texas Historical Association Year Book* 13 (October 1937): 105–11.

Maull, Allen. *Southwest Texas, An Agricultural Empire*. Issued by Passenger Department, Sunset-Central Line. N.p., 1911[?].

McCarty, W. C. *A Few Practical Remarks about Texas, Her Resources, Climate and Soil with Many Important Facts and Extracts from Reliable Sources*. New York: N.p., 1871.

McDaniel, Marylou, comp. and ed. *God, Grass & Grit: History of the Sherman County Trade Area*. Hereford, Tex.: Pioneer Book Publishers, 1971.

McGregor, Stuart. "The Texas Almanac, 1857–1873." *Southwestern Historical Quarterly* 50 (April 1947): 419–30.

McKay, Seth Shepard. *Seven Decades of the Texas Constitution of 1876*. N.p., 1942.

McKay, Seth Shepard, ed. *Debates in the Texas Constitutional Convention of 1875*. Austin: The University of Texas, 1930.

Mehls, Steven F. "Garden in the Grasslands Revisited: Railroad Promotional Efforts and the Settlement of the Texas Plains." *West Texas Historical Association Year Book* 60 (1984): 47–66.

Meister, Chris. "The Texas State Building: J. Reilly Gordon's Contribution to the World's Columbian Exposition." *Southwestern Historical Quarterly* 48 (July 1994): 1–24.

Memorial of the Galveston Chamber of Commerce to the Congress of the United States for the Improvement of the Channels, Bars and Harbors of Galveston Bay. Galveston: Galveston News Steam Book and Job Office, 1870.

Mission Route—The San Antonio and Aransas Pass R'y. St. Louis, Mo.: Woodward and Tiernan Printing Co., n.d.

Moneyhon, Carl H. *Republicanism in Reconstruction Texas.* Austin: University of Texas Press, 1980.

[Morrison, Andrew]. *The Port of Galveston and the State of Texas.* St. Louis, Mo.: Geo. W. Engelhardt & Co., 1890.

The Mortgage Bonds, (7 per cent, Gold or 8 per cent. Currency.) of the New Orleans, Mobile and Texas Railroad Company. New York: Kennard & Hay, n.d.

Mr. Greeley's Letters from Texas and the Lower Mississippi: To which are added his Address to the Farmers of Texas, and His Speech on his Return to New York, June 12, 1871. New York: Tribune Office, 1871.

Myers, Lois E. *Letters by Lamplight: A Woman's View of Everyday Life in South Texas, 1873–1883.* Waco, Tex.: Baylor University Press, 1991.

Nall, Garry L. "Panhandle Farming in the 'Golden Era' of American Agriculture." *Panhandle-Plains Historical Review* 46 (1973): 68–93.

[Neblett, R. S.]. *Texas. Description of Navarro County. Her Resources, and Inducements Offered to Immigrants.* Corsicana, Tex.: Observer Steam Printing House, 1888.

Neugebauer, Janet M., ed. *Plains Farmer: The Diary of William G. DeLoach, 1914–1964.* College Station: Texas A&M University Press, 1991.

New Birmingham, Texas. New Birmingham, Tex.: New Birmingham Development Co., 1891.

New Farming Opportunities in Northwest Texas along the Santa Fe. [Atcheson, Topeka and Santa Fe Railroad]. N.p., 1916[?].

The New Handbook of Texas. 6 Vols. Austin: Texas State Historical Association, 1996.

New York, New Orleans. [Time Tables]. Southern Pacific, Atlantic Steamship Lines. New York: Wynkoop Hallenbeck Crawford Co., 1909.

Northern Settlers' Convention. *Souvenir Program.* Galveston, Tex. April 21, 22, and 23, 1905.

Notes on Texas and the Texas and Pacific Railway. Philadelphia: [Office of President, Texas and Pacific Railway], 1873.

Ousley, Clarence, ed. *Galveston in Nineteen Hundred.* Atlanta: William C. Chase, 1900.

Pennybacker, Anna J. Hardwicke. *A New History of Texas for Schools.* Tyler, Tex.: Published for the author, 1888.

———. *A History of Texas for Schools.* Rev. ed. Austin: Mrs. Percy V. Pennybacker Publisher, 1908.

Peterson, Peter L. "A New Oslo on the Plains: The Anders L. Mordt Land Company and Norwegian Migration to the Texas Panhandle." *Panhandle-Plains Historical Review* 49 (1976): 25–54.

Phillips, Edward Hake. "The Texas Norther." *Southwestern Historical Quarterly* 59 (July 1955): 1–13.

———. "Texas and the World Fairs, 1851–1935." *East Texas Historical Journal* 23 (1985): 3–13.

Pitre, Merline. *Through Many Dangers, Toils and Snares: The Black Leadership of Texas, 1868–1900.* Austin: Eakin Press, 1985.

The Port of Galveston, Texas, U.S.A., 1906–1907. New Orleans: The Southern Manufacturer, 1907.

Proceedings of the Convention of Texian Veterans, held at Houston, May 13, 14, 15, 1873. Galveston: News Steam Book and Job Office, 1873.

Proceedings of the Democratic State Convention, held in the Representative Hall in Austin, on January 23, 24, 25, 26, 1871. [Austin]: State Gazette Job Office, 1871.

Proceedings of the First Annual Session of the Southern Immigration Association of America, held at Nashville, Tenn., on March 11, 12 and 13, 1884. Nashville: R. H. Howell & Co., 1884.

Proceedings of the Immigration Convention, held at the Academy of Music, Charleston, S.C., on May 3, 4, 5, 1870. Charleston, S. C.: Walker, Evans & Cogswell, 1870.

Proceedings of the Immigration Convention of Texas, convened in Dallas, Tex., December 20–21, 1887, and of the State Immigration Committee of Texas, convened in Dallas, Tex., December 29, 1887. Dallas: A. D. Aldridge & Co., 1888.

Proceedings of the Second Annual Session of the Texas State Grange, Patrons of Husbandry, held at the City of Dallas, Tex., Aug., 1875. Waco, Tex.: Waco Examiner and Patron Steam Printing Establishment, 1875.

Proceedings of the Southern Interstate Immigration Convention, convened in Montgomery, Ala., December 12–13, 1888, and of the Southern Interstate Immigration Executive Committee, convened in Montgomery, Ala., December 14, 1888. Dallas: Wilmans Brothers, 1888.

Proceedings of the Third Annual Session of the Texas State Grange, Patrons of Husbandry, held at the city of Tyler, Tex., January, 1877. Waco, Tex.: Examiner and Patron Steam Printing Establishment, 1877.

Proctor, Ben H. *Not without Honor: The Life of John H. Reagan.* Austin: University of Texas Press, 1962.

Profitable Products of East Texas, Orchards and Gardens. Cotton Belt Route. St. Louis, Mo.: Security Printing Co., n.d.

Rathbun, John C. *The "Cephallanographissiment" or a Truthful Description of the Staked Plain.* Midland, Tex.: Staked Plain Job Print., 1886.

Reed, S. G. *A History of the Texas Railroads.* Houston: St. Clair Publishing Co., 1941.

Revised Map of the State of Texas. Houston & Texas Central Railway. N.p.: 1876.

Rice, Lawrence D. *The Negro in Texas, 1874–1900.* Baton Rouge: Louisiana State University Press, 1971.

Riley, B. F. *Alabama as It Is: Or, The Immigrants' and Capitalist's Guide Book to Alabama.* Montgomery, Ala.: W. C. Holt, 1887.

Robertson, Robert J. *Her Majesty's Texans: Two English Immigrants in Reconstruction Texas.* College Station: Texas A&M University Press, 1998.

———. "Texas: *La Terre Promise.*" *West Texas Historical Association* 73 (1997): 11–30.

Rock, James L. and W. I. Smith. *Southern and Western Texas Guide.* [Texas and Pacific Railroad]. St. Louis, Mo.: A. H. Granger, 1878.

Rogers, William Warren, ed. "From Planter to Farmer: A Georgia Man in Reconstruction Texas." *Southwestern Historical Quarterly* 72 (April 1969): 526–29.

San Antonio, Texas: The City of Missions. St. Louis, Mo.: Woodward & Tiernan Printing Co., 1894.

San Antonio as a Health and Pleasure Resort: Climatic Conditions which Have Made this City the Health Seekers Earthly Paradise. St. Louis, Mo.: Woodward & Tiernan Printing Company, n.d.

Scenes along the Houston North Shore Railway. Missouri Pacific Lines. N.p., 1927.

Schlereth, Thomas J. *Victorian America: Transformations in Everyday life, 1876–1915.* New York: Harper Collins Publishers, 1991.

Scott, Larry E. *The Swedish Texans.* University of Texas: Institute of Texans Cultures at San Antonio, 1990.

See Texas Via the H and TC, May, 1890. Houston and Texas Central Railway. Chicago: Rand McNally & Co., 1890.

Shallow Water Country of Northwest Texas. [Atcheson, Topeka and Santa Fe Railway]. N.p., 1913[?].

Simpson, Harold B. *Touched with Valor: Civil War Papers and Casualty Reports of Hood's Texas Brigade.* Hillsboro, Tex.: Hill Junior College Press, 1964.

Smallwood, James M. *Time of Hope, Time of Despair: Black Texans during Reconstruction.* Port Washington, N.Y.: Kennikat Press, 1981.

Smith, Ralph A. "The Grange Movement in Texas 1873–1900." *Southwestern Historical Quarterly* 42 (April 1939): 297–315.

South Western Immigration Company. *Texas: Her Resources and Capabilities.* New York: E. D. Slater, 1881.

Southern Immigration Association of America. *Address of A. J. McWhirter, Pres't, at Vicksburg, Miss. November 21st, 1883 and Proceedings of the First Annual Session of the Southern Immigration Association of America,* held at Nashville, on, March 11, 12 and 13, 1884. Nashville: Albert B. Tavel, Stationer.

Southwest Texas, an Agricultural Empire. Issued by Passenger Department, Sunset-Central Line. Houston: N.p., 1911[?].

Southwest Texas, from San Antonio to El Paso. Issued by Passenger Department, Sunset Route. Houston: N.p., 1908[?].

A Souvenir of Galveston. Galveston: Galveston Evening Tribune, 1893.

Speer, William S., ed. *The Encyclopedia of the New West.* Marshall, Tex.: The United States Biographical Publishing Company, 1881.

Stambaugh, J. Lee and Lillian J. Stambaugh. *The Lower Rio Grande Valley of Texas.* San Antonio: The Naylor Company, 1954.

Stansbury, Norwood. "Letters from the Texas Coast, 1875." James P. Baughman, ed. *Southwestern Historical Quarterly* 69 (April 1966): 499–515.

Statistics and Information Concerning the State of Texas, with Its Millions of Acres of Unoccupied Lands, for the Farmer and Stock Raiser, Unlimited Opportunities for the Merchant and Manufacturer, Great Inducements for the Investment of Capital. . . . With the Compliments of the General Passenger Department of the Missouri Pacific R'y Co., n.d.

The Statistical History of the United States from Colonial Times to the Present. Stamford, Conn.: Fairfield Publishers, 1965.

Stevens, Walter B. *Through Texas, a Series of Interesting Letters.* St. Louis, Mo.: General Passenger Department of the Missouri Pacific Railway Co., 1892.

The Story of San Antonio, as published in "The Mirror" Saint Louis. Reproduced by Passenger Traffic Department of the MK&T. St. Louis, Mo.: Buxton & Skinner, n.d.

Sud und Sudweft Texas. Houston: Sunset Route, 1906[?].

Sugar Lands in Texas. Issued by Passenger Department, Sunset Route. Houston: Cumming & Sons, Printers, 1906[?].

Sunny Southwest Texas. 4th ed. Iron Mountain Route. St. Louis, Mo.: N.p., 1911.

Sweet, Alex E. and J. Armory Knox. *On a Mexican Mustang, Through Texas, From the Gulf to the Rio Grande.* Hartford, Conn.: S. S. Scranton & Company, 1883.

Ten Texas Topics by Texas Tillers and Toilers. Presented by the Passenger Department of the Southern Pacific-Sunset Route. Houston: N.p., 1903[?].

Texas. Houston and Texas Central Railway. N.p., 1880[?].

Texas Almanac. 1867, 1868, 1870, 1872.

Texas Almanac and State Industrial Guide. 1904, 1912.

Texas, along the Line of the Texas and Pacific Ry. Published by the Passenger Department of the Texas and Pacific Railway, Dallas, Tex.

Texas Commercial Secretaries' Association. *Industrial Texas.* Fort Worth: N.p., 1910.

———. *The Master Builder.* Dallas: Johnston Printing & Adv. Co., 1912.

———. *The People, Population 3,896,542.* Fort Worth: N.p., 1912.

Texas, Empire State of the Southwest. Issued by the Missouri, Kansas and Texas Railroad, Passenger Traffic Department. N.p., 1911.

Texas Five Million Club. *Texas from A to Z, A Compendium of Information.* N.p., 1907.

Texas: Her Resources and Attractive Features. Missouri Pacific Railroad. N.p., 1883[?].

Texas: Its Climate, Soil, Productions, Trade, Commerce, and Inducements for Emigration. New York: Martin & Fulkerson, Stationers & Printers, 1870.

Texas Rice Book. Issued by Passenger Department of the Southern Pacific, Sunset Route. N.p., 1901[?].

Texas Rural Almanac. 1876.

Texas Rural Register. 1875.

Texas State Register. 1872, 1876, 1877, 1879.

Texas, the Short Line to Texas is Via the I&GN RR. Chicago: Rand McNally & Co., n.d.

Texas Tourist Points and Resorts, along the Sunset-Central Lines. Houston: N.p., n.d.

Texas Voran! Handbuck von Texas. Houston: Bruck Der State Printing Co., 1907.

The Through Car Line. Missouri, Kansas and Texas Railway, 1879.

Timely Tips to Texas Truckers. Issued by Passenger Department, Southern Pacific—Sunset Route. Houston: N.p., 1910[?].

Trammell, Camilla Davis. *Seven Pines: Its Occupants and Their Letters, 1825–1872.* Houston: Distributed by the Southern Methodist University Press, 1986.

Tyler, Ronnie C. and Lawrence R. Murphy, eds. *The Slave Narratives of Texas.* Austin: Encino Press, 1974.

Van Zant, Lee. *Early Economic Policies of the Government of Texas,* Monograph No. 14 in Southwestern Studies Series, Vol. 4. El Paso: Texas Western Press, 1966.

Vecoli, Rudolph, ed. *Italian Immigrants in Rural and Small Town America.* Staten Island: American Italian Historical Association, 1987.

Vernon's Annotated Constitution of the State of Texas. Vol. 3. Kansas City: Vernon Law Book Co., 1955.

Waco Immigration Society. *The Immigrant's Guide to Waco and McLennan County, Texas by order of the Waco Immigration Society and Approved by City Council of Waco and the Honorable County Court of McLennan County.* Waco: Lambdin & Furmin Printers, 1884.

Waerenskjold, Elise. *The Lady with the Pen: Elise Waerenskjold in Texas.* Edited by C. A. Clausen. Northfield, Minn.: Norwegian-American Historical Association, 1961.

Wallace, Ernest. *Charles DeMorse, Pioneer Editor and Statesman.* Lubbock: Texas Tech University Press, 1943.

———. *The Howling of the Coyotes: Reconstruction Efforts to Divide Texas.* College Station: Texas A&M University Press, 1979.

Walsh & Pilgrim's Directory of the Officers and Members of the Constitutional Convention of the State of Texas, A.D. 1875. Austin: Democratic Statesman Office, 1875.

West Texas beyond the Pecos: Her Health Giving Qualities. Published by Passenger Department, Southern Pacific-Sunset Route. Houston: N.p., 1904[?].

West Texas, Its Soil, Climate and Possibilities, from San Antonio to El Paso. Southern Pacific-Sunset Route. Houston: N.p., n.d.

Western Texas, The Australia of America: Or the Place to Live. By a Six Years' Resident. Cincinnati: E. Mendenhall, 1860.

Whilldin, M., comp. *A Description of Western Texas.* Published by the Galveston, Harrisburg & San Antonio Railway Company, The Sunset Route. Galveston: News Steam Book and Job Office, 1876.

Williams, J. W. "A Statistical Study of the Drouth of 1886." *West Texas Historical Association Year Book* 21 (October 1945): 85–109.

Williams, Robert W. "Thomas Affleck: Missionary to the Planter, the Farmer, and the Gardener." *Agricultural History* 31 (1957): 40–48.

Wilson, Francis W. *Advocate for Texas, Thomas Wilson.* Luling, Tex.: F. W. Wilson, 1987.

[Wilson, James]. *Agricultural Resources of the Texas Pan Handle Country on the Line of the Texas Pan Handle Route.* N.p., 1888[?].

Winkler, Ernest William, ed. *Platforms of Political Parties in Texas.* Bulletin of the University of Texas, No. 53. Austin: The University of Texas, 1916.

Winther, Oscar Osburn. *The Transportation Frontier: Trans-Mississippi West, 1865–1890.* New York: Holt Rinehart and Winston, 1964.

Woodman, David. *Guide to Texas Emigrants.* Waco, Tex.: Texian Press, 1974.

Woodson, Carter G. *A Century of Negro Migration.* 1918. Reprint, New York: Russell & Russell, 1969.

Woodward, C. Vann. *Origins of the New South, 1877–1913.* Baton Rouge: Louisiana State University Press, 1971.

Wygant, Larry J. "The Galveston Quarantine Stations, 1853–1950." *Texas Medicine* 82 (June 1986): 49–52.

Young, Earle B. *Galveston and the Great West.* College Station: Texas A&M University Press, 1997.

———. *Tracks to the Sea: Galveston and Western Railroad Development, 1866–1900.* College Station: Texas A&M University Press, 1999.

Zlatkovich, Charles P. *Texas Railroads: A Record of Construction and Abandonment.* Austin: University of Texas, Bureau of Business Research, 1981.

THESES AND DISSERTATIONS

Adams, Larry Earl. "Economic Development in Texas during Reconstruction, 1865–1875." Ph.D. diss., North Texas State University, 1980.

Baggett, James A. "The Rise and Fall of the Texas Radicals, 1867–1883." Ph.D. diss., North Texas State University, 1972.

Carrier, John Pressley. "A Political History of Texas during the Reconstruction, 1865–1874." Master's thesis, Vanderbilt University, 1971.

Cole, Fred C. "The Texas Career of Thomas Affleck." Ph.D. diss., Louisiana State University, 1942.

Dugas, Vera Lee. "A Social and Economic History of Texas in the Civil War and Reconstruction Periods." Ph.D. diss., University of Texas, 1963.

Huff, Millicent Seay. "A Study of Work Done by Texas Railroad Companies to Encourage Immigration into Texas between 1870 and 1890." Master's thesis, University of Texas, 1955.

Kelly, Ruth Evelyn. "'Twixt Failure and Success': The Port of Galveston in the 19th Century." Master's thesis, University of Houston, 1975.

Marshall, Elmer Grady. "The History of Brazos County, Texas." Master's thesis, University of Texas, 1937.

Mauer, John Walker. "Southern State Constitutions in the 1870's: A Case Study of Texas." Ph.D. diss., Rice University, 1982.

Nolen, Claude Hunter. "Aftermath of Slavery: Southern Attitudes toward Negroes, 1865–1900." Ph.D. diss., University of Texas, 1963.

Rozek, Barbara J. "Words of Enticement: Efforts to Encourage Immigrants to Texas, 1865–1914." Ph.D. diss., Rice University, 1995.

Sandlin, Betty Jeffries. "The Texas Reconstruction Constitutional Convention of 1868–1869." Ph.D. diss., Texas Tech University, 1970.

Turner, Ellis. "In the Trail of the Buffalo: A Descriptive Bibliography of the Oregon, California, and Texas Guidebook, 1814–1860." Ph.D. diss., George Washington University, 1980.

INDEX

———❖———

mittee on Immigration, 52; membership of, 43, 47, 53–54

Grayson County, 41

Greater Galveston Publicity Committee, 185

Greeley, Horace, 93, 115–16

Greenback Labor Party, 110

Gregg, A. W., 185

Gresham, Walter, 181, 182

Grimes County, 6

Grimes County Directory, 128

Grimes County Record, 128

Grinstead, J. E., 128

guidebooks, 64

Gulf Coast Line. *See* St. Louis, Brownsville and Mexico Railroad (SLB&M RR)

Halle, 178

Haltom, R. W., 125

Hamburg-American Packet Company, 178

Handlin, Oscar, 70

Hanford, Albert, 89

Harrison County, 6, 53

Hawaii, 181

healthseeker, 164

Hertzberg, Theodore, 25, 26–27

Hibernians, 71

Hispanics, 128

historical preservation, 111

History and Description of Angelina County, Texas, 125

hogs, 166

Hohenstaufen, 180

Holman, Edward, 180

Holmes, William C., 41, 42, 44

Holt, Alfred, 183

homeseekers, 160, 169, 184; and homeseekers' fares, 145. *See also* immigrants

homestead laws, 30, 36, 56, 72, 84, 107, 141, 144

Hood's Brigade, 32, 33; and Hood's Texas Brigade Association, 33

horses, 166

Hotel Galvez, 165

Houston Age, 56

Houston and Texas Central Railroad (H&TC RR), 33, 146, 147, 148, 156

Houston East and West Texas Railroad (HE&WT RR), 162–63

Houston Post, 195

Houston Telegraph, 59, 62, 71, 81, 95, 102, 191

Houston, Tex., 23, 28, 80, 84, 157

Hubbard, Richard B., 61–62, 75, 173

Humble Oil & Refining Company, 195

Hunt County, 41

Huntington, C. P., 171

Huntsville, Tex., 13, 99, 180

Hurley, C. M., 99

hurricanes: 1900, 177; 1915, 183

Illinois, 30, 49, 55

Illinois Central Railroad, 80–81

immigrant aid societies, 7

immigrant car, 147

Immigrant Homes (railroad), 3, 121, 142, 149–50, 153

immigrant ship, 186. *See also Cassel, Halle, Hohenstaufen*

immigrant train, 156

immigrants, 16, 53, 65–66, 184; and arrival at Galveston, 178, 186; and class issues, 16; and comparison between whites and blacks, 6; and foreign languages, 28; from Alabama, 41; from Asia, 110; from Bohemia, 83; from California, 150; from Canada, 7; from China, 81; from Connecticut, 75; from Czech area of Europe, 149; from Denmark, 80; from England, 60–61; from Europe, 7, 42, 89, 148, 179, 185; from Germany, 8, 14, 16, 22, 23, 41, 50, 71, 80, 81, 83, 93, 148–49, 178; from Germany (Wends), 149; from Illinois, 49, 55; from Iowa, 159; from Ireland, 71; from Italy, 149; from Massachusetts, 75; from North Carolina, 41; from New Jersey, 75; from New York, 14, 75; from northern states, 93; from Norway, 68, 80, 94, 149; from other states, 7, 10, 30; from overseas, 148; from Poland, 9, 148, 149; from Portugal, 150; from Prussia, 41; from Rhode Island, 60; from Scandinavia, 80, 148; from Scotland, 9, 10; from South Carolina, 41, 75, 118; from southern states, 41, 81; from Sweden, 7, 80, 149; from Tennessee, 14, 41; from Vermont, 75; from Virginia, 14, 41; Jewish, 185; and lodging, 21; and statistics, 182, and transportation, 21, travel expenses of, 15, 28; as victims of fraud, 21, 28–29; women, 188. *See also* homeseekers

Immigrant's Guide, 12

immigration, 11, 45–46; financial support for, 51;

ISBN 1-58544-267-4